Teacher Resource Guide

Big Book of Writing Models

Program Authors
Lindamichelle Baron • Sharon Sicinski-Skeans

Modern Curriculum Press
Parsippany, New Jersey

Special thanks to the following schools for providing student writing samples:

Centre Ridge Elementary School, Centreville, VA

DeVargas Elementary School, San Jose, CA

Enterprise Elementary School, Cocoa, FL

Farmington Elementary School
Germantown, TN

Garfield Elementary School, Springfield, VA

Mandarin Oaks Elementary School
Jacksonville, FL

Martin Luther King Elementary School
Lancaster, PA

Mitchell K-6 Elementary School, Atwater, CA

Oak Street School, Basking Ridge, NJ

Red Bug Elementary School, Casselberry, FL

Red Rock Elementary School, Moab, UT

Riverdale Elementary School, Germantown, TN

Russell Primary School, Russell, KY

Shreve Island Elementary School
Shreveport, LA

West University Elementary School
Houston, TX

Special thanks to the following schools for research assistance:

Mount Prospect School, Basking Ridge, NJ

Oak Street School, Basking Ridge, NJ

Sawmill School, Tewksbury Twp., NJ

Special thanks to our Teacher Advisory Board:

Linda Prichard, Murfreesboro, TN

Theresa Langley, Cocoa, FL

Peggy Kearney, Baltimore, MD

Ted Jenes, Fort Collins, CO

Karen Carlson, Ledgewood, NJ

Susie Quintanilla, Houston, TX

Joyce Berube, Norcross, GA

Pat Sears, Virginia Beach, VA

Tracey Gomez, Tracy, CA

Executive Editor: *Betsy Niles*
Editors: *Donna Garzinsky, Barbara Noe*
Designers: *Evelyn O'Shea, Bernadette Hruby*
Cover Design: *Evelyn O'Shea, Bernadette Hruby*
Cover Illustration: *Bernard Adnet*

Credits and Acknowledgments appear on page 224.

Modern Curriculum Press

An imprint of Pearson Learning
299 Jefferson Road, P.O. Box 480 • Parsippany, NJ 07054-0480
www.pearsonlearning.com • 1-800-321-3106

ISBN: 0-7652-2228-0
1 2 3 4 5 6 7 8 9 10   WC   10 09 08 07 06 05 04 03 02 01

Contents

The Forms of Writing

Take Note: Writing to Learn

Once Upon a Time: Writing to Tell a Story

Imagine That: Writing to Describe

Just the Facts: Writing to Inform

Minilessons

Welcome to The Write Direction
For Grades 1-5

Get ready to make the writing process one of the most enjoyable parts of your integrated Language Arts curriculum. *The Write Direction* is a student-centered writing program designed by writing experts. Program authors Sharon Elizabeth Sicinski-Skeans and Lindamichelle Baron are both authorities in the field. Their expertise and child-centered point of view helped to create a program that is not only teacher-friendly, but more important, student-friendly.

Dr. Sharon Elizabeth Sicinski-Skeans received a B.A. degree in English from Sam Houston State University, an M.Ed. in Curriculum and Instruction from the University of Houston-Park, and a Ph.D. at Texas A&M University in Curriculum and Instruction.

Dr. Lindamichelle Baron received a B.A. degree in Education from New York University, an M.A. in Reading, and an Ed.D. in Cross-Categorical Studies from Columbia University Teachers College.

In every lesson, students will see color photos of children their own age or famous authors who demonstrate that it is easy to be successful every step of the way. You will love the many options that appear before every unit in the Teacher Resource Guide for using *The Write Direction* in your classroom.

Look for these teacher-friendly features for support before each unit.

- Overview of Resources and Pacing Suggestions
- Making the Reading-Writing Connection
- The Classroom Writing Center

- Activities for Multiple Intelligences
- Assessment Options including Self-Assessment, Peer, and Teacher Evaluation Checklists, and Benchmark Papers with Rubrics for each Writing Process Lesson

---

Four key benefits of *The Write Direction* ensure writing success for you and your students:

Meets state writing standards

The Write Direction prepares your students for state and standardized writing assessments with more instruction and practice in the stages and forms of writing than any other program.

Guides teachers in teaching writing

The Write Direction's Teacher Resource Guides support teachers by taking the mystery out of teaching writing. Each guide provides simple 3-step core lesson plans for guaranteed success and addresses every writer's needs with proven teaching solutions through Meeting Individual Needs.

Provides easy time management

Whether you have five minutes, one hour, or six weeks, each *Write Direction* Unit Planner provides the teaching options, pacing suggestions, and assessment opportunities to suit diverse teaching styles and schedules.

Integrates the skills of grammar, usage, mechanics, and spelling

Skills for Super Writers practice books and Teacher Guides give third-, fourth-, and fifth-grade writers all the instruction, practice, and application of the skills they need to excel at state tests and become "super writers." In grades 1–5, minilessons at point of use provide meaningful instruction.

Program Components

United at last—a student-centered comprehensive instructional writing program and a fully correlated grammar, usage, mechanics and spelling practice program.

The Write Direction
- ⭐ Big Book of Writing Models
- ⭐ Teacher Resource Guide
- ⭐ Student Book (hardcover)
- ⭐ Transparencies

Skills for Super Writers
Grammar, Usage, Mechanics, and Spelling
- ⭐ Student Book
- ⭐ Teacher Guide

The Write Direction
links to CCC's

Developmentally Appropriate Program Components

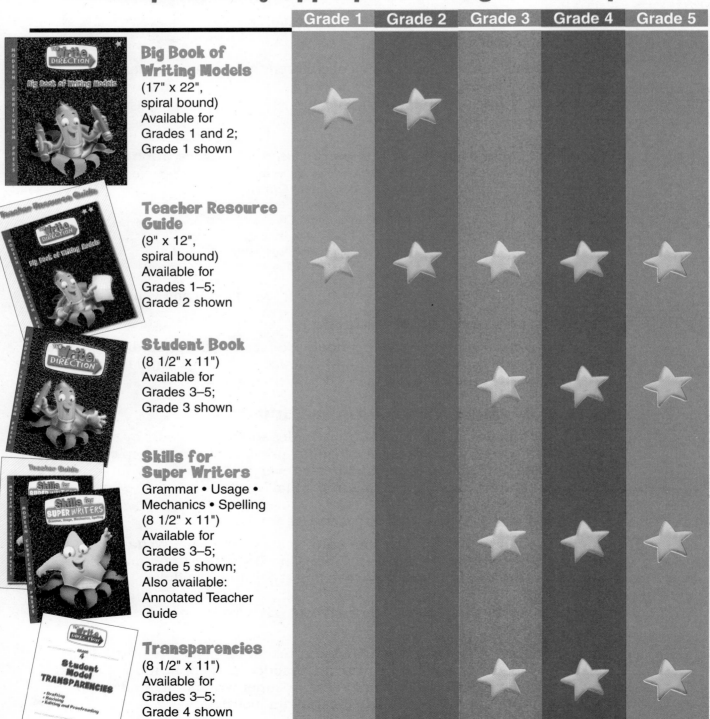

	Grade 1	Grade 2	Grade 3	Grade 4	Grade 5
Big Book of Writing Models (17" x 22", spiral bound) Available for Grades 1 and 2; Grade 1 shown	⭐	⭐			
Teacher Resource Guide (9" x 12", spiral bound) Available for Grades 1–5; Grade 2 shown	⭐	⭐	⭐	⭐	⭐
Student Book (8 1/2" x 11") Available for Grades 3–5; Grade 3 shown			⭐	⭐	⭐
Skills for Super Writers Grammar • Usage • Mechanics • Spelling (8 1/2" x 11") Available for Grades 3–5; Grade 5 shown; Also available: Annotated Teacher Guide			⭐	⭐	⭐
Transparencies (8 1/2" x 11") Available for Grades 3–5; Grade 4 shown			⭐	⭐	⭐

The Write Direction
Scope and Sequence
Grades 1-5

WRITING PROCESS	Grade 1	Grade 2	Grade 3	Grade 4	Grade 5
Prewriting					
Brainstorm	●	●	●	●	●
• Draw	●	●	●	●	●
• Visualize	●	●	●	●	●
Quick Write			●	●	●
Make Lists			●	●	●
Use Journal or Log for Ideas	●		●	●	●
Identify Purpose	●	●	●	●	●
Identify Audience	●	●	●	●	●
Identify Form	●	●	●	●	●
Select Topic	●	●	●	●	●
Narrow Topic/Identify Main Idea					
• Identify Character	●	●	●	●	●
• Identify Setting	●	●	●	●	●
• Identify Problem	●	●	●	●	●
• Identify Plot	●	●	●	●	●
Gather Information					
• Make Lists	●	●	●	●	●
• Read Books, Journals, Logs	●	●	●	●	●
• Interview	●	●	●	●	●
• Research Library, Internet, CD-ROMs	●	●	●	●	●
• Take Notes			●	●	●
•• Summarize			●	●	●
•• Paraphrase				●	●
•• Cite Sources		●			●
• Make Observations	●	●	●	●	●
• Use Charts (KWL Chart)			●	●	●
Organize Information					
• Graphs		●		●	●
• Cluster Diagrams	●		●	●	●
• Information Charts	●	●		●	●
• Diagrams	●	●		●	●
• Story Maps/Charts	●	●		●	●
• Time Lines				●	●
• Venn Diagrams		●		●	●
• Outlines					●
Design a Plan	●				
Conference	●				
• Share With a Partner or Group	●	●	●	●	●
• Listen	●				
• Ask Questions	●		●		
• Take Notes				●	
• Consider/Incorporate Suggestions	●	●	●	●	●
Drafting					
Think About Your Subject	●	●	●	●	●
• Main Idea	●	●	●	●	●
• Character	●	●	●	●	●
• Setting	●	●	●	●	●

	Grade 1	Grade 2	Grade 3	Grade 4	Grade 5
Drafting (continued)					
• Problem	•	•	•	•	•
• Plot	•	•	•	•	•
Think About Your Audience	•	•	•	•	•
Think About Your Purpose	•	•	•	•	•
Think About Your Form	•	•			
Think About Voice, Tone			•	•	•
Think About Language			•	•	•
Review Information			•	•	•
Use Drafting Checklist			•	•	•
Use Charts, Story Maps/Charts, Diagrams	•	•	•	•	•
Follow Plan or Outline	•	•	•	•	•
Include Beginning, Middle, End	•	•	•	•	•
Organize Information Into Paragraphs		•	•	•	•
• Write Topic Sentence That Tells the Main Idea	•	•	•	•	•
• Add Sentences That Support Main Idea: Descriptions (Sensory Details)	•	•	•	•	•
• Add Sentences That Support Main Idea: Facts/Reasons	•	•	•	•	•
• Add Sentences That Support Main Idea: Examples				•	•
• Add Sentences That Support Main Idea: Quotations				•	•
Support Opinions With Facts/Reasons			•	•	•
Sequence Ideas	•	•	•	•	•
Sequence Events	•	•	•	•	•
• Use Time-Order Words	•	•	•	•	•
• Use Transition Words			•	•	•
Write a Beginning That Grabs Reader's Attention	•	•	•	•	•
Write a Conclusion	•	•	•	•	•
• Resolve Problem			•	•	•
• Summarize			•	•	•
• Draw Conclusions			•	•	•
Cite Sources			•	•	•
Write a Title, Headline	•	•	•	•	•
Conference	•	•	•	•	•
• Share With a Partner or Group	•	•	•	•	•
• Listen	•	•	•	•	•
• Ask Questions	•	•	•	•	•
• Take Notes			•	•	•
• Consider/Incorporate Suggestions			•	•	•
Use Handwriting or Word Processing	•	•	•	•	•
Revising					
Review Purpose	•	•	•	•	•
Review Audience	•	•	•	•	•
Review Form	•	•	•	•	•
Review Tone, Voice, Language			•	•	•
Use Revising Marks	•	•	•	•	•
Use Revising Checklist			•	•	•
Revise to Elaborate	•	•	•	•	•
• Add Descriptive Details	•		•	•	•
• Add Facts/Reasons to Support Main Idea/Opinion	•	•		•	•
• Add Examples			•	•	•
• Add Dialogue, Quotation			•	•	•
• Add Sensory Details	•	•	•	•	•
• Add Humor			•	•	•
• Add Flashback			•	•	•

	Grade 1	Grade 2	Grade 3	Grade 4	Grade 5
Revising (continued)					
• Expand Sentences With Adjectives, Adverbs	•	•	•	•	•
Revise to Clarify	•				•
• Rewrite a Confused Sentence or Section to Make Meaning Clear or to Maintain Focus	•	•	•	•	•
• Add Precise Adjectives, Adverbs, Verbs	•	•	•	•	•
• Add Vivid Adjectives, Adverbs, Verbs	•	•	•	•	•
• Add Facts/Reasons and Details to Clarify Opinion/ Point of View			•	•	•
• Add Details to Describe Someone or Explain Something	•				•
• Delete Unimportant Information			•	•	•
• Rewrite to Suit Audience, Purpose, Form			•	•	•
Revise for Variety	•	•	•	•	•
• Vary Length of Sentence	•	•	•	•	•
• Vary Kind of Sentence			•	•	•
• Vary Beginning of Sentence	•	•	•	•	•
• Replace Overused Adjectives, Adverbs, Verbs	•	•	•	•	•
• Combine Short, Repetitive Sentences or Sentences With Similar Ideas			•	•	•
Revise to Create/Maintain Reader Interest	•	•	•	•	•
• Add Title That Makes Reader Want to Continue Reading	•	•	•	•	•
• Add Attention-Grabbing Beginning	•	•	•	•	•
• Include Strong Conclusion That Summarizes, Draws Conclusions, or Resolves Plot/Problem			•	•	•
Revise to Improve Organization	•	•	•	•	•
• Reorder Paragraph With Main Idea in the Beginning Followed by Details and Supporting Facts/Reasons			•	•	•
• Rewrite Beginning to Introduce Characters, Plot, Setting, Main Idea			•	•	•
• Rework Middle to Tell What Happens			•	•	•
• Rearrange Sentences/Paragraphs so Similar Ideas, Facts/Reasons, and Details Are Together	•			•	•
Revise to Improve Sequence	•	•	•	•	•
• Reconsider Sequence of Events and Ideas	•			•	•
• Add Time-Order Words	•	•	•	•	•
• Add Transitional Words				•	•
Conference	•	•	•	•	•
• Share With a Partner or Group	•	•	•	•	•
• Listen	•	•	•	•	•
• Ask Questions	•	•	•	•	•
• Take Notes				•	•
• Consider/Incorporate Suggestions	•	•	•	•	•
Editing and Proofreading					
Use Dictionary	•	•	•		•
Use Thesaurus			•		•
Use Proofreading Marks	•		•		•
Use Proofreading Checklist			•		•
Check Grammar and Usage	•	•	•		•
• Check Sentence Parts, Types, Structure	•		•		•
• Check for Sentence Fragments and Run-Ons			•		•
• Combine Sentences	•	•	•	•	•
• Check Parts of Speech and Their Usage	•	•	•	•	•
• Nouns	•	•	•	•	•
• Verbs	•	•	•	•	•
• Pronouns	•	•	•	•	•
• Adjectives	•	•	•	•	•
• Adverbs	•	•	•	•	•

	Grade 1	Grade 2	Grade 3	Grade 4	Grade 5
Editing and Proofreading (continued)					
• Prepositions			●	●	●
• Conjunctions			●	●	●
• Interjections				●	●
Check Mechanics	●				
• Check Indention		●			
• Check Capitalization	●	●	●	●	●
• Check Abbreviation			●	●	●
• Check Punctuation	●	●	●	●	●
• Period	●	●	●	●	●
• Question Mark	●	●	●	●	●
• Exclamation Point	●	●	●	●	●
• Comma	●	●	●	●	●
• Quotation Marks	●	●	●	●	●
• Apostrophe	●	●	●	●	●
• Italics and Underlining	●	●	●	●	●
• Colon				●	●
• Parentheses				●	●
• Check Handwriting/Neatness	●			●	●
Check Spelling	●	●	●	●	●
Conference	●	●	●	●	●
• Share With a Partner or Group	●	●	●	●	●
• Listen	●	●	●	●	●
• Ask Questions	●	●	●	●	●
• Take Notes			●	●	●
• Consider/Incorporate Suggestions	●	●	●	●	●
Publishing					
Make a List	●	●			
Create Captions	●	●			
Make a Story Silhouette			●	●	
Make Cutouts	●				
Create a Display	●		●		●
Create a Diorama			●		●
Make a Flip Book					●
Create a Bulletin Board	●		●		●
Create a Poster	●	●	●	●	
Make a Classroom Collection/Anthology/Encyclopedia	●	●	●	●	●
Make a Picture Dictionary	●				
Make a Picture Book					
Make a Book/Book Cover	●	●	●	●	●
Make a Notebook/Handbook	●	●			
Create a Storyboard				●	
Make a Mobile		●			
Illustrate Your Writing	●	●	●	●	●
Laminate Your Writing		●			
Frame Your Writing	●				
Create a Multimedia Document		●	●	●	●
Make a Picture Album	●		●		●
Make a Poetry Gallery		●			
Make an Audio Recording	●				●
Make a Video Recording	●	●	●		●
Create a TV Commercial	●				●
Produce a News Broadcast	●				●
Create a Slide Show or Overhead Transparencies Presentation					●

Publishing   (continued)

	Grade 1	Grade 2	Grade 3	Grade 4	Grade 5
Create a Booklet, Pamphlet, or Brochure			●	●	
Print News Stories		●			
Create a Newsletter or Contribute to a Newsletter		●	●		●
Create a Newspaper	●				●
Create a Magazine/Revue			●		●
Create a Resource Rack or Binder	●	●			
Perform a Dramatization or Pantomime	●		●	●	●
Give an Oral Reading or Presentation	●	●	●		●
Have an Authors' Tea	●				
Put On a Puppet Show	●	●	●		
Perform a Radio Play or TV Talk Show					●
Perform a Skit or Stage Play			●	●	●
Perform a Song or Rap		●		●	
Conduct a Panel Discussion			●		●
Give a Speech			●	●	
Make a Map			●		
Send a Letter	●	●		●	●
Send Electronic Mail					●
Submit Writing for Publication					●
Publish Writing Online		●	●	●	●
Make Your Own Letterhead or Stationery	●	●	●		
Make Postcards	●				
Confer With a Published Author					●
Write a Monologue			●		
Present a Video Conference					●
Enter a Contest					●
Present a Science-Fiction Festival					●
Present a Poetry Festival	●				
Present a "Try It" Day	●				

FORMS OF WRITING

Writing to Learn

	Grade 1	Grade 2	Grade 3	Grade 4	Grade 5
Labels	●	●			
Lists	●	●	●	●	●
Captions	●	●			
Posters	●	●			
Picture Dictionary	●				
Notes			●	●	●
Log Entries	●		●	●	●
Journal Entries			●	●	●
Paragraphs			●	●	●
Summaries			●	●	●
Paraphrases			●	●	●
Graphs, Charts, Organizers			●	●	●
Diagrams and Outlines					●

Narrative Writing

	Grade 1	Grade 2	Grade 3	Grade 4	Grade 5
Narrative Paragraph			●	●	●
Story About Me	●				
Story About a Personal Event	●				
Story About a Best Friend	●				
Story About a Pet	●				
Personal Narrative		●	●	●	
News Story	●	●			

	Grade 1	Grade 2	Grade 3	Grade 4	Grade 5
Narrative Writing (continued)					
Folk Tale			•		
Picture Essay			•		
Riddles			•		
Jokes, Puns, and Terse Verse					•
Realistic Story		•	•	•	
Fantasy Story		•	•		
Fable			•		
Comic Strip				•	
Tall Tale				•	
Play Scene				•	
Story From History				•	
Biography					•
Science-Fiction Story					•
Mystery					•
Myth					•
Play					•
Descriptive Writing					
Descriptive Paragraph			•	•	•
Description of a Person	•	•			
Description of a Place	•				
Description of a Story Character	•				
Description of an Event		•			
Character Sketch			•	•	•
Setting			•		
Comparison		•	•		
Quatrain			•		
Free-Verse Poetry	•	•	•	•	
Shape Poem		•			
Haiku				•	
Limerick				•	
Diamante					•
Cinquain			•		•
Concrete Poem					•
Observation Report				•	
Compare-and-Contrast Description				•	
Compare-and-Contrast Essay					•
Eyewitness Account					•
Expository Writing					
Informative Paragraph			•	•	•
Book Report	•	•	•		
Friendly Letter and Envelope	•	•	•	•	
Thank-You Note	•				
Invitation		•			
Interview			•	•	
News Story					•
How-to Paragraph			•		
Report	•	•			
Research Report			•	•	
Research Report With Citations					•
Problem-Solution Essay				•	•
Business or Formal Letter					•
Directions	•				•
Instructions		•			•

	Grade 1	Grade 2	Grade 3	Grade 4	Grade 5
Persuasive Writing					
Persuasive Paragraph			•		•
Book Review			•	•	
Advertisement/Poster				•	
Business Letter			•	•	
Poster					
Brochure			•	•	
Speech					•
Movie Review					•
Editorial Article					•
Point-of-View Essay					•
Commercial					•

INTEGRATED SKILLS

Writer's Craft	Grade 1	Grade 2	Grade 3	Grade 4	Grade 5
Alliteration	•	•	•		•
Analogy			•	•	•
Character	•	•	•		•
Characterization					•
Details—Sensory Words	•	•	•		•
Details—Examples			•	•	•
Dialogue	•	•	•		•
Exaggeration					•
Flashback					•
Foreshadowing and Suspense					•
Humor				•	•
Idioms				•	•
Language—Purpose/Audience	•	•	•	•	•
Language—Formal/Informal			•	•	•
Language—Literal/Figurative				•	•
Language—Slang/Dialect					•
Metaphor				•	•
Mood/Tone			•	•	•
Onomatopoeia			•	•	•
Order of Events and Ideas	•	•	•	•	•
Organization—Beginning, Middle, End	•	•	•	•	•
Organization—Introduction, Body, Conclusion				•	•
Pacing					•
Personification			•	•	•
Plot	•	•	•		•
Point of View—First Person	•	•	•		•
Point of View—Third Person			•		•
Problem	•	•	•		•
Quotations					•
Reader Interest—Titles, Beginnings, Endings	•	•	•	•	•
Repetition					•
Rhyme	•	•	•		•
Rhyme—Assonance and Consonance					•
Rhythm			•	•	•
Sentence Variety—Beginnings			•	•	•
Sentence Variety—Kind, Length			•	•	•
Sentences: Combining and Expanding	•	•		•	•
Sentences: Transitions			•	•	•
Setting	•	•	•		•

	Grade 1	Grade 2	Grade 3	Grade 4	Grade 5
Writer's Craft (continued)					
Simile		•	•	•	•
Voice—Lyric and Narrative			•	•	•
Voice—Dramatic				•	•
Words—Precise Words, Descriptive/Vivid Words			•	•	•
Grammar and Usage					
Sentences					
Sentence Parts	•	•	•	•	•
• Simple Subjects	•	•	•	•	•
• Complete Subjects				•	•
• Compound Subjects			•	•	•
• (*you*) Understood			•	•	
• Simple Predicates	•	•		•	•
• Complete Predicates				•	•
• Compound Predicates			•	•	•
• Direct and Indirect Objects					•
• Phrases					•
• Clauses					•
Sentence Structure	•	•	•	•	•
• Complete Sentences	•	•		•	•
• Simple Sentences			•	•	•
• Compound Sentences			•	•	•
• Complex Sentences				•	•
• Fragments and Run-Ons			•	•	•
• Comma Splices					•
• Combining Sentences			•	•	•
• Expanding Sentences			•	•	•
• Word Order in Sentences				•	•
Sentence Types	•	•	•	•	•
• Declarative Sentences	•	•	•	•	•
• Interrogative Sentences	•	•	•	•	•
• Exclamatory Sentences	•	•	•	•	•
• Imperative Sentences			•	•	•
Nouns					
Common Nouns	•	•	•	•	•
Proper Nouns	•	•	•	•	•
Singular Nouns	•	•	•	•	•
Plural Nouns	•	•	•	•	•
Irregular Plural Nouns	•	•	•	•	•
Possessive Nouns	•	•	•	•	•
Verbs					
Action Verbs	•	•		•	•
Helping Verbs (*be, have, do*)			•	•	•
Linking Verbs			•	•	•
Main Verbs					•
Verb Tenses	•	•			
Present Tense	•	•	•	•	•
Past Tense	•	•	•	•	•
Future Tense					
Irregular Verbs (*bring, say, make*)	•		•	•	•
Principal Parts: Regular Verbs					
Participle					•
Subject-Verb Agreement (Singular and Plural Subjects)	•		•	•	•

	Grade 1	Grade 2	Grade 3	Grade 4	Grade 5
Verbs (continued)					
Subject-Verb Agreement (Simple and Compound Subjects)					●
Change of Tense			●		●
Problem Words (*can, may, doesn't, don't*)			●	●	●
Adjectives					
Common Adjectives	●	●	●		
Proper Adjectives					●
Demonstrative Adjectives				●	●
Predicate Adjectives					●
Comparisons With Adjectives			●	●	●
Articles (*a, an, the*)			●	●	●
Adverbs					
Adverbs That Tell Where, When, and How	●	●	●	●	●
Comparisons With Adverbs			●	●	●
Problem Words (*very/real, good/well*)				●	●
Negatives				●	●
Double Negatives					●
Pronouns					
Personal Pronouns	●	●	●	●	
Subject Pronouns			●	●	●
Object Pronouns			●	●	●
Problem Words: *I* and *me*	●		●	●	●
Possessive Pronouns	●	●	●	●	●
Demonstrative Pronouns					●
Reflexive Pronouns					●
Interrogative Pronouns				●	●
Agreement With Antecedents			●		●
Prepositions					
Prepositions			●	●	●
Prepositional Phrases			●		●
Object of Preposition					●
Conjunctions					
Coordinating Conjunctions			●		●
Interjections					●
Mechanics					
Capitalization					
First Word of Sentence	●	●	●	●	●
Pronoun *I*	●	●	●		●
First Word of Dialogue		●	●	●	●
First Word of Direct Quotations					
Proper Noun	●	●	●		
• Calendar items, days and months, holidays	●	●	●	●	●
• People's first and last names	●	●	●	●	●
• Family relationships				●	●
• Initials			●	●	
Proper Adjectives					●
Titles of People		●	●	●	●
Titles of Books, Stories	●	●	●	●	●
Titles of TV Shows, Movies, Songs, Poems, Headlines			●	●	●
Abbreviations			●	●	●
Place Names	●	●			
Place Names and Geographical Features--streets, cities, states, countries			●	●	●

	Grade 1	Grade 2	Grade 3	Grade 4	Grade 5
Capitalization (continued)					
Organizations, Languages and Nationalities, Names of Historic Events					●
Letter and Envelope Parts	●		●	●	●
Outline Form			●	●	●
Citations					●
Abbreviation					
Streets and Cities, Months and Days			●	●	●
Titles			●	●	●
Kinds of Businesses					
Indention		●	●	●	●
Punctuation					
Period	●	●	●	●	●
• At end of declarative/imperative sentences	●	●	●	●	●
• With abbreviations			●	●	●
• With initials		●	●	●	●
• In outline form			●	●	●
Question Mark	●	●	●	●	●
Exclamation Point	●	●	●	●	●
• Used with interjections				●	●
Comma	●	●	●	●	●
• In dates, addresses, letter parts	●	●	●	●	●
• In compound sentences			●	●	●
• In a series			●	●	●
• With numbers			●	●	●
• After introductory words, phrases			●	●	●
• After clauses				●	●
• With dialogue, direct quotations			●	●	●
Apostrophe	●	●	●	●	●
• In contractions	●	●	●	●	●
• In possessive nouns	●	●	●	●	●
Quotation Marks					
• In conversation	●		●	●	●
• In quotations		●	●	●	●
• In titles of stories, poems				●	●
Underlining/Italics					
• In titles of books, stories	●	●	●	●	●
• In titles of movies, magazines, newspapers				●	●
• In stage directions				●	●
Colon					
• In scripts				●	●
• In business letters after salutation			●	●	●
Parentheses					●
Spelling					
Closed and Open Syllable Constructions			●	●	●
Syllables in CVC and CVCe Words	●	●	●	●	
Long Vowel Sounds and Letter Combinations	●	●	●		
Short Vowel Sounds and Letter Combinations	●	●	●		
Consonant Blends and Digraphs	●	●	●		
Endings *s, es, ed, ing*	●				
Endings *s, es, ed, ing* (Drop Final e)	●	●	●	●	
Endings *s, es, ed, ing* (Double Final Consonant)	●	●		●	●
Endings *s, es, ed, ing* (Words Ending With *y*)			●		●
Endings *s, es, ed, ing* (Words Ending With Vowel + *y*)					●

Spelling (continued)

	Grade 1	Grade 2	Grade 3	Grade 4	Grade 5
Prefixes (*un, dis, re*)	•	•			
Prefixes (*pre, re, im, in, non, co*)			•	•	•
Prefixes (*de, dis, un, ex*)			•	•	•
Rhyming Words	•	•			•
Roots (*drink, speak, read, happy*)		•		•	•
Suffixes		•			
Suffixes (*ness, full, ly, ion, able*)			•	•	•
Schwa *l*			•		
Schwa *n*			•		
Compound Words	•	•	•	•	•
Homonyms and Problem Words (*its/it's; their/they're/there*)		•	•	•	•
Synonyms		•	•	•	•
Antonyms		•	•	•	•
High Frequency Words	•	•			
Phonograms and Word Families	•	•			

Reference Resources

	Grade 1	Grade 2	Grade 3	Grade 4	Grade 5
Table of Contents	•	•			
Index		•			
Graphic Organizers		•			
Almanac				•	•
Map	•	•			
Atlas					•
Card Catalog		•	•	•	•
Computer Software, CD-ROMs, Electronic Media			•	•	•
Internet			•	•	•
Dictionary	•	•	•	•	•
Encyclopedia	•	•		•	•
Magazines			•	•	•
Outline		•	•	•	•
Thesaurus			•	•	•

The Write Direction: Grades 1 and 2 at a Glance

Teaching writing to young children is both a joy and a challenge. Children have vivid imaginations and a unique perspective on the world. They have thoughts, opinions, and feelings waiting to be given form. Your job as a teacher is to help children learn how to use words and language to express themselves through writing. The job of *The Write Direction* is to give you the tools and support you need to lead children to become independent, successful writers.

The Write Direction is a complete program that teaches writing using the writer's workshop model and the 5-stage writing process. Grades 1 and 2 cover the appropriate forms of writing: Writing to Learn, Writing to Tell a Story, Writing to Describe, and Writing to Inform. Under each category you will find the forms of writing most commonly covered in state standards and assessment tests.

The Write Direction contains writing-process lessons that invite children to write in various forms and for various purposes. The real student models, literature models, and graphic organizers in the *Big Book of Writing Models*, as well as blackline masters in the *Teacher Resource Guide* provide plenty of opportunity for instruction and practice. First- and second-grade children need interactive, hands-on materials. The Big Book allows children to experience a finished piece of writing done by someone their own age. Throughout the lessons, children have the opportunity to read and analyze these models and to use them as inspiration for their own writing.

The Write Direction for grades 1 and 2 includes:

Big Book of Writing Models features

- real student writing models
- literature models
- write-on/wipe-off charts

Teacher Resource Guide features

- a how-to section on using the writing process, including
  - assessment
  - journal writing
  - conferencing
  - minilessons
- lesson plans for every form of writing in the Big Book
- related literature titles
- suggestions for meeting the individual needs of children, including:
  - Minilessons
  - Writer's Block
  - ESL Strategy
  - Home-School Connection
  - Writing Across the Curriculum
- expanded section of minilessons

How Does a Writer Grow?

Every Writer Is Different

It's the end of September—another new school year has begun. Joan Bennett, a first-grade teacher, is reading her class's first attempts at writing. As usual she is surprised by the wide range of abilities among children who are within a year of the same age.

◆ Take Sam, for instance. It's hard to believe that those random symbols, some of which look like letters, really mean anything. Yet Joan remembers that when she asked Sam to tell her about his writing he recounted a whole story about his cat. Sam has quite an imagination, and once his writing skills catch up, everyone will be able to enjoy his stories.

◆ Next, she looks at Maya's paper. In the middle of the page is a carefully drawn house with two small figures outside. Under the picture are several neatly written words that are phonetically spelled but accurate enough that Joan is able to read them. Maya has written about playing soccer with her sister. Maya is definitely ready for first grade.

◆ Then there's Todd. Todd is one of the older children in the class. Joan is impressed as she reads his account of a summer camping trip. Many of the words are spelled correctly, and Todd has included some interesting details and attempts at dialogue. He is clearly one of the more advanced writers in the class, and Joan hopes he will be an inspiration to the other children.

Writers Grow One Step at a Time

As an experienced teacher Joan knows that even though children of the same age can have widely different skills, research has demonstrated that they all learn to write by moving through specific developmental stages. On the following pages are real student writing models that show the natural development of writing skills.

The stages are based on the research of Joetta Beaver, Kathleen Taps, Mark Carter, and E. Jane Williams, authors of the *Developing Writer's Assessment (DWA). DWA*, which is available from Celebration Press, is a complete assessment program that enables teachers to evaluate the strengths and needs of each writer and then use the information to plan instruction that moves children to the next level. By comparing your students' writing to the writing models that represent each level, you can see where your students are on target and where they may need extra help.

Student Writing Samples

On the following pages are levels 1 through 9 of the *DWA Continuum*, followed by student writing samples that represent each of those levels. These are the levels that correspond to kindergarten, first, and second grade.

Emerging Writers

Emerging writers create brief written messages of one simple sentence or less, which are based on their pictures. These writers are learning about the relationship of letters to sounds and the correspondence of written words to spoken words, as well as how to spell a few high-frequency words conventionally. They generally form a mixture of uppercase and lowercase letters that are, for the most part, the same size. Some of their words are unreadable without dictation. Emerging writers covers levels 1, 2, and 3.

Level 1

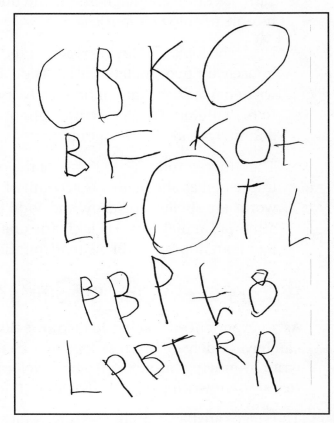

Spider was blue.
My other spider is black.
They are swinging.

Conventions

Sentence Structure Includes no evidence of intended message.

Directionality, Spacing, and Punctuation Places squiggles, other shapes, letterlike shapes, and/or letters randomly.

Letter Formation and Capitalization Forms squiggles, other shapes, and/or letterlike shapes.

Spelling Represents words using letterlike shapes and/or letters with no letter-sound correspondence to the intended word. Dictation needed to read all words.

Content

Supporting Details Includes no evidence of intended articles or modifiers.

Word Choice Includes no evidence of intended words.

Emerging Writers
Level 2

My baby chicken

Conventions

Sentence Structure Includes 1 *intended* word or phrase.

Directionality, Spacing, and Punctuation Places letterlike shapes or letters in a left to right direction and may have a space between 2 words.

Letter Formation and Capitalization Forms mostly uppercase letters, may form 1 word using lowercase letters.

Spelling Represents 1–2 words by recording at least 1 dominant sound. May spell 1 word conventionally. Dictation needed to read most words.

Content

Supporting Details Includes 1 intended article and/or modifier.

Word Choice Uses 1–3 intended routine words.

Emerging Writers
Level 3

Title _____ Sakx _____
<small>snakes</small>

Sakx kn liv in the
<small>snakes</small>

zoo.

Snakes can live in the zoo.

Early Writers

Early writers create short stories or informational pieces. They use a few compound and complex sentences and spell many one-syllable and some two-syllable words conventionally. These writers develop their ideas using primarily one strategy. They are learning to create stories that have simple beginnings, middles, and ends, and to use basic punctuation and capitalization. Early writers covers levels 4, 5, and 6.

Level 4

 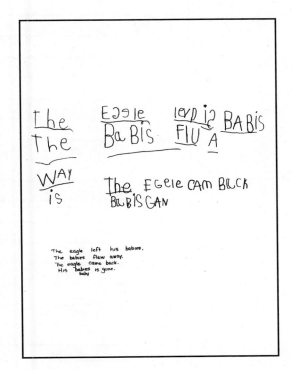

The eagle left his babies.
The babies flew away.
The eagle came back.
His babies (baby) is gone.

Conventions
Sentence Structure Includes 2–3 simple sentences or 1 complex / compound sentence.
Sentence Variation Begins all sentences with the same word.
Punctuation Ends 1 sentence or the story with a period.
Capitalization Capitalizes first word in 1 sentence; other letters may be inappropriately capitalized.
Spelling Spells 4–8 different words conventionally; dictation needed to read a few words.

Content
Opening Begins with an action or a fact in the first of 2–3 related thoughts or sentences.
Transitions Uses 1 transitional word or phrase to connect thoughts.
Development of Ideas Uses a glimmer of at least 1 strategy to develop an idea.
Supporting Details Includes 3–4 modifiers.
Word Choice Uses 1 precise word that is more exact in meaning.
Closing Stops abruptly with no ending after 2 or more related thoughts or sentences.

Early Writers
Level 5

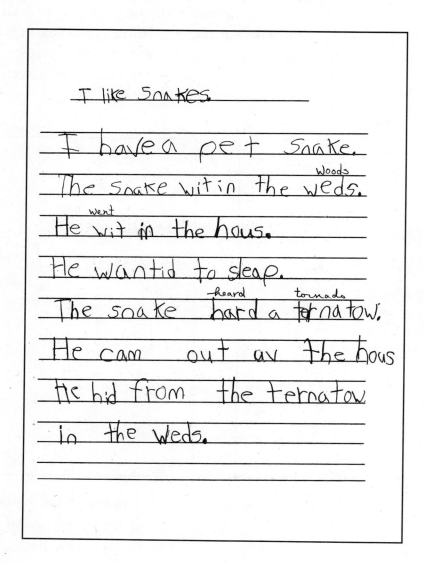

I like snakes.

I have a pet snake.

The snake witin the weds. [woods]

He wit in the hous. [went]

He wantid to sleap.

The snake hard a ternatow. [heard] [tornado]

He cam out av the hous

He hid from the ternatow

in the weds.

Conventions

Sentence Structure Includes 4 or more simple sentences and/or 2 compound or complex sentences.

Sentence Variation Varies the way 2–3 sentences begin.

Punctuation Ends 2 to 6 sentences with periods.

Capitalization Capitalizes first word in 2 or more sentences. Other letters may be capitalized.

Spelling Spells 9 or more different one-syllable words conventionally.

Content

Opening Begins with an action or a fact in the first of 4 or more sentences.

Transitions Uses 2 different transitional words and/or phrases to connect thoughts or ideas.

Development of Ideas Uses 1 strategy somewhat effectively to develop an idea.

Supporting Details Includes 5 or more different modifiers.

Word Choice Uses 2 precise words that are more exact in meaning.

Closing Signals ending with "The End."

Early Writers
Level 6

> The Butterfly Who
> Had Beautyful Wings
> One day I was going for
> a walk. And then I saw
> a Butterfly so I decited
> to catch it And when I
> did I took it home and
> I got it in a jar
> for my pet and then
> I made hole in it so
> it could breath air.
> And when I was eating
> dinner it flaped it's
> wings to try to fly
> but it couldn't get
> away and when I went
> into my room I saw it's
> cool wings.
>
> And that is the end.

Conventions

Sentence Structure Includes 3 compound and/or complex sentences.

Sentence Variation Varies the way 4–5 sentences begin.

Punctuation Ends at least 7 sentences with periods or uses 2 or more forms of punctuation appropriately at times.

Capitalization Uses 2 or more forms of capitalization appropriately at times.

Spelling Spells 4 to 5 different two-syllable words conventionally.

Content

Opening Creates a brief context or introduction with 1 opening sentence.

Transitions Uses 3 different transitional words and/or phrases to connect thoughts or ideas.

Development of Ideas Uses 1 strategy somewhat effectively and at least a glimmer of 1 other strategy to develop ideas.

Supporting Details Supports 1 idea with details in at least 3 sentences.

Word Choice Uses 3–4 precise words that are more exact in meaning.

Closing Creates a logical ending or resolves the problem in at least 1 sentence; may include "The End."

Transitional Writers

Transitional writers begin their compositions by creating an introduction or a context. They use a variety of sentence structures. They spell many two-syllable and some multisyllable words conventionally, and they use basic punctuation and capitalization. These writers generally create brief endings. They are learning to use more than one strategy to develop ideas, to support and clarify ideas with details, and to organize their ideas into paragraphs. Transitional writers covers levels 7, 8, and 9.

Level 7

> A   Friend
> One day a Horse was grazing on some
> grass when an Elephant Shrew came
> along on the ground. The Horse said
> "Hello!" to the Elephant Shrew. The
> Elephant Shrew said "Hello!" back.
> Then they became friends. Then
> they went on a walk together.
> The Elephant Shrew went on
> the Horse's back! Then they went into

> a meadow where the Horse stoped
> to eat. Then the Horse said "Bye!" to
> the Elephant Shrew. The Elephant
> Shrew said "Bye!" to the Horse.
> Then the Horse went back to eating.
> And the Elephant Shrew went on a
> path to walk some more.

Conventions

Sentence Structure Includes 4–6 compound and/or complex sentences.

Sentence Variation Varies the way 6–7 sentences begin.

Punctuation Uses 3 forms of punctuation appropriately most of the time.

Capitalization Uses 3 forms of capitalization appropriately most of the time.

Spelling Spells 6 to 8 different two-syllable words conventionally.

Content

Opening Creates a context or introduction with 2 opening sentences.

Transitions Uses 4–5 different transitional words, phrases, and/or clauses to connect thoughts or ideas.

Development of Ideas Uses at least 2 strategies somewhat effectively to develop ideas.

Supporting Details Supports 2 ideas with details in at least 3 sentences; may be paragraphed.

Word Choice Uses 5–6 precise words or phrases that are more exact in meaning.

Closing Creates a brief closing (wrap-up, summary, conclusion) with at least 1 sentence. May include "The End."

Transitional Writers
Level 8

Title: Niagara Falls.

10/21/99

Dear Friend,

Have you been to Niagara Falls? I have. My whole family did. We stayed there for 3 days. We went to the Falls in the summer of "99". We got there at 12:00 at night. We stayed in a motel called Horse Shoe Motel. Our motel was right next to a tower. The next day we went to the Maid of the Mist and the Cave of the Winds trip, it was cool. Then we went to a tourist store. My mom bought a picture of the Niagara Falls. After that we went out of the store and took a glaze at the Falls. My dad said the Canadian Falls real name is Horse Shoe Falls beca-use it is shaped like a horse shoe. When it was 8:00 we started to go back to the motel. When we entered to motel, my dad asked the person at the information desk what time the light show at the Falls would

begin. They said it started at 11:00 pm. Then we went to our room. We went back to the Falls at 11:08, and watched the light show. It was beautiful. After the light show we went back to our room and went to bed. The next day was our last day to stay at Niagara Falls. We all woke up early and took a quick bath. We got in our van and went to the Falls and took a last glaze and started home.

Conventions

Sentence Structure Includes 7–9 compound and/or complex sentences.

Sentence Variation Varies the way 8–9 sentences begin.

Punctuation Uses 4 forms of punctuation appropriately most of the time.

Capitalization Uses 4 forms of capitalization appropriately most of the time.

Spelling Spells 9 or more different two-syllable words conventionally.

Content

Opening Creates a context or introduction somewhat effectively with at least 3 opening sentences. May be paragraphed.

Transitions Uses 6–7 different transitional words, phrases, and/or clauses to connect thoughts or ideas.

Development of Ideas Uses 1 strategy generally effectively and at least 1 other strategy somewhat effectively to develop ideas.

Supporting Details Supports 3 ideas with details in at least 3 sentences. May be paragraphed.

Word Choice Uses 7–9 precise words or phrases that are more exact in meaning.

Closing Creates a somewhat effective closing (wrap-up, summary, conclusion) with at least 2 sentences.

Transitional Writers
Level 9

The Pretty Butterfly

One summer day in the woods, Nadeine the catapillar said, "I wish I could fly like the rest of you." Billy the fly, Jesse the wasp, Daniel the bumble bee and Nathan the moth all said, "keep dreaming!" Nadeine said, "I know but I just can't help it!"

One day Nathan said, "Come on Nadeine. Lets play throw the rock." But Nadeine said, "I can't I feel funny!" Then all of a sudden Nadeine was rolling up in something happend to Nadeine! She was wraped up into a big brown ball!

A couple days later Jesse said, "It's not fun around here

any more" because Nadeine's gone. "Yeah" said Billy "nothing is fun any more." "I remember when she always..." Then all of a sudden Nadeine popped out of the big brown ball! Every one said, "It's Nadeine." Nadeine looked at herself "I have wings." said Nadeine, "I can fly!" "Great," said Nathan "now we can play throw the rock!" Then Daniel said, "now she is Nadeine the Butterfly!"

Conventions

Sentence Structure Uses a variety of sentences, including 10 or more compound and /or complex sentences.

Sentence Variation Varies the way 10–12 sentences begin.

Punctuation Uses 5–6 forms of punctuation appropriately most of the time.

Capitalization Uses 5 forms of capitalization appropriately most of the time.

Spelling Spells 4–5 different multisyllabic words conventionally.

Content

Opening Creates a context or introduction generally effectively with at least 3 opening sentences. May be paragraphed.

Transitions Uses 8–9 different transitional words, phrases, and/or clauses to connect thoughts or ideas.

Development of Ideas Uses 1 strategy generally effectively and at least 2 other strategies somewhat effectively to develop ideas.

Supporting Details Supports 4 ideas with details in at least 3 sentences; may be paragraphed.

Word Choice Uses 10–12 precise words and a few vivid or figurative phrases to clarify ideas and/or create a clearer image.

Closing Creates a generally effective closing (wrap-up, summary, conclusion) with at least 2 sentences.

Introducing the Writing Process in Grade 1

The writing process is made up of five stages: prewriting, drafting, revising, editing/proofreading, and publishing. In *The Write Direction* Grade 1 revising and editing/proofreading have been combined into one stage to simplify the process. Children do not move straight through the stages. They move back and forth as they rethink and revise their writing. You may wish to make a chart like the one below to hang in the classroom so that children become familiar with the stages of the writing process.

Prewriting — Get ready to write

1. dog

2. fish

3. cat

♦ Make a list.

1. dog

2. fish

3. cat

♦ Choose what you want to write about.

♦ Make a plan.

Drafting — Write, write, write

♦ Use your plan to help you.

My Cat

My cat is funy. He chases his tail

♦ Write as much as you can think of.
♦ Don't worry about mistakes.

Revising and Editing — Make your writing the best it can be

♦ Read your writing again.
♦ Add a word. ⟶
♦ Check your spelling. ⟶
♦ Fix mistakes. ⟶

My Cat

My cat is very funny. He chases his tail⊙

Publishing — Share your work

♦ Draw a picture.
♦ Make a book.
♦ Read aloud.

My Funny Cat
by John

Using The Write Direction

The Extra Help First Graders Need

Because first graders are just beginning to read and write, they need extra support and repeated exposure to the process of writing. Students begin with modeled writing, where they analyze and discuss a student writing model or a literature model, and then move to shared and interactive writing, where they contribute either verbally or by writing themselves to create a group story. Finally they are ready for independent writing where they write on their own.

In each stage of the writing process:

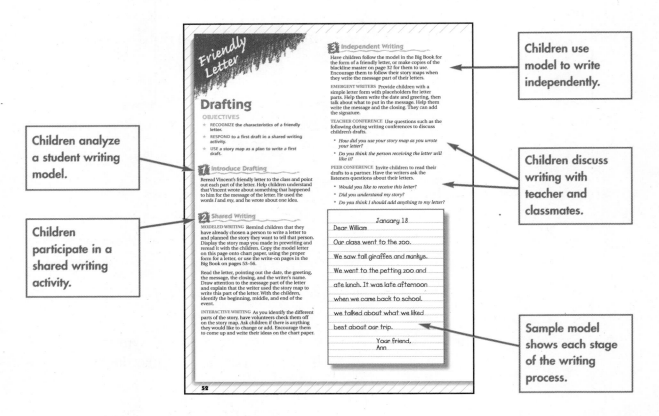

The Role of Literature in Writing

Children learn about writing through example. They can watch other people write, read books, or have books read to them. In grade 1, lessons begin with writing models written and illustrated by real first graders. The model is shown in the child's own handwriting with the child's drawings to show the range of ability among children at this age and to make the writing more authentic.

Literature plays an important role in writing both as a model and as an inspiration. In the *Big Book of Writing Models*, student models are interspersed with literature models from noted children's authors.

Additional literature titles related to each form of writing are listed at the beginning of each unit. These books can serve as a springboard for the writing lesson, another example of a particular form of writing, or a source for a writing topic.

The Flexibility Second Graders Need

Like grade 1, grade 2 of *The Write Direction* features real student writing models as well as literature models. In grade 2, however, there are two kinds of lessons:

◆ lessons that model each stage of the writing process; and
◆ lessons that show only the finished model.

The lessons that model each stage of the writing process show the student writer's work at every stage of the writing process and can be used to guide children through the process with their own writing. These lessons generally take longer to complete.

The lessons that show only the finished model serve as examples of different forms of writing and can be used when time is a concern or when you don't want to take children through the whole process.

Lessons That Work for You

One of the strengths of *The Write Direction* is its flexibility. The forms of writing can be taught in the order they are presented or they can be adapted to fit your classroom curriculum. You may choose to work through the program in the order we suggest, or you may wish to teach some or all the forms of writing in a particular category. You may also pick and choose individual lessons as they relate to other subjects or classroom themes. Make a copy of the following chart to help you keep track of the forms of writing you've taught throughout the year.

Grade 1	
Form of Writing	**Date Taught**
Writing to Learn	Unit 1
Labels	
Lists	
Captions	
Posters	
Picture Dictionary	
Literature Log	
Writing to Tell a Story	Unit 2
Friendly Letter	
Story About Me	
Story About a Best Friend	
Story About a Pet	
News Story	
Writing to Describe	Unit 3
Description of a Person	
Description of a Place	
Free-Verse Poem	
Description of a Story Character	
Writing to Inform	Unit 4
Book Report	
Thank-You Note	
Report	
Directions	

Grade 2	
Form of Writing	**Date Taught**
Writing to Learn	Unit 1
Lists	
Captions	
Posters	
Literature Log	
Learning Log	
Observation Log	
Writing to Tell a Story	Unit 2
News Story	
Personal Narrative	
Folk Tale	
Realistic Story	
Fantasy	
Writing to Describe	Unit 3
Shape Poem	
Description of an Event	
Description of a Person	
Free-Verse Poem	
Comparison	
Writing to Inform	Unit 4
Instructions	
Invitation	
Friendly Letter	
Book Report	
Report	

The Writer's Workshop Model

The typical writer's workshop is a block of time scheduled each day for students to work on writing. The time block begins with a teacher-directed minilesson followed by children writing on their own. The teacher's role shifts from whole class instructor to a facilitator and promoter of writing. The instruction becomes individualized as children work at their own pace on different pieces of writing at different stages in the process.

Components of the Writer's Workshop

Whole Class Meeting/Minilesson – Many teachers begin the writer's workshop with a minilesson. *The Write Direction* provides a minilesson in each of the writing process lessons as well as many additional minilessons in the back of the *Teacher Resource Guide*. Minilesson topics can be an introduction to the lesson, an extension or a review of a topic, or a spontaneous discussion generated by the class.

Independent Writing/Teacher-Student Conferences – Suggested questions for teachers to ask during conferencing are provided for each stage of the writing process. Checklists to guide children as they work are offered for drafting, revising, and editing/proofreading.

Peer Conferences – Pairs or small groups of children share their writing with one another, exchanging ideas, asking questions, and making suggestions. Children listen and make comments in a way that other children understand and respect.

Group Share – This is one of the most important parts of the writer's workshop because it gives children the opportunity to validate their writing by sharing it with others. You may want to have an Author's Chair or a Share Chair in your room when several children are scheduled to share their writing on a given day. Sharing and publishing ideas are suggested for each lesson in *The Write Direction*.

Pacing the Writer's Workshop in Your Classroom

Whole Class Meeting	5 minutes
Shared & Independent Writing/ Teacher-Student Conferences	10–15 minutes
Peer Conferences	5 minutes
Group Share	5 minutes

Journal Writing

Why Write in a Journal?

A journal is a special place for children to write—words, lists, feelings, questions, ideas, drawings, even doodles. A journal can be a notebook, a composition book, or a few sheets of paper stapled together.

Why is journal writing important, even as early as first grade? Not only do writers get many of their ideas from their journals, but for young children, journal writing promotes fluency in thinking, writing, and reading. Putting words on paper makes thinking "visible." When a young child has a thought and writes it in words, he or she is thrilled when someone else can actually read those words and knows what the child is thinking. Writing that someone else can read validates the child's personal experiences and feelings.

Journal writing also encourages risk taking. When children write in their journals where spelling, grammar, and punctuation don't count, they try out new words and stretch their writing. As one teacher said, "When spelling doesn't count, I get a lot more stories about alligators and elephants than I do about cats."

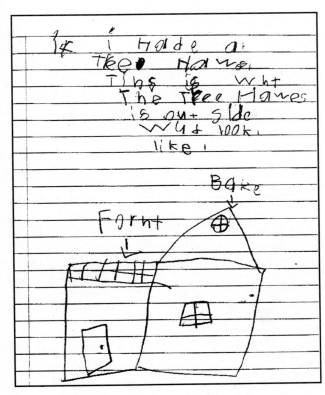

Early first-grade journal entry

If I had a
treehouse
this is what
the tree house
is outside
would look like.
Front. Back.

Late first-grade journal entry

Journal Writing

How to Get Started

Children should have the opportunity to write in their journals every day, even if it's just for a few minutes. Start with five minutes and gradually expand it to fifteen. Sometimes children will write a lot, other times they may write one sentence or just draw a picture.

How do you encourage children who are reluctant to write? Model writing for them. Share a few sentences from your own journal with the class. Let them see you write. Write in your journal when they are writing in theirs. For children whose writing skills are not developed, allow them to draw pictures in their journals and dictate the words while you write them down.

Some teachers use a prompt to start journal writing, but an even more effective approach is a short group prewriting session. Talk about journals and why you write in them—to remember important experiences and to express your thoughts and feelings. Then ask, "What can we write about today?" Share an idea with the class and encourage them to come up with others. Before long, everyone will have something to write about.

Journals as a Record of Progress

In addition to being a good source for writing ideas, journals are also a valuable assessment tool. Over the year a journal provides a longitudinal record of a child's writing development. It can help you identify children's strengths and needs. For example, if children can read back what they have written, it is a good indication of their ability to match letters and sounds.

On Thursday me and my dad wetnt to the Bronx Zoo. We sar a poler bare. It was siting on a rock and then a duck flow in the water. The poler bare sirckiled

the water. Then he jumped in the water. When he jumped in the water the duck flue out. It was so funny. I hyd a gruet time.

Second-grade journal entry

Conferencing

Making the Most of the Teacher Conference

Listening, really listening, is the key to a good conference. Listening means not only hearing the words but reading body language and voice tone, knowing the history of the current piece of writing, and the child's progress with this piece. Your ultimate goal is to help the writer. Respond to the writer, not to the writing.

Conferencing can happen quickly as you walk around the room stopping at a few children's desks, or it can be a more formal discussion at a neutral table or desk elsewhere in the room. Try to conference with each child at least once a week—more frequently if possible.

Here are some suggestions for successful conferencing.

- ◆ Keep conferences short.
- ◆ Listen and learn from the children. Allow them to do the talking.
- ◆ Tell the child what you've understood. Ask questions to find out what you don't understand.
- ◆ Give encouraging and genuine responses. Avoid overpraising.
- ◆ Keep the conference focused by talking about only one or two issues.
- ◆ Emphasize the child's accomplishments, rather than focusing on the deficiencies.
- ◆ Use the conference to gently nudge the child—to keep the writer writing.

Sample Teacher/Student Conference

EMILY: I'm stuck.

MISS F: Is this the same story you were stuck on yesterday?

EMILY: Yes. (*sigh*)

MISS F: Emily, I have an idea. You seem to be stuck on this piece, so why don't you put it away for a while? See if you can write about something else. Look in your journal for ideas.

EMILY: There is one thing I could write about.

MISS F: What's that?

EMILY: I went to a restaurant last night. It had flowers by the front door. (*Emily's thoughts ramble, and one topic leads to another and another.*)

MISS F: Is there something about the restaurant you'd like to write about?

EMILY: Yes, I just remembered. I got a dollhouse for my birthday, and my dad made some furniture to go in it.

MISS F: Could you write about that? Your dollhouse? And the new furniture?

EMILY: Yes, I think I will.

Making the Most of Peer Conferencing

Peer conferencing, even for first and second graders, is a beneficial experience and an important part of the writing process. It gives children an opportunity to share their writing with their peers, exchange ideas, ask questions, and offer suggestions. By helping other writers, they are learning about writing and honing their own skills.

Establish guidelines for peer conferencing from the beginning so that children know what is expected of them. As a group, discuss how to act in a conference. Make a chart and post it in the classroom.

How to Conference

★ Listen quietly.

★ Tell what you like about the writing.

★ Ask questions about things you don't understand.

★ Make suggestions if the writer wants them.

Start by modeling a conference during group sharing. Give each child in the group an index card with a question mark drawn on one side and a smiling face drawn on the other. When the writer has finished sharing his or her story, hold up your card— the smiling face if you liked the story, the question mark if there's something more you want to know or something that isn't clear. Children will model your behavior and hold up the same card. When they do, ask them why they liked the story or what they have a question about.

When children are ready to conference in small groups or in pairs they can use the cards. Children need to learn to listen to each other when they read. This may take some time with young children but as one teacher explained, even if a child is not listening the writer still benefits by hearing his or her own writing read aloud.

As children take turns reading their writing, they will learn to listen to and appreciate each other's writing. Eventually the index cards can be replaced with written questions or checklists children can use to evaluate their own and others' writing.

Sample Peer Conference

A classmate listens as six-year-old Adam reads the beginning of his story out loud.

ADAM: We go on a big bus. It took us to the game. The Cougars and the Knights played. The score was 35 to 21. We saw men with painted faces at the game. There was a bathroom on the bus. There were lots of people on the bus. I ate a hot dog with ketchup at the game.

SARAH: It isn't about one thing. It goes hippie-hop from one thing to the next. It's all mixed up.

Sarah assured Adam that with Jaws's (the classroom stapler) help, he could take his book apart and put the pages in a more logical order.

Minilessons

What Is a Minilesson?

Minilessons are exactly what the name implies—brief instructional lessons that last sometimes only a minute and rarely over five minutes. The benefit of minilessons is that children are learning skills in context and when they need them. Good minilessons respond to the situation and the needs of the writer at a particular point in time.

Let the children lead you. Observe and listen to discover opportunities for learning. When children want to add information but give up because their page is full, recognize the opportunity to teach several minilessons on adding information. When the glue is disappearing and everyone wants to use the stapler at once, a minilesson on managing materials would be appropriate. When children don't know what to write next, present a minilesson on ways to get back on track.

Remember, minilessons are not just lessons that are presented once and then forgotten. The same topic can be covered again and again—in other lessons, in different contexts, from a new perspective. These lessons help children develop and become more skillful writers. *The Write Direction* provides minilessons in each lesson at point of use. These are generally related to a skill in the lesson. There is also a collection of minilessons on related writing skills at the end of the *Teacher Resource Guide*. These can be used at any time and are ideal for reviewing skills or expanding a lesson.

Minilessons can be broken down into four areas.

◆ **Basic Skills** These are fundamental skills that all young children need to learn in order to read and write, such as
- left-to-right progression
- spacing between sentences
- size of words

◆ **Writing Process** These are strategies and skills that facilitate the writing process, such as
- conferencing
- managing time
- making revisions

◆ **Writer's Craft** These are techniques that improve writing, such as
- using dialogue
- adding colorful vivid words
- varying the beginning of sentences

◆ **Language Skills** These are the conventions of grammar, usage, mechanics, and spelling that clarify the writer's words for the reader. They include
- capitalizing the first word in a sentence
- using punctuation marks at the end of sentences
- making subjects and verbs agree

Minilessons

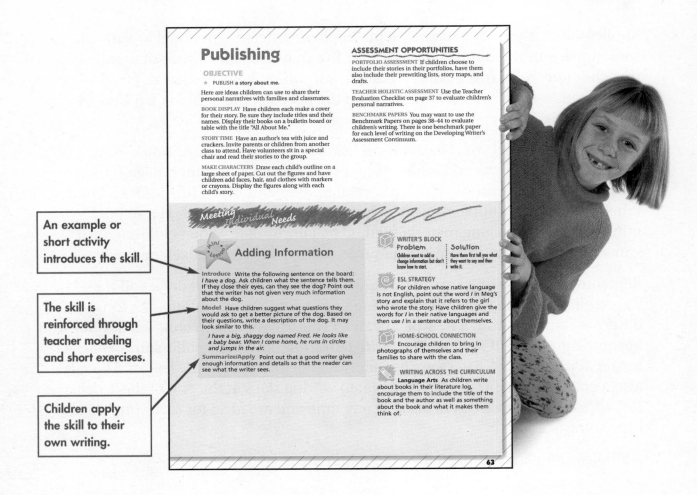

An example or short activity introduces the skill.

The skill is reinforced through teacher modeling and short exercises.

Children apply the skill to their own writing.

Publishing

OBJECTIVE

★ PUBLISH a story about me.

Here are ideas children can use to share their personal narratives with families and classmates.

BOOK DISPLAY Have children each make a cover for their story. Be sure they include titles and their names. Display their books on a bulletin board or table with the title "All About Me."

STORY TIME Have an author's tea with juice and crackers. Invite parents or children from another class to attend. Have volunteers sit in a special chair and read their stories to the group.

MAKE CHARACTERS Draw each child's outline on a large sheet of paper. Cut out the figures and have children add faces, hair, and clothes with markers or crayons. Display the figures along with each child's story.

ASSESSMENT OPPORTUNITIES

PORTFOLIO ASSESSMENT If children choose to include their stories in their portfolios, have them also include their prewriting lists, story maps, and drafts.

TEACHER HOLISTIC ASSESSMENT Use the Teacher Evaluation Checklist on page 37 to evaluate children's personal narratives.

BENCHMARK PAPERS You may want to use the Benchmark Papers on pages 38–44 to evaluate children's writing. There is one benchmark paper for each level of writing on the Developing Writer's Assessment Continuum.

Meeting Individual Needs

Mini Lesson — Adding Information

Introduce Write the following sentence on the board: *I have a dog.* Ask children what the sentence tells them. If they close their eyes, can they see the dog? Point out that the writer has not given very much information about the dog.

Model Have children suggest what questions they would ask to get a better picture of the dog. Based on their questions, write a description of the dog. It may look similar to this.

I have a big, shaggy dog named Fred. He looks like a baby bear. When I come home, he runs in circles and jumps in the air.

Summarize/Apply Point out that a good writer gives enough information and details so that the reader can see what the writer sees.

WRITER'S BLOCK

Problem	Solution
Children want to add or change information but don't know how to start.	Have them first tell you what they want to say and then write it.

ESL STRATEGY For children whose native language is not English, point out the word *I* in Meg's story and explain that it refers to the girl who wrote the story. Have children give the words for *I* in their native languages and then use *I* in a sentence about themselves.

HOME-SCHOOL CONNECTION Encourage children to bring in photographs of themselves and their families to share with the class.

WRITING ACROSS THE CURRICULUM **Language Arts** As children write about books in their literature log, encourage them to include the title of the book and the author as well as something about the book and what it makes them think of.

63

Ways to Present Minilessons

Minilessons should be short and fun and grab children's attention. There are many ways to present minilessons.

◆ Direct presentation

◆ Role play

◆ Demonstration by a child

◆ Compiling lists from the group

◆ Teacher writing in front of the class

◆ Telling past classroom experiences

Some minilessons should be presented to the entire class; others might be better presented to a small group. In some cases, one particular child may be in need of an individual minilesson. If you see that several children are struggling with a concept such as dialogue, take them aside and present a quick minilesson on quotation marks. If one child is misusing the writing center, he or she should have a minilesson about caring for and using the supplies at the center. Minilessons are flexible and can be taught as the need arises.

Take Note: Writing to Learn

Contents

RESOURCES

TEACHING PLANS

Writing to Learn

WRITING FORM	MINILESSONS				
	Basic Skills/ Writing Process/ Writer's Craft	Grammar, Usage, Mechanics, Spelling	Writing Across the Curriculum	Meeting Individual Needs	Assessment
Lesson 1 LABELS pp. 14–15 (2–3 days)	• Writing Your Name and Date on Paper, 15		• Science, 15	• Writer's Block, 15 • ESL Strategy, 15 • Home-School Connection, 15	• Teacher Checklist, 11 • Teacher Conferencing, 14
Lesson 2 LISTS pp. 16–17 (2–3 days)	• Numbering a List, 17		• Social Studies, 17	• Writer's Block, 17 • ESL Strategy, 17 • Home-School Connection, 17	• Teacher Checklist, 11 • Teacher Conferencing, 16
Lesson 3 CAPTIONS pp. 18–19 (2–3 days)	• Left-to-Right Progression, 19		• Art, 19	• Writer's Block, 19 • ESL Strategy, 19 • Home-School Connection, 19	• Teacher Checklist, 11 • Teacher Conferencing, 18
Lesson 4 POSTERS pp. 20–21 (2–3 days)	• Size of Words, 21		• Social Studies, 21	• Writer's Block, 21 • ESL Strategy, 21 • Home-School Connection, 21	• Teacher Checklist, 11 • Teacher Conferencing, 20
Lesson 5 PICTURE DICTIONARY pp. 22–23 (2–3 days)	• Letters: Uppercase and Lowercase, 23		• Math, 23	• Writer's Block, 23 • ESL Strategy, 23 • Home-School Connection, 23	• Teacher Checklist, 11 • Teacher Conferencing, 22
Lesson 6 LITERATURE LOG pp. 24–25 (2–3 days)	• Using Books and Stories to Get Ideas, 25		• Science, 25	• Writer's Block, 25 • ESL Strategy, 25 • Home-School Connection, 25	• Teacher Checklist, 11 • Teacher Conferencing, 24

Making the Reading-Writing Connection
Writing to Learn

You may want to add the following books to your classroom library. Each category of book represents one form of writing children will be introduced to in *Writing to Learn*. The books serve as models for good writing and are valuable resources to use throughout each lesson. The suggested titles offer opportunities for you to read to the class as well as for children to read themselves.

Use literature to introduce a writing form, to show a model of successful writing, to enhance minilessons, to focus on grammar and usage, or to expand each lesson.

LABELS

Mice Squeak, We Speak
by Arnold Shapiro. Illustrated by Tomie de Paola. Putnam, 1997. In this rhyming romp, children review animal sounds and the uniqueness of human language.

Who's Who in My Family
by Loreen Leedy. Holiday House, 1999. Family trees are explored with vivid illustrations and supportive text.

Sounds All Around
by Wendy Pfeffer. Illustrated by Holly Keller. Harpercollins, 1999. The science of sound is explained in this easy-to-read text.

LISTS

Frog and Toad Together
by Arnold Lobel. Harperfestival, 1999. More adventures in the beloved Frog and Toad series.

When Momma Comes Home Tonight
by Eileen Spinelli. Illustrated by Jane Dyer. Simon & Schuster, 1998. A rhyming story that lists all the warm and cozy things Momma will do for her child when she gets home from work.

Sector 7
by David Wiesner. Houghton Mifflin, 1999. Just where do clouds come from? This wordless book offers an imaginative possibility.

CAPTIONS

The Best Book of the Moon
by Ian and Aan Graham. Kingfisher, 1999. An informative reference book about the moon.

How to Be a Friend
by Laurie Krasny Brown and Marc Brown. Little Brown, 1998. Everything you wanted to know about making and maintaining friendships—just for children.

A Book of Kisses
by Dave Ross. Illustrated by Laura Rader. Harpercollins, 2000. Describes all the kinds of kisses there are—from the Good Morning kiss to the I'm Sorry kiss.

POSTERS

A Dollar for Penny
by Julie Glass. Illustrated by Joy Allen. Random House, 2000. Learning to count money has never been so much fun.

Curious Cats in Art and Poetry
edited by William Lach and The Metropolitan Museum of Art. Atheneum, 1999. Cats are the subject of poetry and fine art in this collection of prose and images.

Memories
by Teresa O'Brien. Child's Play, 1995. Many of the pleasant things that we can experience with our five senses are recalled in pictures and text.

PICTURE DICTIONARY

The American Heritage Picture Dictionary
edited by Maggie Swanson. Houghton Mifflin, 1998. Includes categorized vocabulary lists at the end of the book.

The Children's Visual Dictionary
by Jane Bunting. Illustrated by Dave Hopkins. Dorling Kindersley, 1995. This lavishly illustrated first dictionary is designed to build vocabulary.

Scholastic First Dictionary
edited by Judith S. Levey. Scholastic, 1998. Multiple-meaning words and sample sentences address beginning reader needs.

LITERATURE LOG

Flip's Fantastic Journal
by Angelo DeCesare. Dutton, 1999. Designed to look like a real notebook, this is a high-spirited introduction to the joys of creativity, especially writing and drawing.

Franklin Goes to Day Camp
by Paulette Bourgeois. Illustrated by Brenda Clark. Scholastic, 1998. In five fun-filled days, Franklin overcomes his shyness about attending day camp.

Pepper's Journal: A Kitten's First Year
by Stewart J. Murphy. Illustrated by Marsha Winborn. Harpercollins, 2000. Readers will learn all about days, weeks, months, and years as they find out just how much fun a new kitten can be.

The Classroom Writing Center

Writing to Learn

As your children learn about different ways they will be *Writing to Learn*, you can use your classroom writing center to support and extend their writing experiences.

- ◆ Display many examples of environmental print in your writing center and throughout the classroom.

- ◆ Post a chart with children's names and times for center use.

- ◆ Include a tape recorder and blank tapes in the listening center near your writing center. Children can record lists of words or labels and captions.

- ◆ Provide blank books of different sizes for children to decorate and use for literature logs, picture dictionaries or ABC books, and journals.

Create a Bulletin Board for Writing to Learn

Create an interactive bulletin board that focuses on writing to learn. It could be headed "Write On!"

- ◆ One section can be devoted to a list made by you and the children, such as the daily lunch menu or a special "to-do" list for the day.

- ◆ Post a picture or photo representing some area of study for the day and have children write a label or caption.

- ◆ Display a poster announcing an upcoming event or a birthday for that day.

Connecting Multiple Intelligences
Writing to Learn

The following activities focus on specific independent writing ideas for children who demonstrate intelligence in different ways: talent and skill with words (linguistic), with numbers (logical-mathematical), with pictures (spatial), with movement (bodily/kinesthetic), with people (interpersonal), with self (intrapersonal), with music (musical), and/or with nature (environmental or naturalist).

Writing to Learn

Linguistic
Independent Writing — Read a story and make a poster to tell about it. Present your poster to a group.

Logical-Mathematical
Independent Writing — Include numbers and names of shapes in a picture dictionary.

Spatial
Independent Writing — Draw a series of pictures illustrating a book you have read for a literature log entry.
Include color words in a picture dictionary.

Bodily Kinesthetic
Independent Writing — List five favorite games you play.
Make a poster showing one favorite game you play.
Demonstrate it for the class.

Environmental (Naturalist)
Independent Writing — Collect objects from nature. Make a label for each piece and display for others to enjoy.
Make a picture dictionary with words that focus on an animal, plant, or nature theme.

Intrapersonal
Independent Writing — Write a list of favorite things to tell others about you, such as favorite foods, games to play, or favorite toys.
Include these things in a picture dictionary.

Interpersonal
Independent Writing — Interview others or work with a partner to collect words for a picture dictionary.

Musical
Independent Writing — Listen to a musical selection. Write a list of all the things the music makes you think about.
Include the names of musical instruments in your picture dictionary.

List

A list can help you when you write.

_____

1. _____

2. _____

3. _____

4. _____

5. _____

Captions

Draw pictures. Then write captions for them.

Picture Dictionary

Write words you want to remember on this page.

_____ _____

Name _____ **Date** _____

Literature Log

Write about books you've read.

Title _____

_____

Author _____

This book is about _____

_____

_____

_____

_____

I like the book because _____

_____

_____

Evaluating Student Writing

Writing to Learn

The Write Direction offers a variety of assessment options. The following are short descriptions of the assessment opportunities available in this unit. Just select the assessment option that works best for you.

Types of Assessment	Writing Lessons
Checklists The Teacher Evaluation Checklist helps track children's progress as their writing skills develop.	• Teacher Evaluation Checklist, page 11
Teacher Conferencing Throughout each lesson in this unit, there are opportunities to interact with children, informally questioning them about their progress and concerns.	• Labels, page 14 • Lists, page 16 • Captions, page 18 • Posters, page 20 • Picture Dictionary, page 22 • Literature Log, page 24

Teacher Evaluation Checklist
Writing to Learn

Name of Writer _____

Date _____

Writing Mode _____

Use this checklist when you are evaluating a child's
- **labels**
- **lists**
- **captions**
- **posters**
- **picture dictionary**
- **literature log entries**

	YES	NO	Recommendations to Child
Is the writing developed according to the model of the writing mode?	❑	❑	
Does the writing include appropriate content from the source?	❑	❑	
Does the writing include enough information?	❑	❑	
Is the information recorded accurately?	❑	❑	
Is the writing organized?	❑	❑	
Is the information recorded in such a way that the student will be able to understand and use it later?	❑	❑	
Is the handwriting legible?	❑	❑	
Was the work done neatly?	❑	❑	

11

Home Letter

Dear Family,

Your child is learning about ways we all write to learn. Writing labels and lists is something we do every day. Making a poster and writing captions is a way to share information. Our class will work together to create a picture dictionary. Your child will also begin to keep a special notebook called a Literature Log to write what he or she thinks and feels about books that are read.

You can look forward to having your child bring home samples of writing to share with the family. Here are some ways to help your child use writing to learn.

1 Ask your child to help you write lists, such as a things-to-do list, grocery list, things-to-take-to-camp list, or people-to-call list.

2 Help your child put together a writing box with writing supplies. Your child can label containers to store various supplies.

3 As photos are added to a family album, have your child help you write captions for them.

4 Make posters for special family celebrations such as birthdays and anniversaries. These can be made on a computer.

5 Visit the library with your child. Find books you can read together. Here are some books to look for.
- *A-Zenith of Creatures* by Angie Raiff. Bear Lake Publishing, 1997. One of many alphabet books your child would enjoy. This book combines rhymed text and a letter search with interesting animal facts about each creature.
- *What Food Is This?* by Rosemarie Hausherr. Econo-Clad Books, 1999. A question-answer format is used for children to survey and label kinds of foods.
- *Who's Who in My Family* by Loreen Leedy. Holiday House, 1995. Check out how to make your own family tree.

Sincerely,

Carta para el hogar

Estimada familia,

Su hijo/a está estudiando las maneras que tenemos de aprender a escribir. Escribir etiquetas y listas es algo que hacemos todos los días de la vida. Hacer un cartel o escribir pies de grabados son maneras de comunicar información. Nuestra clase va a crear un diccionario pictográfico. Su hijo/a también comenzará un Diario de Literatura que mantendrá consigo para escribir lo que él o ella piensa y siente acerca de los libros que lee.

Ustedes pueden participar en la diversión estando atentos a las muestras de escritura que su hijo/a traerá a casa para compartirlas con la familia. He aquí algunas sugerencias que le servirán a su hijo/a para usar la escritura para aprender.

1. Pídanle a su hijo/a que los ayude a escribir listas tales como listas de cosas que hacer, la lista del supermercado, una lista de cosas que llevar al campamento o una lista de personas que llamar.

2. Ayuden a su hijo/a a confeccionar una caja de suministros de escritura. Su hijo puede rotular envases para almacenar los diversos útiles de escritura.

3. Pídanle pida a su hijo/a que los ayude a escribir pies para las fotos álbum familiar.

4. Hagan carteles de fiestas especiales de la familia, tales como cumpleaños y aniversarios. Estos se pueden hacer en una computadora.

5. Visiten la biblioteca con su hijo/a. Busquen libros que puedan leer juntos. He aquí algunos libros que pueden buscar.
   A-Zenith of Creatures por Angie Raiff. Bear Lake Publishing, 1997. Uno de muchos abecedarios que su hijo/a disfrutará. Este libro combina textos con rima y una búsqueda de letras con datos interesantes acerca de cada animal.
   What Food Is This? por Rosemarie Hausherr. Econo-Clad Books, 1999. Un formato de preguntas-respuestas que se usa para que los niños estudien y rotulen diferentes tipos de alimentos.

Sinceramente,

13

Labels

OBJECTIVES

★ RECOGNIZE the characteristics and purposes of labels.

★ RESPOND to model labels written by a student writer.

★ WRITE labels.

Michael Donnelly
Virginia

1 Introduce Writing Labels

Display cans of food, one with the label removed. Discuss how cans have labels to let people know what is inside. Ask children to identify the contents of each can. Conclude that the can without a label cannot be identified. Invite children to name things in the classroom with labels. Point out that a label is often one word that names a thing or each part of a thing.

MEET THE WRITER Show children the bicycle on page 2 of the Big Book of Writing Models and introduce the writer, Michael Donnelly. Explain that Michael uses labels to name the picture, bicycle, and the parts of a bicycle. Michael labeled the parts of the bicycle to show what each part is called. Michael uses the labels to show what he knows about bicycles.

2 Shared Writing

MODELED WRITING Ask children to tell which label names the object that Michael drew. Read aloud the other labels as you point to each part of the bicycle. Note that each label is a single word. Direct children's attention to the line that connects the word to the part. Point out that each label is written alongside the thing it names, not on it, as on the cans.

When you finish, ask children why they think Michael's labels are helpful. Reinforce the idea that using labels is a good way to identify and remember the names of things.

INTERACTIVE WRITING Have children help draw a simple scene to show where they might ride a bicycle. Begin by drawing a path on chart paper. Children can add details such as trees, a pond, a park, and houses and then suggest a label for each thing they would see along the way. Invite volunteers to write the words. Remind children to use lines to connect the labels to the pictures.

3 Independent Writing

Invite children to write words to label a picture they have drawn or cut out of a magazine. Have them choose a picture of a familiar thing, such as a plant, an animal, or a house. After drawing or pasting the picture on paper, children can write one label to name the picture and additional labels to name the parts of the picture.

EMERGENT WRITERS Provide children with blank stick-on labels. Have children slowly say each word they wish to use for a label. Help children use what they know about letters and sounds to contribute letters as each label is written. Slowly read together each label before having the child attach it to the picture in its place.

TEACHER CONFERENCE As children label their pictures, ask questions such as the following. Make sure children understand that labels are used to identify a picture and/or the important parts of a picture.

• *What label names your picture?*

• *How did you decide which parts of the picture to label?*

• *How are your labels helpful?*

Writing Your Name and Date on Paper

Introduce Show children a mock homework page that is missing the student's name and the date. Invite children to tell you what is missing. Explain that the student's name and the date tell whose work is on the paper and when the work was done.

Model Use lined chart paper to demonstrate how children should write their names and the date on paper. Then guide children in writing their names and date on paper at their desk. Point out a calendar in your classroom as a resource for writing the name of the current month.

Summarize/Apply Have children look at the labeled picture they finished making to make sure they have written their names and the date at the top of the paper. Remind children to always put their names and the date on work they do in school and on homework.

WRITER'S BLOCK

Problem	Solution
Children write too few labels on their pictures or they label unimportant parts.	Provide a picture with write-on lines connected to the important parts. Have children fill in the blanks with the correct labels.

ESL STRATEGY

Provide students with blank stick-on labels. Have students work with a partner who is proficient in English to make labels for items throughout the classroom. Labels can be written in the students' native language, then in English. Monitor children closely, assisting as needed.

HOME-SCHOOL CONNECTION

Have children share their labeled pictures with family members. Invite families to work together to label items in or around their homes. Families might make labels to identify plants in a garden or items stored in boxes.

WRITING ACROSS THE CURRICULUM

Science As children learn about topics in science, have them draw and label pictures to summarize what they have learned.

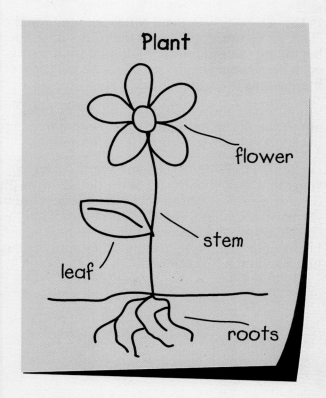

Lists

OBJECTIVES

★ **RECOGNIZE** the characteristics and purposes of lists.

★ **RESPOND** to a model list written by a student writer.

★ **WRITE** a list.

1 Introduce Writing Lists

Ask children how their family members remember what they need to pack when they go on a vacation. Have the class pretend they are going on a trip and let each child suggest an item to pack. Number and list their responses on the board. Point out that a list is a good way to remember things.

MEET THE WRITER Show children the list of ways to travel on page 3 of the Big Book of Writing Models and introduce the writer, Nina Saito. Explain that Nina wrote the list to help her think about and remember different ways to travel.

2 Shared Writing

MODELED WRITING Read Nina's list aloud to the class. As you read, point out the numbers at the beginning of each line. Explain that numbering each item keeps the list in order and tells how many items there are altogether.

When you finish, ask children what they think about Nina's list. Reinforce the idea that making a list is a good way to remember information.

INTERACTIVE WRITING Encourage children to suggest other items to add to the list. Write as they dictate, or invite volunteers to write letters or entire words on the board. Ask children to tell what they should do every time an item is added to the list. Lead children to recognize that they should start a new line and add a numeral.

3 Independent Writing

Have children write their own lists. Encourage them to select a topic from something they are studying in class. If needed, suggest a few topics. Remind children to number their lists or have them use the blackline master on page 6. Encourage children to include drawings.

EMERGENT WRITERS Once children have decided on a topic, have them draw or cut out pictures of items for their lists. Have them use the sounds and letters they know to write the names of the pictures.

TEACHER CONFERENCE As children write their lists, ask the following questions.

- *Why did you choose this idea for a list?*
- *How might you use your list?*

Mini Lesson

Numbering a List

Introduce Write the numerals from 1 to 5 in a column on the board. Invite children to name five different ways they move. Write each response next to a numeral. As you read the list together, invite children to demonstrate each movement.

Model Point out the numerals on Nina's list, drawing attention to the fact that the numbers are in order starting at the top and going down the page. The numbers show how many ways of travel Nina is listing.

Summarize/Apply Make certain children know that using numerals keeps the items of a list in order and tells how many items there are altogether.

WRITER'S BLOCK

Problem	Solution
Children write their lists all over the paper or run items together.	Provide lined paper that's already numbered, or make a colored dot on each line to indicate where children should begin writing.

ESL STRATEGY

Have children whose first language is not English draw pictures for their numbered lists. Then have them work with a partner who is proficient in English to write the words next to the pictures. Partners should slowly say the words in English while the ESL student writes them.

HOME-SCHOOL CONNECTION

Have children share their lists with family members and ask if there is any other information they can add.

WRITING ACROSS THE CURRICULUM

Social Studies As children learn about their school and community, suggest that they make a list to remember important information, such as the names of community helpers. Encourage children to add to their list throughout the unit. Then invite partners to share and compare their lists.

People Who Help Us

1. police officers
2. firefighters
3. crossing guards
4. nurses
5. doctors

Captions

OBJECTIVES

★ RECOGNIZE the characteristics and purposes of captions.

★ RESPOND to a model caption written by a student writer.

★ WRITE a caption.

1 Introduce Writing Captions

Invite children to share one of their drawings or paintings with the class and tell something about the picture. Write their words as a sentence on the board or on a strip of paper and display the picture with the caption. Point out that the sentence, which is called a caption, tells about the picture.

MEET THE WRITER Have children look at the pictures and the captions on page 4 of the Big Book of Writing Models. Introduce the writer, Rosa Martinez, and explain that Rosa wrote the captions to tell what is happening in her pictures.

2 Shared Writing

MODELED WRITING As you read Rosa's captions aloud, point out that each caption is written below the picture and tells important things about it. Lead children to express that the captions tell who or what is in each picture and what Rosa is doing.

Ask children how Rosa's captions make the pictures more interesting. Point out that a caption can add information that a picture doesn't show, such as how Rosa feels about her writing. Talk about the difference between a caption and a label. Lead the children to understand that a label is usually only one word and does not give as much information as a caption.

INTERACTIVE WRITING If possible, show photographs or drawings of the children engaged in a variety of activities. Talk about what is shown in each picture. Invite children to dictate and to contribute letters and words to write short, simple captions. Compile the pictures in an album that can be added to throughout the year.

Rosa Martinez
Ohio

3 Independent Writing

Have children write captions for some of the drawings in their portfolios or use the blackline master on page 7. You can also distribute magazine photos for children to use. Remind children to describe who or what is in the picture and what's happening.

EMERGENT WRITERS Help children orally compose a caption. Have them remember what they want to write by repeating it. As you write for them, talk about how to form letters and words as children say them slowly. Then have them copy the captions below their pictures.

TEACHER CONFERENCE Ask children the following questions as they work on their captions. Make sure children understand that a caption gives special information about a particular picture.

- *How did you decide what to write for a caption?*

- *How does your caption help someone understand your picture?*

Left-to-Right Progression

Introduce Review the meaning of *left* and *right* with the class and help children think of ways to distinguish between the two sides. For example, have children form the letter *L* with the thumb and forefinger of their left hand.

Model Have children look at Rosa's captions on page 4 of the Big Book. Invite volunteers to point out the beginning of each sentence. Then point to each word as you read the captions aloud, drawing attention to the left-to-right progression. Afterward, demonstrate how to write sentences from left to right.

Summarize/Apply Explain that sentences in English are always written from left to right. For children having difficulty with the concept, use green dots to indicate the beginning of each sentence and a red dot for the end. You may choose to explain that some other languages, such as Arabic and Chinese, are written differently.

WRITER'S BLOCK

Problem	Solution
Children are having difficulty thinking of captions to write.	Invite partners to discuss the pictures before they write the captions, or provide partially written captions for children to complete.

ESL STRATEGY

Have children write captions for photographs that are labeled. Choose large photographs with simple themes. Talk about the people, places, and/or things shown and use self-stick notes to label them. Help children read and understand the labels. Guide children as they add words to each label to write their own captions.

HOME-SCHOOL CONNECTION

Have children work with their family members to write captions for a family photo album. Invite children to share their results with the class. Encourage children and their families to look for and discuss captions written in newspapers, magazines, and books.

WRITING ACROSS THE CURRICULUM

Art Show children a print of a painting by a famous artist. Prompt children to describe the details of the painting. Then have children write a caption that tells what they think the artist wanted to share. Invite children to read their captions aloud, or display the captions with the picture if possible.

The Circus
by Georges Seurat

Riding on a horse is a great circus act.

Posters

Gregory Wilkes
Idaho

Posters 5

OBJECTIVES

★ **RECOGNIZE** the characteristics and purposes of posters.

★ **RESPOND** to a model poster written by a student writer.

★ **MAKE** a poster.

 Introduce Making Posters

Display a variety of posters in the classroom. Invite children to vote for their favorite poster and tell why they like it. Talk about ways all posters are alike. List ideas on the board, such as large words, pictures, and bright colors. Point out that a poster is a big sign that gives information.

MEET THE WRITER Show children the poster on page 5 of the Big Book of Writing Models and introduce the writer, Gregory Wilkes. Read what Gregory says about making the poster to remind students to use the trash can at school.

 Shared Writing

MODELED WRITING Read aloud and talk about Gregory's poster. Ask children what catches their attention. Talk about what Gregory uses to share his message—words, pictures, and colors. Point out that Gregory's poster is easy to read because the letters are big and the message is short.

Ask children why they think Gregory chose to make a poster to share his message. Reinforce the idea that a poster catches people's attention and is an interesting way to share information.

INTERACTIVE WRITING Work with children to make a poster about keeping schools, parks, or beaches clean. First, brainstorm what to write and draw. Then work with children to organize and make the poster on unlined chart paper, using the poster in the Big Book as a model. Invite children to contribute drawings and write letters, words, and punctuation.

3 Independent Writing

Have children work alone or with a partner to make a poster. Suggest that children choose a simple message to remind others about class rules, healthy eating, pet care, or another idea. Encourage children to talk about their plan to help them focus on one idea. Remind children to write a short message that is easy to read.

EMERGENT WRITERS For children who need extra support, suggest that they draw their pictures first and then try to write the words. Provide writing resources that children can refer to as they make their posters.

TEACHER CONFERENCE As children work on their posters, ask the following questions.

- *What is your poster about? Why did you choose this idea to write about?*

- *How did you determine what words and pictures to use?*

- *What do you think others will learn from reading your poster?*

Size of Words

Mini Lesson

Introduce Display several posters in the classroom. Encourage children to look at the posters up close and from far away. Draw children's attention to the words on each poster. Invite volunteers to share their opinions about the size and spacing of the words.

Model Have children look at the size of the words on Gregory's poster. Help them understand that Gregory wrote words large enough to read from a distance but small enough to fit on the poster. Have children suggest ways they can decide how big to write words on a poster of their own.

Summarize/Apply Emphasize the importance of choosing the right size words for their writing. Have them compare the size of the words on a poster with the size of the words in a book or in their journals.

WRITER'S BLOCK

Problem	Solution
Children are having difficulty with the organization and spacing of the words and pictures on their poster.	Mark off children's posters in advance by using a pencil to lightly draw write-on lines and boxed art space. Or have children cut and paste their sentences and pictures onto the poster paper. Children can arrange the parts before pasting them onto the paper.

ESL STRATEGY

Give children posterboard to create their posters. Pair students with other students who are proficient in English. Encourage both students to add their words and pictures to the poster.

HOME-SCHOOL CONNECTION

Have children take their posters home to share with family members. Families can also look at posters they might have at home or see in their communities and then talk about how words and pictures are used to give information.

WRITING ACROSS THE CURRICULUM

Social Studies As children are reminded of safety rules at school, it might be helpful to have them create posters with words and pictures to remind everyone of each rule. The posters can be displayed throughout the school.

Picture Dictionaries

Shannon O'Brien
Indiana

6 Writing to Learn

OBJECTIVES

★ RECOGNIZE the characteristics and purposes of picture dictionaries.

★ RESPOND to a model picture dictionary written by a student writer.

★ WRITE entries for a picture dictionary.

1 Introduce Picture Dictionaries

Make picture/word cards for the words *ant, apple, art, bed, big, boy, car, cat, cup* and display the cards in random order. Using pictures as clues, have children read the words with you. Invite children to suggest ways to group the words into lists. Lead them to see that grouping words that begin with the same letter is one way. Talk about how word lists such as these would be helpful when writing.

MEET THE WRITER Have children look at the dictionary entries on page 6 of the Big Book of Writing Models. Introduce the first-grade writer, Shannon O'Brien, and explain that Shannon made a picture dictionary to help her spell and use words correctly.

2 Shared Writing

MODELED WRITING As you look together at Shannon's picture dictionary, point out that she grouped words together that begin with the same letter and that the letters that label each group of words are in the same order as the alphabet. Stress how Shannon used the correct spelling of each word and included pictures that help show the meanings of some words.

Reinforce the idea that a picture dictionary helps a writer remember new words and how to spell them correctly. Invite children to suggest others words they know that begin with the letters *b* and *c* that could be added to Shannon's lists.

INTERACTIVE WRITING Have children make a page for a picture dictionary, listing words beginning with *d*. Have a volunteer write the letters *Dd* at the top of chart paper. As children name words, have them suggest how to spell each word. Invite volunteers to write words or parts of words on the chart paper. Other children can draw a picture for each word.

3 Independent Writing

Children can make picture dictionaries by stapling together sheets of plain or lined paper or by using notebooks. You may also use the blackline master on page 8. Have them write a letter of the alphabet at the top of each page and add pictures of words that begin with that letter. Names of pictures can be added. As children discover new words they want to remember, the words can be added to the appropriate page.

EMERGENT WRITERS Have children focus on finding pictures of words that begin with a particular letter. Help them use the letters and sounds they know to write the words. Provide the correct spelling if necessary.

TEACHER CONFERENCE As children write words in their picture dictionaries, ask questions such as these.

• *How will your picture dictionary help you?*

• *When will you add words to your picture dictionary?*

• *How does the picture help you when you read the words in your picture dictionary?*

Capital and Lowercase Letters

Introduce Display an alphabet chart that shows both capital and lowercase letters. Invite the class to recite the alphabet or sing "The Alphabet Song" as you point to the letters. Review the differences between capital and lowercase letters.

Model Have children look at Shannon's picture dictionary entries. Direct children's attention to the capital and lowercase letters that label each list, and review the purpose of these headings. Help children understand that the capital and lowercase letter on each page tells them the letter that each word begins with on that page. The pages in the picture dictionary go from A to Z.

Summarize/Apply Have children look again at the picture dictionaries they have made. Using the alphabet chart as a resource, they can check the formation of the capital and lowercase letters they have written at the top of each page and check that the letters have been written in the same order as the alphabet.

WRITER'S BLOCK

Problem	Solution
Children can't think of any words to add to their picture dictionaries	Suggest that they look through their portfolios for words they used in their writing but had trouble spelling, or interesting words they read in books and want to remember.

ESL STRATEGY

Have ESL students create picture dictionary entries, writing the word in their native language. Then pair them with English-proficient students to help write the English entry on the page.

HOME-SCHOOL CONNECTION

Invite children to share their picture dictionaries with family members. Encourage family members to help children add more words. Children can write words they discover at home or during family outings.

WRITING ACROSS THE CURRICULUM

Math Have children keep a content-specific picture dictionary for each area of the curriculum throughout the year. For example, children can work together to create math picture dictionaries that include new math terms, pictures, and examples. Place the dictionary pages in a ring binder so that new pages can easily be added.

S s

square

4−2=2
subtract

Literature Logs

Lottie's New Beach Towel
by Petra Mathers
Lottie is a chicken. One
day she gets a beach
towel. She takes it to the
beach. The towel helps her.
The book is very funny.

Writing about books helps me remember them.

Bryson Chandler
West Virginia

OBJECTIVES

★ **RECOGNIZE** the characteristics and purposes of literature logs.

★ **RESPOND** to a model literature log written by a student writer.

★ **WRITE** entries in a literature log.

1 Introduce Literature Logs

Read a story to the children. After reading, distribute paper strips for children to make bookmarks. On one side, model how children are to write the book title and author's name. On the other side, children can draw a picture to show a favorite part and write a caption. Point out how the bookmark will remind them of the story. Explain that now they will learn another way to write about books.

MEET THE WRITER Show children the log entry on page 7 of the Big Book of Writing Models and introduce the first-grade writer, Bryson Chandler. Explain that Bryson writes in a special notebook called a literature log to tell about books and stories he has read or heard. Bryson wrote about the book *Lottie's New Beach Towel* because he liked it and wanted to remember it.

2 Shared Writing

MODELED WRITING Read aloud Bryson's log entry and then point out what the writer did. Bryson began by writing the date, the title of the book, and the author's name. Then he wrote about the character and what happens. He also tells how he feels about the book.

When you finish, ask children why they think writing about a book the way Bryson did is a good idea. Have them share ways Bryson can use what he writes in his literature log. Stress that a literature log is a special place to write what you think and how you feel. Your log is also a good place to get ideas for writing stories.

INTERACTIVE WRITING Read a story aloud to the class. Then have children help you write the title of the book and the author's name on the board. Invite children to share their thoughts about the story, and encourage them to explain what they liked and didn't like about it. Write their responses on chart paper or on page 53 of the Big Book. Invite children to come up and write words or parts of words.

3 Independent Writing

Have children read a book or listen to a story you read aloud. Provide each child with a blank book or notebook to write a log entry. You may also use the blackline master on page 9. Display the Big Book model and give oral prompts such as these: *Tell who (or what) the story is about. Tell what you like or do not like. Tell how the story makes you feel.*

EMERGENT WRITERS Have children talk freely about the book. Then ask them what they would like to write in their log. Guide children's writing so that what they write can be easily remembered and read. Write for children but have them contribute letters and words they know.

TEACHER CONFERENCE As children write in their logs, ask questions such as the following.

* *Why should you write the title and author?*

* *What did you write first?*

* *Do you tell what you think and feel about the story?*

Using Books and Stories to Get Ideas

Mini Lesson

Introduce Have children help you collect a few favorite books you have shared from your classroom library. As you talk briefly about the stories and characters, invite children to express what they are reminded of. List their ideas on the board. Point out that each of these ideas can be used to write stories of their own.

Model Turn to page 7 of the Big Book and look again at what Bryson wrote in his literature log. Ask children if they are reminded of another idea that they might use to write a story of their own. If necessary mention key words from the story, such as *chicken, beach towel,* and *picnic*.

Summarize/Apply Explain that books and stories can be a source of ideas for writing. Encourage children to review their literature logs to get ideas for writing stories of their own.

WRITER'S BLOCK

Problem

Children have difficulty organizing their thoughts and deciding what to write.

Solution

Before children write their entries, encourage them to talk about the story and characters and tell how they feel about the story. Encourage them to write what they think is important to remember.

ESL STRATEGY

Have children draw pictures in their literature logs if they are having difficulty writing sentences. Then encourage them to write a label or caption below each picture to help explain what they read.

HOME-SCHOOL CONNECTION

Have children share their literature logs with their families. Encourage family members to help children read stories and write more entries in the literature logs.

WRITING ACROSS THE CURRICULUM

Science Have students read nonfiction picture books about topics they are learning in science. Then have them write about the books in their literature logs.

September 17

Fabulous Frogs
by Linda Glaser

The book is about frogs. Frogs hop and swim. Baby frogs are tadpoles. Tadpoles look like fish! I like the pictures a lot.

Revising and Editing Marks

≡	capitalize
∧ or ∨	add
⎯	remove
⊙	add a period
/	make lowercase
◯	spelling mistake
↻	move

Once Upon a Time: Writing to Tell a Story

Contents

RESOURCES

TEACHING PLANS

Writing to Tell a Story

MINILESSONS

WRITING FORM	Basic Skills/ Writing Process/ Writer's Craft	Grammar, Usage, Mechanics, Spelling	Writing Across the Curriculum	Meeting Individual Needs	Assessment
Lesson 1 FRIENDLY LETTER pp. 48–55 (7–9 days)	• Brainstorming, 48 • Choosing a Topic, 51 • Sequence Events by Cutting & Pasting Sentences, 53 • Draft vs. Final Copy, 55		• Science/Math, 51 • Art, 53 • Language Arts, 55	• Writer's Block, 51, 53, 55 • ESL Strategy, 51, 53, 55 • Home-School Connection, 51, 53, 55	• Teacher Checklist, 37 • Benchmark Papers, 38–44 • Portfolio, 55 • Teacher and Peer Conferencing, 50, 52, 54
Lesson 2 STORY ABOUT ME pp. 56–63 (7–9 days)	• Title and Author, 56 • Double-spacing a Draft, 61 • Expand Sentences by Adding Information, 63	• Using Pronoun I, 59	• Science/Social Studies, 59 • Science/Social Studies, 61 • Language Arts, 63	• Writer's Block, 59, 61, 63 • ESL Strategy, 59, 61, 63 • Home-School Connection, 59, 61, 63	• Teacher Checklist, 37 • Benchmark Papers, 38–44 • Portfolio, 63 • Teacher and Peer Conferencing, 58, 60, 62
Lesson 3 STORY ABOUT A BEST FRIEND pp. 64–71 (7–9 days)	• Using Illustrations in Writing, 64 • Problem, 67 • Sequence Events Using a Story Map, 69	• Exclamation Point, 71	• Social Studies, 67 • Language Arts, 69 • Social Studies, 71	• Writer's Block, 67, 69, 71 • ESL Strategy, 67, 69, 71 • Home-School Connection, 67, 69, 71	• Teacher Checklist, 37 • Benchmark Papers, 38–44 • Portfolio, 71 • Teacher and Peer Conferencing, 66, 68, 70
Lesson 4 STORY ABOUT A PET pp. 72–79 (7–9 days)	• Setting, 72 • Organization: Beginning, Middle, End, 75 • Reader Interest: Write a Strong Conclusion, 79	• Capital Letter at Beginning of a Sentence, 77	• Social Studies, 75 • Language Arts, 77 • Math, 79	• Writer's Block, 75, 77, 79 • ESL Strategy, 75, 77, 79 • Home-School Connection, 75, 77, 79	• Teacher Checklist, 37 • Benchmark Papers, 38–44 • Portfolio, 79 • Teacher and Peer Conferencing, 74, 76, 78
Lesson 5 NEWS STORY pp. 80–87 (7–9 days)	• Identify Form: Real vs. Make-Believe, 80 • Reader Interest: Writing a Strong Title, 83 • Order of Events and Ideas, 87	• Capitalization: Days and Dates, 85	• Social Studies, 83 • Music, 85 • Language Arts, 87	• Writer's Block, 83, 85, 87 • ESL Strategy, 83, 85, 87 • Home-School Connection, 83, 85, 87	• Teacher Checklist, 37 • Benchmark Papers, 38–44 • Portfolio, 87 • Teacher and Peer Conferencing, 82, 84, 86

Making the Reading-Writing Connection
Writing to Tell a Story

You may want to add the following books to your classroom library. Each category of book represents one form of writing children will be introduced to in *Writing to Tell a Story*. The books serve as models for good writing and are valuable resources to use throughout each lesson. The suggested titles offer opportunities for you to read to the class as well as for children to read themselves.

Use literature to introduce a writing form, to show a model of successful writing, to enhance minilessons, to focus on grammar and usage, or to expand each lesson.

FRIENDLY LETTER

The Jolly Postman: Or Other People's Letters
by Janet and Allan Ahlberg. Little, Brown & Co., 1986. Children open envelopes to peek at real mail as the jolly postman covers his route.

Yours Truly, Goldilocks
by Alma Flor Ada. Illustrated by Leslie Tryon. Atheneum, 1998. As familiar storybook characters write letters to plan a party, some bullies write about plans to cause trouble.

Good-bye, Curtis
by Kevin Henkes. Illustrated by Marisabina Russo. Greenwillow, 1995. When the mail carrier retires, the neighbors give him presents and a party.

STORY ABOUT ME

When I Was Five
by Arthur Howard. Harcourt Brace & Co., 1996. A six-year-old reminisces about what he liked when he was a five-year-old.

My Name Is Georgia
by Jeanette Winter. Silver Whistle, 1998. From the time she was a young girl, Georgia O'Keefe knew she wanted to be an artist.

Owl Moon
by Jane Yolen. Illustrated by John Schoenherr. Philomel Books, 1987. Late one winter night, a little girl and her father go owling.

STORY ABOUT A BEST FRIEND

My New Boy
by Joan Phillips. Illustrated by Lynn Munsinger. Random House, 1986. A little black puppy "acquires" a boy and shares his feelings about his new best friend.

Lizzy and Skunk
by Marie-Louise Fitzpatrick. Dorling-Kindersley, 2000. Lizzy learns to overcome her fears with the help of her friend.

We Are Best Friends
by Aliki. Morrow, 1982. Two friends learn to get along in this narrative.

STORY ABOUT A PET

Daddy, Could I Have an Elephant?
by Jake Wolf. Illustrated by Marylin Hafner. Puffin Books, 1998. At first Tony wants a pet elephant or a gorilla, but after talking with Daddy, he decides a puppy would be better.

The Best Pet Yet
by Louise Vitellaro Tidd. Photographs by Dorothy Handelman. Millbrook Press, 1998. After considering various pets in the pet shop, a young boy finally chooses a pet rabbit.

Any Kind of Dog
by Lynn Reiser. Greenwillow, 1992. Mom says dogs are too much trouble and offers many other kinds of pets before she finally gives in.

NEWS STORY

Some Good News
by Cynthia Rylant. Illustrated by Wendy Anderson Halperin. Simon & Schuster, 1999. Three cousins put together a neighborhood newspaper.

The Furry News: How to Make a Newspaper
by Loreen Leedy. Holiday House, 1993. Inside information about how a newspaper is put together.

Mr. Duvall Reports the News
by Jill D. Duvall. Photographs by Lili Duvall. Children's Press, 1997. A TV reporter gathers facts, writes his story, and delivers it on air.

The Classroom Writing Center
Writing to Tell a Story

Children are probably feeling more comfortable with different kinds of writing. As children learn about *Writing to Tell a Story*, promote story writing in the writing center.

◆ Create a dramatic play area near your writing center. Include props, puppets, and costumes for reenacting stories written by the children.

◆ Make available drawing software that enables children to add text to drawings they have made or from stamps they have used.

◆ Display books that model the kinds of writing in this unit. See the list of suggested books at the beginning of the unit.

◆ Include a prominent Author's Chair in your writing center. Make the chair special by putting a decorative label on it.

Create a Bulletin Board for Writing to Tell a Story

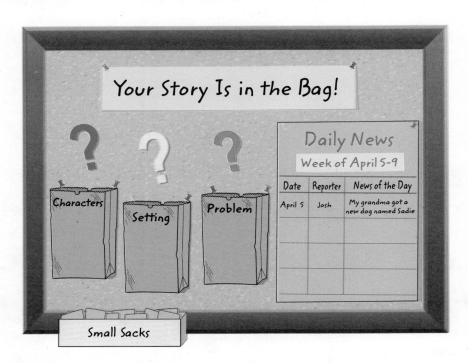

Create a bulletin board that focuses on writing stories with characters as well as news stories. Here are some ideas.

◆ For the "Daily News" corner, make a chart that allows one child each day to be the reporter and write news he or she would like the class to know.

◆ Attach three large paper bags to the board. Label each with one of the following: Character, Setting, Problem. Fill the Character and Setting bags with pictures and the Problem bag with simple story problems. Children select one or more character pictures, a setting picture, and a problem and then work on a story.

Connecting Multiple Intelligences
Writing to Tell a Story

The following activities focus on specific prewriting, drafting, revising, and publishing ideas for children who demonstrate intelligence in different ways: talent and skill with words (linguistic), with numbers (logical-mathematical), with pictures (spatial), with movement (bodily/kinesthetic), with people (interpersonal), with self (intrapersonal), with music (musical), and/or with nature (environmental or naturalist).

Linguistic
Prewriting — Talk with a partner about your plan for a story.
Publishing — Make a tape recording of your letter to send to a friend or family member.

Logical-Mathematical
Prewriting — Draw a series of numbered boxes for the scenes of your story.
Drafting/Revising — Talk with a partner about problems your story characters are having and how they could be solved.

Spatial
Prewriting — Use three colors of paper to write the beginning, middle, and end of a story.
Publishing — Add drawings to your news story to show what happened.

Bodily Kinesthetic
Publishing — Design special stationery to write your friendly letter.
Perform a story you have written for classmates.

Writing to Tell a Story

Environmental (Naturalist)
Prewriting — Plan to write a news story about animals or people who are saving the environment.
Publishing — Add photos or drawings of a pet animal to your story.

Intrapersonal
Prewriting — Look through family photo albums to find an idea for a story about yourself.
Drafting — Find a quiet place to write. Read your writing aloud to see if it sounds all right.

Interpersonal
Prewriting — Talk with your best friend to plan ideas for your story about him or her.
Revising — Conference with one or more peers to decide ways to improve a story about yourself.

Musical
Prewriting — Write a story about yourself that tells about an experience you had with music.
Publishing — Use simple sound effects to tell or read aloud a story you have written.

Name _____ Date _____

Letter

Use this page to write a letter.

Date _____

Dear _____,

_____

_____

_____

_____

_____

_____

 **Your friend,**

_____

Name _____ Date _____

Story Web

Use the web to plan your story.

Story Chart

Use the chart to plan your story.

Characters

Setting

Problem

Ending

Name _____ Date _____

Story Map

Write about what happens in your story.

Beginning

Middle

End

Evaluating Student Writing

Writing to Tell a Story

The Write Direction offers a variety of assessment options. The following are short descriptions of the assessment opportunities available in this unit. Just select the assessment option that works best for you.

Types of Assessment	Writing Lessons
Benchmark Papers Annotated student writing models are provided as benchmarks for evaluating children's writing. Children's writing can be compared to these models, which represent different developmental stages as specified in the Developing Writer's Assessment Continuum.	Student samples for writing to tell a story, levels 1–7, pages 38–44
Checklists The Teacher Evaluation Checklist helps track children's progress as their writing skills develop.	• Teacher Evaluation Checklist, page 37
Portfolio Assessment Children's work generated throughout the writing process may be used in creating individual portfolios illustrating children's progress as writers. Suggested pieces for a portfolio include completed works and works-in-progress, graphic organizers, logs, and journals.	• Friendly Letter, page 55 • Story About Me, page 63 • Story About a Best Friend, page 71 • Story About a Pet, page 79 • News Story, page 87
Teacher and Peer Conferencing Throughout each lesson in this unit, there are opportunities to interact with children, informally questioning them about their progress and concerns. Children also have opportunities to interact with one another to ask questions, share ideas, and react to the partner's writing.	• Friendly Letter, pages 50, 52, 54 • Story About Me, pages 58, 60, 62 • Story About a Best Friend, pages 66, 68, 70 • Story About a Pet, pages 74, 76, 78 • News Story, pages 82, 84, 86

Teacher Evaluation Checklist
Writing to Tell a Story

Name of Writer _____

Date _____

Writing Mode _____

Use this checklist when you are evaluating a child's
- **friendly letter**
- **story about me**
- **story about a best friend**
- **story about a pet**
- **news story**

	YES	NO	Recommendations to Child
Is the topic appropriate for the story line?	☐	☐	
Is the writing focused on the topic?	☐	☐	
Does the writing have a clear beginning, middle, and end?	☐	☐	
Is the sequence of events clear?	☐	☐	
Are the events presented in the right order?	☐	☐	
Does the writer adhere to the conventions of grammar? usage? spelling? punctuation? capitalization?	☐ ☐ ☐ ☐ ☐	☐ ☐ ☐ ☐ ☐	
Is the handwriting legible?	☐	☐	
Was the work done neatly?	☐	☐	

37

Emerging Writer: Level 1

Writing to Tell a Story

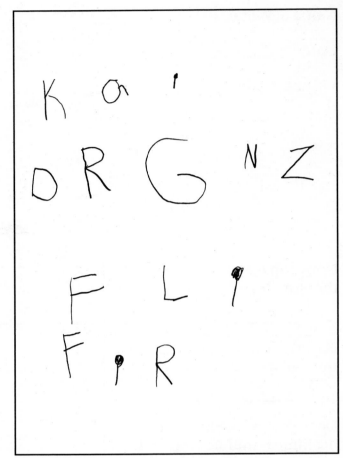

The dragon flies.

Conventions

Sentence Structure Includes no evidence of intended message.

Directionality, Spacing, and Punctuation Places squiggles, other shapes, letterlike shapes, and/or letters randomly.

Letter Formation and Capitalization Forms squiggles, other shapes, and/or letterlike shapes.

Spelling Represents words using letterlike shapes and/or letters with no letter-sound correspondence to the intended word; dictation needed to read all words.

Content

Supporting Details Includes no evidence of intended articles or modifiers.

Word Choice Includes no evidence of intended words.

Emerging Writer: Level 2
Writing to Tell a Story

My baby chicken.

Conventions

Sentence Structure Includes 1 intended word or phrase.

Directionality, Spacing, and Punctuation Places letterlike shapes or letters in a left to right direction and may have a space between 2 words.

Letter Formation and Capitalization Forms mostly uppercase letters; may form 1 word using lowercase letters.

Spelling Represents 1–2 words by recording at least 1 dominant sound; may spell 1 word conventionally; dictation needed to read most words.

Content

Supporting Details Includes 1 intended article and/or modifier.

Word Choice Uses 1–3 intended high-frequency routine words.

a cat   scratched   me and my mom

acatSXaN meMmom

A cat scratched me and my mom.

Conventions

Sentence Structure Includes 1 intended simple sentence.

Directionality, Spacing, and Punctuation Places letters and/or words in a left to right direction and leaves spaces between 3 or more words; may attempt punctuation.

Letter Formation and Capitalization Forms 2 or more words using lowercase letters.

Spelling Represents most words by recording 1 or more dominant sounds; may spell 2–3 different words conventionally; dictation needed to read some words.

Content

Supporting Details Includes 2 intended modifiers.

Word Choice Uses 4 or more intended high-frequency routine words.

Emerging Writer: Level 4
Writing to Tell a Story

Title The cat is hom. [Home]

The cat is in the
cage [cage]
caegse, [cage]
It guht oht. [got] [out]
It fuand is Wa [found] [it's] [way]
hom.. [home]

Conventions

Sentence Structure Includes 2–4 simple sentences and/or 1 compound or complex sentence.

Sentence Variation Begins all sentences with the same word.

Punctuation Ends 1 sentence or the story with a period.

Capitalization Capitalizes first word in 1 sentence; may capitalize other letters inappropriately.

Spelling Spells 4–8 different words conventionally; dictation needed to read a few words.

Content

Opening Begins with an action or a fact in the first of 2–3 related thoughts or sentences.

Transitions Uses 1 transitional word or phrase to connect thoughts. (Note: No transitional word or phrase is scored level 3.)

Development of Ideas Uses a glimmer of at least 1 strategy to develop an idea.

Supporting Details Includes 3–4 different modifiers.

Word Choice Uses 1 precise word that is more exact in meaning.

Closing Stops with no ending after 2 or more related thoughts or sentences.

Emerging Writer: Level 5

Writing to Tell a Story

ouns a por a time
there was a woof.
nambd roofis he was
all a lone he was a
teenajre.
nambd he met a ber
a Jiyent casy. casy was
echuthr they Plad with
frens. they wer troo
sumpthig they hrd a nos
went boom they
ran a way the nos was a
man wus in the Jugol
they hid they wr saf

Conventions

Sentence Structure Includes at least 5 simple sentences and/or 2 compound or complex sentences.

Sentence Variation Varies the way 2–3 sentences begin.

Punctuation Ends 2 to 4 sentences with periods; may use other forms of punctuation appropriately at times.

Capitalization Capitalizes first word in 2–4 sentences; may use other forms of capitalization appropriately at times.

Spelling Spells 9 or more different one-syllable words conventionally.

Content

Opening Begins with an action or a fact in the first of 4 or more related sentences.

Transitions Uses 2 different transitional words or phrases to connect thoughts or ideas.

Development of Ideas Uses 1 strategy somewhat effectively to develop an idea.

Supporting Details Includes 5 or more different modifiers.

Word Choice Uses 2 precise words that are more exact in meaning.

Closing Signals ending with "The End."

Emerging Writer: Level 6
Writing to Tell a Story

The snake and the boy.
Once there was a boy.
His name was Jacb.
He wanted a snake
for a pet. When he
went by the pet shop he said
mom can I have a snake for
a pet yes you may
have a snake for a pet. But
she could not buy it

because it was too much
mony to buy it. That
night a house was doing
a yard sale Jacb went
to it. Jacb fianlley
got a snake for his pet.

Conventions

Sentence Structure Includes 3 compound and/or complex sentences.

Sentence Variation Varies the way 4–5 sentences begin.

Punctuation Ends at least 5 sentences with periods; or may use other forms of punctuation appropriately at times.

Capitalization Capitalizes first word in at least 5 sentences; may use other forms of capitalization appropriately at times.

Spelling Spells 3–5 different two-syllable words conventionally.

Content

Opening Creates a brief context or introduction with 1 opening sentence.

Transitions Uses 3 different transitional words or phrases to connect thoughts or ideas.

Development of Ideas Uses 1 strategy somewhat effectively and at least a glimmer of 1 other strategy to develop ideas.

Supporting Details Supports 1 idea with details in at least 3 sentences.

Word Choice Uses 3–4 precise words that are more exact in meaning.

Closing Creates a logical ending or resolves the problem in at least 1 sentence; may include "The End."

Emerging Writer: Level 7
Writing to Tell a Story

Title: The whale and the poler bear.

Once upon a time there lived a poler bear and a whale. They were best friends. The poler bear's name is Polly. The whale's name is Wally. Polly is a female. Wally is a male. They lived in the Artic togther. The Artic was very cold. There was many snow in the Artic. One day

when Polly and Wally were playing hide and seek a hanter was near by watching. The hanter had a net with him. But then when Polly said time out the hanter jumped out of his hiding place and throgh the net on Polly. Wally was scarred so he went to hide in the water. Then the hanter draged the net witch Polly was in. Then the hanter throgh the net in his truck, then he drove away.

Wally gasped. Wally swam next to to the truck and when the truck stpped Wally got his tail up and slam slammed it on the water facing the truck and splash!

Conventions

Sentence Structure Includes 4–6 compound and/or complex sentences.

Sentence Variation Varies the way 6–7 sentences begin.

Punctuation Ends at least 6 sentences with periods and uses 2 other forms of punctuation appropriately most of the time.

Capitalization Capitalizes first word in at least 6 sentences and uses 1 other form of capitalization appropriately most of the time.

Spelling Spells 6–8 different two-syllable words conventionally.

Content

Opening Creates a context or introduction somewhat effectively with 2 opening sentences.

Transitions Uses 4–5 different transitional words, phrases, and/or clauses to connect thoughts or ideas.

Development of Ideas Uses at least 2 strategies somewhat effectively to develop ideas.

Supporting Details Supports 2 ideas with details in at least 3 sentences; may be paragraphed.

Word Choice Uses 5–6 precise words or phrases that are more exact in meaning.

Closing Creates a brief closing (wrap-up, summary, conclusion) with at least 1 sentence; may include "The End."

Home Letter

Dear Family,

Do you enjoy telling a great story at a family dinner? Maybe you'd rather curl up with a good book or read about the community in a newspaper. Some people are great at writing funny stories in a letter.

During the next few weeks your child will learn about writing to tell a story by learning how to write a friendly letter and write stories about topics they know quite well—themselves, a best friend, and a pet. Your child will even become an ace news reporter to write a news story. You can look forward to reading these stories as your child works on drafting them and publishing them.

Here are some ways you can support your child's story writing.

1 A travel log will keep your child writing whenever you take a trip. Together you can write stories about what you experienced. Include photos, drawings, and travel memorabilia with the writing.

2 If your child has use of a computer at home, send E-mail messages to family and friends who live at a distance.

3 Create a family newsletter to send out periodically. Involve all family members by having them write articles and choose photos.

4 Check out these books that reinforce story writing.
- ◆ *Don't Forget to Write* by Martina Selway. Econo-Clad Books, 1999. While visiting Grandad's farm, Rosie expresses her feelings as she adds to the letter she is writing home.
- ◆ *Lucy's Summer* by Donald Hall. Harcourt Brace, 1995. Seven-year-old Lucy spends the summer of 1910 on a farm in New Hampshire. She helps with canning, enjoys a train trip, and makes a special visit to Woolworth's toy counter.
- ◆ *Our Granny* by Margaret Wild. Tichnor & Fields, 1994. Two children present a list of all types of grandmothers interspersed with loving comments about their own granny.

Sincerely,

Carta para el hogar

Estimada familia,

¿Les gusta hacer buenos cuentos a la hora de la cena? O tal vez prefieran acurrucarse con un buen libro o leer los acontecimientos del barrio en el periódico. A alguna gente le encanta escribir cuentos divertidos en sus cartas. Durante las próximas semanas su hijo/a va a estudiar cómo se escribe para relatar un cuento por medio de cartas amistosas y cuentos acerca de temas bien conocidos —ellos mismos, un mejor amigo y un animalito de mascota. Su hijo/a también se convertirá en reportero estrella escribiendo para un noticiero. Puede participar en la lectura de estos cuentos en todas las etapas, mientras su hijo/a redacta el borrador y luego los publica.

He aquí algunas maneras en que pueden ayudar a su hijo/a en la escritura de cuentos.

1 Llevar un diario de viaje sirve para mantener a su hijo/a escribiendo cada vez que toman un viaje. Juntos pueden redactar cuentos de lo que hayan experimentado. Al escribir, incluyan fotos, dibujos y recuerdos del viaje.

2 Si su hijo/a tiene una computadora en clase, envíen mensajes por correo electrónico a familiares y amistades que viven lejos.

3 Creen un boletín de la familia para ser enviado periódicamente. Involucren a todos los familiares pidiéndoles que escriban artículos y que elijan fotos.

4 Busquen libros en la biblioteca que sirvan para reforzar los conceptos de la escritura de cuentos.
   - *Don't Forget to Write* por Martina Selway. Econo-Clad Books, 1999. En una visita a la finca de la abuela, Rosie expresa sus sentimientos íntimos agregando cosas a la carta que le escribe a la familia.
   - *Lucy's Summer* por Donald Hall. Harcourt Brace, 1995. Lucy, de siete años de edad, pasa el verano de 1910 en una finca en New Hampshire. Ayuda a preservar alimentos en lata, disfruta de un viaje en tren y de una visita al mostrador de los juguetes del almacén Woolworth.
   - *Our Granny* por Margarey Wild. Tichnor & Fields, 1994. Dos niños presentan una lista de todos los tipos de abuelas que hay, intercalando comentarios de cariño acerca de su propia abuelita.

Sinceramente,

Teacher Notes

Friendly Letter

Introduction

OBJECTIVES

★ **RESPOND** to a student model of a friendly letter.

★ **RECOGNIZE** the characteristics of a friendly letter.

1 Building Background

Invite children to name friends or relatives who live far away, such as grandparents or friends who have moved. Ask children to tell different ways they keep in touch with these people. Point out that one way is to write letters and send them in the mail.

2 Meet the Writer

Direct children's attention to the friendly letter on page 8 of the Big Book of Writing Models. Point to Vincent's signature and explain that he is the letter's author. Read the text in the speech bubble. Discuss why Vincent wrote the letter.

3 Respond to a Model

Read Vincent's letter aloud to the class. Point to and name each part of the letter (date, greeting, message, closing, and writer's name). Ask children to retell Vincent's story in their own words. List their responses in a story map titled "What Happened to Vincent." You can use the Story Map on page 51 of the Big Book.

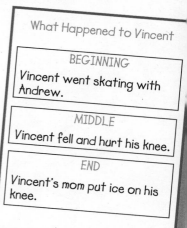

What Happened to Vincent

BEGINNING
Vincent went skating with Andrew.

MIDDLE
Vincent fell and hurt his knee.

END
Vincent's mom put ice on his knee.

Meeting Individual Needs

LITERATURE CONNECTION

Before children write their friendly letters, you may want to introduce them to one of these books.

1. *The Jolly Postman: Or Other People's Letters* by Janet and Allan Ahlberg. Little, Brown & Co., 1986. Children open envelopes to peek at real mail as the jolly postman covers his route.

2. *Yours Truly, Goldilocks* by Alma Flor Ada. Illustrated by Leslie Tryon. Atheneum, 1998. As familiar storybook characters write letters to plan a party, some bullies write about plans to cause trouble.

3. *Good-bye, Curtis* by Kevin Henkes. Illustrated by Marisabina Russo. Greenwillow, 1995. When the neighborhood mail carrier retires, the neighbors give him presents and a party. What does Curtis do on his first day of retirement? He writes thank-you letters!

Mini-Lesson

Brainstorming

Introduce Introduce brainstorming by naming a general topic, such as school. Ask children to name as many words as possible that tell about "school." Tell children that what they are doing is called brainstorming. Explain that there are no right or wrong ideas in brainstorming. The purpose is to think of as many different ideas as possible.

Model Reread Vincent's letter and point out that he wrote about something interesting that he did. Write *Things Our Class Has Done* on chart paper, and have children contribute ideas about activities the class has done together. List all the ideas they suggest.

Summarize/Apply Explain that one of the hardest things about writing is deciding what to write about. Brainstorming is one way to find an idea to write about. Ask children to create their own personal lists titled *What I've Done*. They can list ideas from the class chart as well as add ideas from their own lives with friends and families.

Friendly Letter

from the

Big Book of Writing Models

page 8

Friendly Letter

Prewriting

OBJECTIVES

★ **BRAINSTORM** and **SELECT** an idea for a friendly letter.

★ **RECOGNIZE** the use of a story map for prewriting.

★ **CONTRIBUTE** to a story map in a shared prewriting activity.

★ **MAKE** a story map to identify information to be included in a friendly letter.

1 Introduce Prewriting

Recall something the class recently did together, such as visit the library or attend a school play. Encourage children to tell what you did step by step. Write their responses on the board in the order that the events happened. Reread the list, pointing out what happened in the beginning, the middle, and the end. Explain that stories or events you write about in a letter also have a beginning, a middle, and an end.

2 Shared Writing

Explain that choosing something to write about is one of the first things a writer does. Ask children to think about letters they have received and what the writer said. Was the letter fun to read? Did they write back? Tell children you are going to share a plan with them for a letter about a trip to the zoo.

MODELED WRITING Use the information on the sample story map on this page to fill in the story map on page 51 of the Big Book. Point out that good writers plan what they are going to write about before they begin. Share the story map with the class and discuss how an event has a beginning, a middle, and an end.

INTERACTIVE WRITING Explain that writers sometimes talk with other writers, or brainstorm, to get ideas. Invite children to ask questions or suggest other information to add to the chart. Have volunteers come up and write their ideas on the chart. Point out that writers often include a lot of information in their charts and then choose the best ideas to write about.

3 Independent Writing

Have children choose a person to write a letter to. Make copies of the blackline master on page 35 for children to use to tell about something fun or interesting that happened to them. Remind them that they can get ideas from their brainstorming list, their journals, or the school activity calendar. Encourage them to use the story map you made as a guide.

EMERGENT WRITERS Have children draw pictures on the story map to show each part of their story. Then guide them as they write simple phrases to tell about each picture. Guide their composition to be sure the text is one that can be remembered and repeated.

TEACHER CONFERENCE You may want to use the following questions during your conferences with children to discuss their story maps.

- *How did you decide whom to write to?*
- *How did you choose one idea to write about?*
- *Do you have a beginning, a middle, and an end?*

PEER CONFERENCE Select pairs of children to share their story maps with one another. Suggest that writers ask listeners the following questions.

- *What do you think about my idea?*
- *Do I need to tell any more?*

BEGINNING
class trip to zoo
rode on bus

MIDDLE
saw big giraffes
played in petting zoo
saw funny monkeys

END
came home on bus
talked about field trip

Mini Lesson

Choosing a Topic

Introduce Show the brainstorming chart titled *Things Our Class Has Done* from page 48. Remind children that brainstorming helps writers think of many different ideas. Some of the ideas are interesting and some are not. Some ideas are too big to write about in a short letter, and some will be just right.

Model Discuss whom the letter might be written to: a friend, a relative, or a parent. Talk about how to decide which idea will be a good topic for a letter. Explain why some topics would be too long or not interesting to the person who will read the letter.

Summarize/Apply Remind children that their ideas should be interesting but just long enough to write about in a short letter. Have children review their personal *What I've Done* lists, cross out ideas that will not work, and circle their favorite ideas before beginning their story maps.

WRITER'S BLOCK

Problem	Solution
Children can't decide whom to write to.	Ask children to think about a person they would like to share a story with or someone who would enjoy receiving a letter or whom they would like to get a reply from. Then they can choose the best story to share with that person.

ESL STRATEGY

Encourage English-language learners to complete their story maps by drawing pictures of what happened. Then help them label and number the pictures in order.

HOME-SCHOOL CONNECTION

Have children ask family members for ideas about whom to write to and then to supply the addresses.

WRITING ACROSS THE CURRICULUM

Science/Math One way for children to recall what they learned by doing a science experiment is to tell what happened in their own words. Children can use a story map to recall the steps in the correct order.

Measuring Rain

BEGINNING

I got a cup.

I put the cup outside.

MIDDLE

Rain fell into the cup.

When rain stopped, I brought the cup back inside.

END

I measured the water with a ruler.

I wrote the number on a chart.

Friendly Letter

Drafting

OBJECTIVES

★ **RECOGNIZE** the characteristics of a friendly letter.

★ **RESPOND** to a first draft in a shared writing activity.

★ **USE** a story map as a plan to write a first draft.

1 Introduce Drafting

Reread Vincent's friendly letter to the class and point out each part of the letter. Help children understand that Vincent wrote about something that happened to him for the message of the letter. He used the words *I* and *my*, and he wrote about one idea.

2 Shared Writing

MODELED WRITING Remind children that they have already chosen a person to write a letter to and planned the story they want to tell that person. Display the story map you made in prewriting and reread it with the children. Copy the model letter on this page onto chart paper, using the proper form for a letter, or use the write-on pages in the Big Book on pages 53–56.

Read the letter, pointing out the date, the greeting, the message, the closing, and the writer's name. Draw attention to the message part of the letter and explain that the writer used the story map to write this part of the letter. With the children, identify the beginning, middle, and end of the event.

INTERACTIVE WRITING As you identify the different parts of the story, have volunteers check them off on the story map. Ask children if there is anything they would like to change or add. Encourage them to come up and write their ideas on the chart paper.

3 Independent Writing

Have children follow the model in the Big Book for the form of a friendly letter, or make copies of the blackline master on page 32 for them to use. Encourage them to follow their story maps when they write the message part of their letters.

EMERGENT WRITERS Provide children with a simple letter form with placeholders for letter parts. Help them write the date and greeting, then talk about what to put in the message. Help them write the message and the closing. They can add the signature.

TEACHER CONFERENCE Use questions such as the following during writing conferences to discuss children's drafts.

- *How did you use your story map as you wrote your letter?*

- *Do you think the person receiving the letter will like it?*

PEER CONFERENCE Invite children to read their drafts to a partner. Have the writers ask the listeners questions about their letters.

- *Would you like to receive this letter?*

- *Did you understand my story?*

- *Do you think I should add anything to my letter?*

January 18

Dear William

Our class went to the zoo.

We saw tall giraffes and munkys.

We went to the petting zoo and

ate lunch. It was late afternoon

when we came back to school.

we talked about what we liked

best about our trip.

Your friend,
Ann

Mini Lesson

Sequencing Events by Cutting and Pasting Sentences

Introduce Remind children that the events in the story that Vincent tells in the message of his letter are told in the order in which they happened. Sometimes when writing a draft, it's easy for a writer to forget the exact order in which things happened. An easy way to fix this problem is to cut the sentences apart and move them around.

Model Copy Vincent's letter onto chart paper. Begin each sentence on a separate line and skip a space between each sentence. Write one or two sentences out of order. Demonstrate how to cut apart the sentences. Then invite children to use a pocket chart to put the sentences in the correct order. Read them together in the new order.

Summarize/Apply Remind children that it is easy to forget the right order in which things happened when writing a first draft. Suggest that they try writing each sentence on a separate line in case they need to cut their sentences apart and put them in a different order.

WRITER'S BLOCK

Problem	Solution
Children worry more about letter form than content.	Remind children that during revising and editing they will have the opportunity to make changes.

ESL STRATEGY

Invite children with varying language proficiencies to read their letters to a partner. Partners can react to the letter's message and offer a response.

HOME-SCHOOL CONNECTION

Encourage children to read aloud their drafts to family members. They can also show family members their story maps and ask if they should add any other interesting details to the message of their letters.

WRITING ACROSS THE CURRICULUM

Art Tell children that writing a draft is like making a sketch before painting or coloring a picture. A draft in art class would be the pencil sketch that they make and can then erase and change before completing the picture with paint or crayons.

Friendly Letter

Revising/Editing

OBJECTIVES

★ **RECOGNIZE** that writing can be improved by revising it.

★ **CONTRIBUTE** to the revision of a friendly letter in a shared writing activity.

★ **REVISE** a first draft of a friendly letter.

★ **RECOGNIZE** that story events need to be told in the order in which they happened.

1 Introduce Revising and Editing

Explain to children that now is the time for them to add ideas, make changes, or fix mistakes in their letters. They need to revise to make sure their letter makes sense and has all the letter parts.

Reread Vincent's letter to the class, pointing out the date, greeting, message, closing, and writer's name. Ask children if there's anything else they would add to Vincent's letter. Record children's suggestions on the board.

2 Shared Writing

MODELED WRITING Use the model on this page to make changes to the letter about the zoo. Reread the letter, pointing out the changes the writer made as you go. Point out the different parts of a letter: date, greeting, message, closing, writer's name.

Model how to draw a line through a word you want to replace or change. Then show children how to use a caret to add a word or missing information. Give each child a copy of the revising and editing marks on page 26 of the Teacher Resource Guide.

INTERACTIVE WRITING After discussing and modeling one or two changes, invite volunteers to make other changes on the chart, following your example. As children become more familiar with revising, you may want to present the draft without the revisions and have children find the mistakes and make changes using the revising marks they've learned.

3 Independent Writing

Allow time for children to quietly reread their drafts aloud to themselves. As they read, suggest that they ask themselves questions such as the following.

* *Have I told all the important events?*
* *Did I include a closing and signature?*
* *Will my story be clear to my reader?*

EMERGENT WRITERS Have children who need extra help read their letters to you. Select one thing, such as the order of the events, for them to correct. Show them how to write the sentences on individual strips of paper and put them in order.

TEACHER CONFERENCE You may wish to use the following questions when children share their revised drafts with you.

* *Do you show the date, greeting, message, closing, and your name in the letter?*
* *Does your message make sense?*
* *Did you check the spelling in your letter?*

PEER CONFERENCE Invite children to read their revised letter to partners. Suggest that the writers ask the listeners the following questions.

* *How do you like my letter?*
* *Do you have any questions about my story?*

January 18

Dear William,

Our class went to the zoo.

We saw tall giraffes and (munkys). *monkeys*

We went to the petting zoo and ate lunch. It was late afternoon when we came back to school.

we talked about what we liked best about our trip.

Your friend,
Ann

Publishing

OBJECTIVE

★ **PUBLISH** a friendly letter.

Children will need to make clean copies of their letters if they publish them. Invite children to use these suggestions to share their friendly letters.

AUTHOR'S CHAIR Supply children with a variety of colorful stationery for them to use to publish their letters. Invite children to read their letters from the Author's Chair before mailing them.

IT'S IN THE MAIL Have children bring in the addresses of the people to whom they wrote. Provide envelopes and stamps. Walk children to the nearest mailbox or mail the letters from the school office.

SHOW AND TELL Distribute copies of children's letters to partners. While one child reads, the letter's author can act out his or her narrative.

ASSESSMENT OPPORTUNITIES

PORTFOLIO ASSESSMENT If children choose to include their letters in their portfolios, have them also include their prewriting charts and drafts.

TEACHER HOLISTIC ASSESSMENT Use the Teacher Evaluation Checklist on page 37 to evaluate children's friendly letters.

BENCHMARK PAPERS You may want to use the benchmark papers on pages 38–44 to evaluate children's writing. There is one paper for each level of writing on the Developing Writer's Assessment Continuum.

Meeting Individual Needs

Mini Lesson — Draft vs. Final Copy

Introduce Remind children that writing is so much more than putting marks on paper. Once a good writer plans what he or she will write, the writer then makes a draft by putting ideas into sentences. Writing doesn't end there. A good writer goes back to make changes to make the writing clearer and to check for capital letters, spelling, and punctuation. Then the writer is ready to make a final copy to share.

Model Display the revised/edited draft and final copy of your friendly letter. Ask children to describe ways the draft is different from the final copy. Talk about the changes that were made before making the final copy.

Summarize/Apply Remind children that a draft is supposed to be a "first try" at writing a story, poem, or letter. They should not worry about making mistakes. Have children compare their revised/edited drafts to their published pieces to see how much their writing improved.

WRITER'S BLOCK

Problem
Children have difficulty checking the form of their letters.

Solution
Display Vincent's letter from page 8 of the Big Book. Use self-stick notes to label the date, greeting, message, closing, and writer's name.

ESL STRATEGY

Help English-language learners with the terms *date, greeting, message, closing,* and *writer's name* by writing each word on self-stick notes and then cutting a letter into the matching parts. Have children rebuild the letter and use the self-stick notes as labels.

HOME-SCHOOL CONNECTION

Children may wish to mail letters to family members. Invite the family to write letters back, showing their appreciation or praising children's accomplishments.

WRITING ACROSS THE CURRICULUM

Language Arts Encourage children to use a letter format to retell a favorite part of a story the class has shared. The letter can be written from the child to one character. The message will summarize the story or part of the story.

Story About Me

Introduction

OBJECTIVES

★ **RESPOND** to a student model of a story about me.

★ **RECOGNIZE** the characteristics of a story about me.

1 Building Background

To introduce the idea of writing a story about me (personal narrative), have children draw a picture of themselves doing something they like or are good at. When they have finished, have them tell about their pictures. Encourage them to use the word *I* when they talk about themselves. Display their pictures in the classroom.

2 Meet the Writer

Direct children's attention to the story "All About Me" on page 9 of the Big Book of Writing Models and introduce the writer, Meg Morris. Explain that Meg is in first grade and this is a story she wrote. Read the title "All About Me" and ask children what they think the story is about. Point out Meg's name at the bottom of the page. Explain that writers put their names on their work so that readers know who wrote the stories.

3 Respond to a Model

Read Meg's story aloud to the class. As you read each page, focus children's attention on the pictures and text. When you finish the story, encourage the class to tell what they learned about Meg from her writing. List their responses in a chart titled "What We Learned About Meg."

> **What We Learned About Meg**
> blonde hair
> brown eyes
> 6 years old
> birthday is April 17
> one brother
> one sister
> house is gray
> likes to color
> favorite colors are light blue and light green
> favorite sports are soccer, basketball, hockey
> good at riding bike up a hill

Meeting Individual Needs

LITERATURE CONNECTION
Before your students write their personal narratives, you may want to introduce them to one of these books.

1. *When I Was Five* by Arthur Howard. Harcourt Brace & Co., 1996. A six-year-old reminisces about what he liked when he was a five-year-old.

2. *My Name Is Georgia* by Jeanette Winter. Silver Whistle, 1998. From the time she was a young girl, Georgia O'Keefe knew she wanted to be an artist.

3. *Owl Moon* by Jane Yolen. Illustrated by John Schoenherr. Philomel Books, 1987. Late one winter night a little girl and her father go owling.

Mini Lesson

Title and Author

Introduce Display several familiar books and point out the titles. Explain that the title is the name of the book and tells something about the book. Next, point out the authors' and illustrators' names. Explain that the author is the person who wrote the book and that the illustrator is the person who drew or painted the pictures.

Model Discuss the books you've displayed. Point out that titles can be one or several words and can be serious, funny, or unusual. Encourage children to tell which titles would want to make them read the books and why.

Summarize/Apply Explain that writers try to make their titles interesting so people will want to read the books. Then remind children that when they write books and stories they are the authors and their names will go on the covers.

Story About Me

from the

Big Book of Writing Models

pages 9–16

All About Me

by Meg Morris

My story tells about me and what I like

Meg Morris
New Jersey

My name is Meg. I have blonde hair and brown eyes.

I am 6 years old. My birthday is April 17th.

I have one brother and one sister.

My house is gray, but it doesn't look gray. It looks white.

I like to color. My favorite colors are light blue and light green.

My favorite sports are basketball, soccer and hockey.

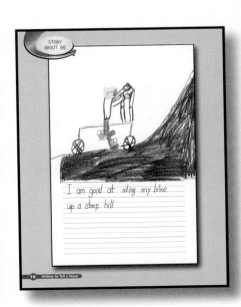

I am good at riding my bike up a steep hill.

Story About Me

Prewriting

OBJECTIVES

★ RECOGNIZE the use of a list for prewriting.

★ CONTRIBUTE to a list in a shared prewriting activity.

★ MAKE a list to identify information to be included in a story about me.

 1 Introduce Prewriting

Have children look around the classroom to find examples of lists, such as a list of children's names or classroom jobs. Encourage them to think of other kinds of lists they or their families might use at home. Point out that lists are important because they help people remember things.

 2 Shared Writing

MODELED WRITING Introduce the idea that good writers plan what they are going to write about before they begin writing. Explain that you are going to write a story about yourself. The first thing you are going to do is make a list of the information you want to share with a reader.

On chart paper, model writing a list similar to the one shown, including information about yourself. Point out that every time you add information to your list you start a new line. Include more information in your list than you will use in your story.

INTERACTIVE WRITING Invite children to suggest information they know about you that they think should be included in your story. Invite them to add the information to your list.

3 Independent Writing

Have children make their own lists of information they would want a reader to know about them. Encourage them to look at their journals for ideas and to use the list you wrote with them as a guide.

EMERGENT WRITERS You may want to suggest that children draw pictures of what they want classmates to know about them and then write the words.

TEACHER CONFERENCE You may want to use the following questions during your conferences with children to discuss their lists.

- *How are you doing?*
- *Was it hard to think of information about yourself?*
- *Is there any more information you want to add?*

PEER CONFERENCE Select pairs of children and have them share their lists with each other. Suggest that the writers ask the listener questions.

- *What do you think of my list?*
- *Do I need to add anything?*

ABOUT ME

brown hair
glasses
teach first grade
live with husband, son,
    and daughter
went to Disney World
dog named Sam
live in a house
play catch with Sam
favorite sports are running
    and fishing
caught a big fish
don't like to clean fish

Using the Pronoun I

Introduce Show children Meg's story in the Big Book along with other books or stories written in the first person. Ask children to name the word writers use to tell about themselves. Conclude that the word is *I*.

Model Use the list of facts about you to model writing sentences using the pronoun *I*. Explain that the word *I* is used when an author is writing to tell about herself or himself. Remind children of Meg's sentences in the Big Book.

Summarize/Apply Invite volunteers to say sentences to tell about themselves, using the word *I* and ideas from the prewriting list they have written. Point out that these are the kinds of sentences they can write in their stories that tell about themselves.

WRITER'S BLOCK

Problem	Solution
Children write too few items in their lists.	If children are having trouble thinking of enough items for their lists, encourage them to look at their journals or find a partner to share ideas with.

ESL STRATEGY
Pair children with varying language proficiencies and have them work together to make their lists.

HOME-SCHOOL CONNECTION
Have children share their lists with their families, and have family members suggest other information or details that could be added.

WRITING ACROSS THE CURRICULUM
Science/Social Studies As children add to the science and social studies sections of their learning logs, encourage them to make lists when appropriate. You may wish to share this example.

What I Know About Frogs

green and brown
can jump
can swim
eat flies
start as tadpoles

Story About Me

Drafting

OBJECTIVES

★ **RECOGNIZE** the characteristics of a story written in the first person.

★ **RESPOND** to a first draft in a shared writing activity.

★ **USE** a list as a plan to write a first draft.

1 Introduce Drafting

Reread Meg's story about herself to the class, encouraging children to tell what happens on each page. Point out how Meg drew pictures of herself, her family, and things she likes to do to help tell her story. She also included details about herself, such as the color of her hair and eyes and some of her favorite things.

2 Shared Writing

MODELED WRITING Explain that just like Meg you are going to write a story about yourself. The list you made will help you remember what you want to say. Point out that you may not use every item on the list.

Write your story on chart paper or use the write-on pages on pages 53–56 of the Big Book. Explain that what you are writing is a draft and that the purpose of a draft is to get your ideas on paper.

A sample story based on the list on page 58 is shown. Notice that not all the items in the list were included in the story.

INTERACTIVE WRITING As you read through your story, have children check off each item included from your list. Ask them if they have any additions or corrections. Encourage them to write their ideas on the chart paper.

3 Independent Writing

Encourage children to put a mark by the items on their lists that they think are important to include and draw a line through items they want to leave out. Have them use their lists as they write their drafts. Reassure them that a first draft is the time to get their ideas on paper and not to worry about spelling or punctuation.

EMERGENT WRITERS Help children who need extra support pick out just two or three items to write about.

TEACHER CONFERENCE You may want to use these questions during your conferences with children to discuss their drafts.

- *How is your writing going?*
- *Why did you decide to start your story this way?*
- *Did you include all the items you marked in your list?*

PEER CONFERENCE Pair children and have them read their stories to one another. Remind them how to behave in a conference.

- *Listen quietly to the other person's story.*
- *Tell what you like about the story.*

A Story About Me
by Mrs. Green

My name is Mrs. Green. I teach first grade. I have brown hair and glasses. I love to teach. I live with my husband, my son, and my daughter. We live in a nice house. We have a dog named Sam. I like to play catch with him in the park. My favorite sports are running and fishing. Last summer we went camping. I caught the biggest fish!

Double-spacing a Draft

Introduce Explain that writers go back and make changes in their writing, so they often leave an extra space between the lines so they have room to make changes.

Model Show children your first draft of a personal narrative and point out the extra line between each line of writing. Explain that you purposely wrote on every other line so you could go back and add information or fix mistakes.

Summarize/Apply Encourage children to double-space their drafts. Suggest they make a small mark at the beginning of every other line so they will remember to skip lines.

WRITER'S BLOCK

Problem	Solution
Children are having difficulty getting started with their first drafts.	Suggest that children look at their lists and pick one piece of information they want to start with.

ESL STRATEGY
Have children speak what they want to write into a tape recorder first. They can replay the recording to help them write their first drafts.

HOME-SCHOOL CONNECTION
Communicate to family members that the purpose of a draft is to get ideas down on paper and that changes and corrections will be made later. Family members can help by recalling details about the experiences children are writing about.

WRITING ACROSS THE CURRICULUM
Science/Social Studies As children write about topics in science and social studies, encourage them to write on every other line so they can go back and add information or make changes later. You may wish to share this example.

Frogs
Frogs are green.

Sometimes they are brown.

They can jump very far because

they have strong back legs.

They can also swim very well.

Story About Me

Revising/Editing

OBJECTIVES

★ **RECOGNIZE** that writing can be improved by revising it.

★ **CONTRIBUTE** to the revision of a story in a shared writing activity.

★ **REVISE** a first draft of a story about me.

★ **RECOGNIZE** the use of the word *I* in a story about me.

1 Introduce Revising and Editing

Introduce the idea that good writers reread their drafts and often go back and make changes or corrections. Writers revise their writing so that it will be clear and make sense to their readers.

Reread Meg's story with the class. Ask if they have any questions about the story. Is there anything else they want to know about Meg? Record children's responses on chart paper.

2 Shared Writing

MODELED WRITING Revisit the story you wrote about yourself with the class. Explain that you want to publish this story and you need to know if it is finished or if it needs any changes. Reread the story to the class. Ask them if there is anything missing or if there is anything else they want to know.

Using a caret, demonstrate how to insert a word to describe someone or something or add a detail that gives more information. Draw a line through any words you want to change or delete.

INTERACTIVE WRITING You may wish to have volunteers draw a line through a word that needs to be changed. They could also show where in the story a word should be inserted and then make the caret.

3 Independent Writing

Have children quietly reread their first drafts aloud to themselves. Encourage them to ask themselves these questions.

- *Have I told enough about myself?*
- *Is there anything I want to add?*

Remind them to use a caret to add words and to draw a line through words they want to change. Suggest that they use the model you revised in Shared Writing as a guide.

EMERGENT WRITERS Have children who need extra support read their drafts to you. Select one thing, such as the spacing between words or the omission of a word, for them to correct.

TEACHER CONFERENCE You may wish to use the following questions when children share their revised drafts with you.

- *What is the most important thing you want your readers to know?*
- *Do you have enough information about it?*

PEER CONFERENCE Have pairs of children read their drafts to one another. Suggest that the writer ask the listener the following questions.

- *Does my story make sense to you?*
- *Is there anything else you want to know?*

A Story About Me
by Mrs. Green

My name is Mrs. Green. I teach first

grade. I have brown hair and glasses. *(new)*

I love to teach. I live with my husband,

my son, and my daughter. We live in a

nice house. We have a dog named Sam. *(blue)* *(with a garden)*

I like to play catch with him in the park.

My favorite sports are running and *(sailing,)*

fishing. Last summer we went camping.

I caught the biggest fish!

Publishing

OBJECTIVE

★ PUBLISH a story about me.

Here are ideas children can use to share their personal narratives with families and classmates.

BOOK DISPLAY Have children each make a cover for their story. Be sure they include titles and their names. Display their books on a bulletin board or table with the title "All About Me."

STORY TIME Have an author's tea with juice and crackers. Invite parents or children from another class to attend. Have volunteers sit in a special chair and read their stories to the group.

MAKE CHARACTERS Draw each child's outline on a large sheet of paper. Cut out the figures and have children add faces, hair, and clothes with markers or crayons. Display the figures along with each child's story.

ASSESSMENT OPPORTUNITIES

PORTFOLIO ASSESSMENT If children choose to include their stories in their portfolios, have them also include their prewriting lists, story maps, and drafts.

TEACHER HOLISTIC ASSESSMENT Use the Teacher Evaluation Checklist on page 37 to evaluate children's personal narratives.

BENCHMARK PAPERS You may want to use the Benchmark Papers on pages 38–44 to evaluate children's writing. There is one benchmark paper for each level of writing on the Developing Writer's Assessment Continuum.

Meeting Individual Needs

Mini Lesson — Adding Information

Introduce Write the following sentence on the board: *I have a dog.* Ask children what the sentence tells them. If they close their eyes, can they see the dog? Point out that the writer has not given very much information about the dog.

Model Have children suggest what questions they would ask to get a better picture of the dog. Based on their questions, write a description of the dog. It may look similar to this.

> *I have a big, shaggy dog named Fred. He looks like a baby bear. When I come home, he runs in circles and jumps in the air.*

Summarize/Apply Point out that a good writer gives enough information and details so that the reader can see what the writer sees.

WRITER'S BLOCK

Problem	Solution
Children want to add or change information but don't know how to start.	Have them first tell you what they want to say and then write it.

ESL STRATEGY

For children whose native language is not English, point out the word *I* in Meg's story and explain that it refers to the girl who wrote the story. Have children give the words for *I* in their native languages and then use *I* in a sentence about themselves.

HOME-SCHOOL CONNECTION

Encourage children to bring in photographs of themselves and their families to share with the class.

WRITING ACROSS THE CURRICULUM

Language Arts As children write about books in their literature log, encourage them to include the title of the book and the author as well as something about the book and what it makes them think of.

Story About a Best Friend

Introduction

OBJECTIVES

★ **RESPOND** to a literature model of a story about a best friend.

★ **RECOGNIZE** the characteristics of a story about a best friend.

 Building Background

To inspire children to write a story about a best friend, have them draw a picture of themselves doing something special with a best friend. As children share their pictures with the class, talk about what a friend is and what friends like to do together. Display the pictures for all to enjoy.

2 Meet the Writer

Direct children's attention to "Kat's Good Idea" on pages 17–27 of the Big Book of Writing Models and introduce the writer, Tomie dePaola. Tell children that he wrote this story and drew the pictures to tell about two friends who are also brother and sister. Read the title and preview the illustrations. Ask children what they think the story is about.

3 Respond to a Model

Read "Kat's Good Idea" aloud. As you read, focus children's attention on the illustrations and text. When you finish the story, encourage children to retell the story in their own words. Record responses on the chart on page 52 of the Big Book.

> **Kit and Kat**
>
> **Characters**
> Kit and Kat
>
> **Setting**
> outside
>
> **Problem**
> Kit and Kat want to ride bikes.
> Kit's feet don't reach the pedals.
>
> **Ending**
> Kat put two blocks on Kit's pedals. Kit wins the race.

Meeting Individual Needs

LITERATURE CONNECTION

Before your students write their stories about a best friend, you may want to introduce them to one or more of these books.

1. *My New Boy* by Joan Phillips. Illustrated by Lynn Munsinger. Random House, 1986. A little black puppy "acquires a boy" and shares his feelings about his new best friend.

2. *Lizzy and Skunk* by Marie-Louise Fitzpatrick. Dorling-Kindersley, 2000. Lizzy learns to overcome her fears with the help of her friend.

3. *We Are Best Friends* by Aliki. Morrow, 1982. Two friends learn to get along in this narrative.

Mini-Lesson: Using Illustrations in Writing

Introduce Share a favorite picture book with children. Talk about the illustrations. Discuss what readers can learn about a story by looking at the illustrations, such as where the story takes place (the setting), what events happen, and what the characters look and act like or how they feel. Explain that writers use pictures to give more clues to the reader and to make a story more interesting.

Model Look again at the illustrations from "Kat's Good Idea" on pages 17–27 of the Big Book. Invite children to share anything they learned about the story of Kit and Kat that was shown in the pictures but not told in the text. Ask children what they would add to any of the illustrations if they were the writer.

Summarize/Apply Have children share why they would want to use illustrations in the stories they will write about a best friend.

Story About a Best Friend
from the
Big Book of Writing Models
pages 17–27

Kat's Good Idea

One day, Kit and Kat got a big surprise from Mom and Dad.

Two bikes!
Kat got a red bike.

Kit got a blue bike.

"Let's race!"
said Kat.
She got on the red bike.
Off she went.
"I WIN!"
said Kat.

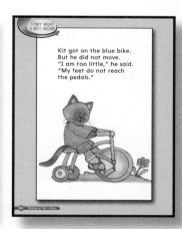

Kit got on the blue bike.
But he did not move.
"I am too little," he said.
"My feet do not reach
the pedals."

Kat had an idea.
She got two blocks.

Kat put the blocks
on the pedals.

"Your feet will reach now,"
said Kat.
Then Kit got on his bike.
His feet did reach!

Off he went.
"I WIN!" said Kit
to Kat.

Prewriting

OBJECTIVES

★ BRAINSTORM and SELECT a topic for a story about a best friend.

★ RECOGNIZE the use of a story chart for prewriting.

★ CONTRIBUTE to a story chart in a shared prewriting activity.

★ MAKE a story chart to plan details to be included in a story about a best friend.

1 Introduce Prewriting

Invite children to name any charts they see in the classroom or use at home, such as a classroom helper chart, a homework chart, or a chore chart. Explain that charts are used to organize and keep track of information. Tell children that writers also use charts as they think of ideas for stories.

2 Shared Writing

Explain that choosing a topic is one of the first things a writer does. Have children talk about experiences or adventures they've had with a best friend. Ask if anyone has ever gone on a picnic with their best friend. Tell them that you're going to share a plan with them for a story about two best friends who go on a picnic.

MODELED WRITING Use the information on the sample chart on this page to fill in the story chart on page 52 of the Big Book. Remind children that good writers plan what they are going to write about before they begin writing. Share the chart with the class and discuss how a story needs characters, a setting, and a problem to work out.

INTERACTIVE WRITING Invite children to ask questions or suggest other information to add to the chart. Have volunteers come up and write their ideas on the chart. Point out that writers often include a lot of information in their charts and then choose the best ideas for their stories.

3 Independent Writing

Encourage children to look at their journals or brainstorm with each other to select an idea to write about. Make copies of the blackline master on page 34 for children to use to plan their own story about a best friend.

EMERGENT WRITERS Have children who need extra support use a tape recorder as they talk about their story ideas. Slowly repeat the words children say and talk about how to write them to list ideas on their charts.

TEACHER CONFERENCE You may want to use the following questions during your conferences with children to discuss their charts.

- *How did you decide what to write about?*

- *What was the hardest part about writing your chart? What was the easiest?*

- *How will you use your chart to write your story?*

PEER CONFERENCE Have children share their charts with a partner. Partners can ask questions such as the following.

- *Is this a true story about you and your best friend?*

- *Tell me about each part of your chart.*

Characters
Katie and Brad

Setting
park the neighborhood

Problem
They planned a picnic. It rained. They felt sad.

Ending
They went anyway. They ate lunch under a shelter. They splashed in puddles.

Problem

Introduce Play a game of "What would you do if ...?" Provide children with obvious story plots such as the one in "Kat's Good Idea." Explain that many stories have a character or characters with a problem. How the characters work out the problem is what makes a story interesting.

Model Revisit "Kat's Good Idea" on pages 17–27 of the Big Book. Help children identify the character with the problem (Kit), the problem (Kit's feet can't reach the bike pedals), and the way the problem is solved (Kat puts blocks on the pedals).

Summarize/Apply Invite children to describe problems and how they are worked out in other familiar stories. Make a chart listing the problem and how it was solved.

WRITER'S BLOCK

Problem	Solution
Children can't think of a problem they shared with a best friend.	Provide children with a sentence frame to prompt thinking: *My friend _____ and I wanted to _____, but _____.*

ESL STRATEGY

Have children draw pictures on the story chart rather than write words. As children tell about their drawings, partners can help them label their pictures with words to use when writing.

HOME-SCHOOL CONNECTION

Suggest that children share their charts with their families and discuss how they plan to use them when writing. To spark ideas, suggest that children ask family members to share stories about their own best friends.

WRITING ACROSS THE CURRICULUM

Social Studies Explain that a story chart can be helpful as children record information about historical events such as the development of inventions. You may wish to share this example.

Characters

Crayola Crayon Company

Setting

Easton, Pennsylvania, in 1958

Problem

not enough colors for children
crayons became flat with coloring

Ending

16 colors were added to the box of 48

the 64-crayon box had a built-in sharpener

Story About a Best Friend

Drafting

OBJECTIVES

★ **RECOGNIZE** the characteristics of a story about a best friend.

★ **RESPOND** to a first draft in a shared writing activity.

★ **USE** a story chart as a plan to write a first draft.

1 Introduce Drafting

Ask if anyone in the class knows how to ride a two-wheeled bicycle. Discuss how much practice it takes before you can finally ride without training wheels or someone helping you. Point out that writing is the same. Writers often write several drafts of a story before it is finished and ready to be published.

2 Shared Writing

MODELED WRITING Display the story chart you made in prewriting and reread it with children. Copy the model draft on this page onto chart paper or use the write-on pages on pages 53–56 of the Big Book. Explain that the writer used the information on the chart to write the first draft of the story. Read the story with children. Discuss the characters, the setting, and what happens in the story.

INTERACTIVE WRITING As you identify the different parts of the story, have volunteers check them off on the chart. Ask children if there is anything they would like to change or add. Encourage them to come up to the chart and write their ideas at the end of the story.

3 Independent Writing

Have children follow their charts as they write their own stories. They may want to put a checkmark by each item as they use it in the story. Remind them that the purpose of a first draft is to get their ideas on paper.

EMERGENT WRITERS Invite children who need extra support to dictate their stories as you write. Reread each sentence as it is written. Then ask children to read the story to you so they know what they have written.

TEACHER CONFERENCE You may want to use these questions during your conference with children to discuss their drafts.

- *How did you use your chart to write your draft?*
- *Did you include all the ideas from your chart? Why or why not?*
- *How did you decide which items on your chart to include and which ones to leave out?*

PEER CONFERENCE Have pairs of children read their stories to one another and ask questions such as the following.

- *Does my story make sense to you?*
- *Can you picture my story in your mind as I read it to you?*

Katie and Brad are six. they are best friends. One day they decided to have a picnic in the park. Suddenly, it started to rain. They were sad. Then Katie had an idea. They put on their raincotes and boots They went anyway. They ate lunch under a little roof. They splashed in puddles. They had a great picnic!

Sequencing Events Using a Story Map

Introduce Tell children that the events in a story take place in a certain order. As you recall the events in a familiar story, use the story map on page 51 of the Big Book to focus on the beginning, middle, and end of the story.

Model Look back at "Kat's Good Idea" and ask children to recall the important story events. Help children organize the events of the story by telling what happens in the beginning, middle, and end. As you retell the story, use words such as *first, next, then,* and *last*.

Summarize/Apply Suggest that children make a story map of their own stories about a best friend. Telling or writing what happens in the beginning, middle, and end of the story will help them double-check if the events are in the correct order.

WRITER'S BLOCK

Problem	Solution
Children are having difficulty beginning to write their first draft.	Have children begin their stories by telling about the characters or what happened first. They can go back and change the beginning later if they wish.

ESL STRATEGY

Have children point to each item on their chart while telling their story aloud. If they have difficulty telling a part of the story, offer a sentence or phrase using the detail in the chart to model how to use the chart.

HOME-SCHOOL CONNECTION

Encourage children to share their drafts with their families and to show how they used their prewriting charts as plans to write their first drafts. Remind children to tell family members that this is just a draft and does not need to be perfect.

WRITING ACROSS THE CURRICULUM

Language Arts After reading "Kat's Good Idea," children may enjoy other Tomie dePaola stories. Have children use a story chart or a story map to keep track of the events in the other books they read.

Revising/Editing

OBJECTIVES

★ **RECOGNIZE** that writing can be improved by revising it.

★ **CONTRIBUTE** to revising a story about a best friend in a shared writing activity.

★ **REVISE** a first draft of a story about a best friend.

★ **RECOGNIZE** that every story has a beginning, a middle, and an end.

1 Introduce Revising and Editing

Remind children that good writers reread their drafts many times to make changes or fix mistakes.

Reread "Kat's Good Idea" with the class. Ask if children have any questions about the story. Is there anything else they want to know? What kinds of changes might Tomie dePaola have made to his story? Record children's responses on chart paper.

2 Shared Writing

MODELED WRITING Use the model on this page to make changes to the draft of a story about friends going on a picnic. Reread the story with children, drawing attention to the changes the writer made. Point out the title the writer added and ask what the children think about it. Does it make them want to read the story?

Demonstrate how to circle a misspelled word and insert the correctly spelled word above it. Also model how to mark a capital letter at the beginning of a sentence and add a period at the end. Give each child a copy of the revising and editing marks on page 26 of the Teacher Resource Guide.

INTERACTIVE WRITING As children become more familiar with revising, you may want to present the draft without the revisions and have children find the mistakes and make changes using the revising marks they've learned.

3 Independent Writing

Have children reread their drafts aloud to themselves. Encourage them to ask these questions.

- *Did I remember to add an interesting title?*
- *Do I tell what happens first, next, and last?*
- *Do any sentences need a capital letter or an end mark?*

Remind children to circle misspelled words they want to correct and to use a caret to add new words.

EMERGENT WRITERS Have children who need extra support read their drafts aloud to you. Focus on one skill at a time, such as checking for capital letters.

TEACHER CONFERENCE You may use the following questions when children share their revised drafts.

- *Have you given your story a title?*
- *Does your story have a beginning, middle, and end?*
- *Tell me about the changes you have made.*

PEER CONFERENCE Pair children and have them read their drafts to one another. Suggest that the writer ask the listener the following questions.

- *What do you like about my story?*
- *Do you have any questions?*

A Rainy Day Picnic

Katie and Brad are six. they are best friends. One day they decided to have a picnic in the park. Suddenly, it started to rain. They were sad. Then Katie had an idea. They put on their raincoats and boots. They went anyway. They ate lunch under a little roof. They splashed in puddles. They had a great picnic!

Publishing

OBJECTIVE

★ PUBLISH a story about a best friend.

After making a clean copy of their stories, here are some ideas children can use to share their stories with family and classmates.

BOOK TALK Have children write their story sentences on separate sheets of paper and illustrate each page. Have them bind the pages with a cover they have illustrated. Then they can share their published books with a kindergarten class in your school.

WRITE A LETTER Have children send a copy of the finished story to the friend they wrote about.

FRAME IT Have children frame their stories inside decorative tagboard frames they have made. Have them display their framed stories in a prominent place along with pictures showing friendship.

ASSESSMENT OPPORTUNITIES

PORTFOLIO ASSESSMENT If children choose to include their stories in their portfolios, have them also include their prewriting charts and drafts.

TEACHER HOLISTIC ASSESSMENT Use the Teacher Evaluation Checklist on page 37 to evaluate children's stories about a best friend.

BENCHMARK PAPERS You may want to use the benchmark papers on pages 38–44 to evaluate children's writing. There is one paper for each level of writing on the Developing Writer's Assessment Continuum.

Meeting Individual Needs

Exclamation Point

Introduce Write three sentences on the board, one with a period, one with a question mark, and one with an exclamation point.

I see my best friend.

Do you want to play a game?

Let's play hide-and-seek!

Read aloud the sentences with exaggerated expression. Circle the ending punctuation marks and discuss with children why each one was used.

Model Write the following sentences from "Kat's Good Idea" on the board.

Two bikes!

His feet did reach!

Remind children that an exclamation point is used at the end of a sentence that shows strong feeling. Model how to read each sentence and then let children read them.

Summarize/Apply Point out how you ended the final sentence in your story with an exclamation point. Have children look through their stories. Ask them to decide if they can find or add a sentence that shows strong feeling and end it with an exclamation point.

WRITER'S BLOCK

Problem
Children end every sentence with a period.

Solution
Help children look back at their sentences and decide if any ask a question or make an exclamation. Show your draft as an example.

ESL STRATEGY
Children can work with a partner to check each sentence in their stories as they prepare to make a clean copy. Partners can make sure they have copied all the sentences correctly from the revised/edited draft.

HOME-SCHOOL CONNECTION
Compile children's stories into a class "Friendship Newsletter" for children to send home to families. Children will be able to share their own stories as well as those of their classmates.

WRITING ACROSS THE CURRICULUM
Social Studies As children learn about families, neighborhoods, and communities, suggest that they work together to make a list of how people help each other.

Story About a Pet

Introduction

OBJECTIVES

★ **RESPOND** to a student model of a story about a pet.

★ **RECOGNIZE** the characteristics of a story about a pet.

1 Building Background

Invite children to name pets they have or would like to have. Talk about what kinds of fun a child and a pet can have together. Encourage children to talk about how to take care of a pet and what you can teach a pet to do.

2 Meet the Writer

Show children "My Dog" on pages 28–29 of the Big Book of Writing Models, and ask what kind of pet the story is about. Introduce first-grade author Myles Smith. Read aloud the text in the speech bubble and ask how they think Myles feels about his dog. Then by using the drawing Myles made, have them predict what might happen in the story.

3 Respond to a Model

Read the story aloud to the class. Remind children that a story has a beginning, a middle, and an end. Explain that in the beginning of a story, the author tells who the characters are and where the story happens. In the middle, the author tells about a problem the characters have. In the end, the author shows how the problem is solved. Ask children to tell what happens in each part of "My Dog." Record their responses on a story chart, like the one on page 52 of the Big Book.

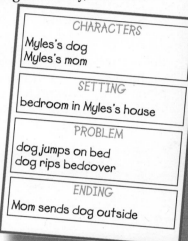

CHARACTERS
Myles's dog
Myles's mom

SETTING
bedroom in Myles's house

PROBLEM
dog jumps on bed
dog rips bedcover

ENDING
Mom sends dog outside

Meeting Individual Needs

LITERATURE CONNECTION

Before your students write their stories about a pet, you may want to introduce them to one or more of these books.

1. *Daddy, Could I Have an Elephant?* by Jake Wolf. Illustrated by Marylin Hafner. Puffin Books, 1976. At first Tony wants a pet like an elephant or a gorilla, but after talking with Daddy, he decides a puppy would be better.

2. *The Best Pet Yet* by Louise Vitellaro Tidd. Photographs by Dorothy Handelman. Millbrook Press, 1976. After considering various pets in the pet shop, a young boy finally decides on a pet rabbit.

3. *Any Kind of Dog* by Lynn Reiser. Greenwillow, 1772. Mom says dogs are too much trouble and offers many other kinds of pets before she finally gives in.

Mini Lesson — Setting

Introduce Tell children that the setting of a story is the place where it happens. Play a game to get children thinking about places by saying, "I'm thinking about a beach." Then invite children to tell how the place looks and what is happening there. Continue with a new place (farm, city, classroom, field, and so on).

Model Show the story "My Dog." Ask children to look at the second drawing and find words in the text to name the story's setting (bedroom in Myles's house). Point out that the setting is important to know because this is where Myles's dog gets into trouble.

Summarize/Apply Remind children that every story has a setting. Tell children that when they write stories, they should make sure to tell about the setting so readers can understand where things happen in the story.

Story About a Pet

from the

Big Book of Writing Models

pages 28–29

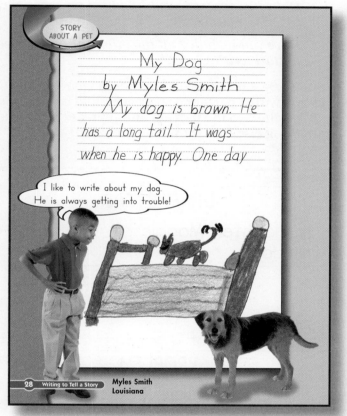

Story About a Pet

Prewriting

OBJECTIVES

★ BRAINSTORM and SELECT a topic for a story about a pet.

★ RECOGNIZE the use of a story chart for prewriting.

★ CONTRIBUTE to a story chart in a shared prewriting activity.

★ MAKE a story chart to plan details for a story about a pet.

1 Introduce Prewriting

Show pictures of animals that people keep as pets. Include common pets, such as cats, dogs, gerbils, fish, and parakeets, as well as unusual pets, such as iguanas, snakes, and tarantulas. Ask children to identify pictures that show pets like those they have or would like to have.

2 Shared Writing

To help children think about a writing topic, share an experience you have had with a pet. Encourage children to do the same. Then point out that thinking about experiences they have had with pets might give them some good ideas for a story. Tell them you are going to share a writing plan with them for a story about a pet hamster.

MODELED WRITING Use the information on the sample chart on this page to fill in the story chart on page 52 of the Big Book. Point out that good writers use a plan like this to decide what they want to include in a story. As you fill in the chart, reinforce the idea that a story needs characters, a setting, and a problem.

INTERACTIVE WRITING Based on what children know about pets, invite them to look at the chart and ask questions or suggest other details that might be added. Invite volunteers to write their ideas on the chart. Remind children that even though writers don't use every idea in their plans, they try to include as much information as they can.

3 Independent Writing

Encourage children to discuss their experiences with pets with classmates before deciding on a topic for their story. Make copies of the blackline master on page 34 so children can use the chart to plan a story about a pet. Display the chart you made as a guide.

EMERGENT WRITERS Have children plan a story by drawing a picture. As children tell about their picture, help them write words on their story charts. Read together what has been written.

TEACHER CONFERENCE You may want to use the following questions during your conferences with children to discuss their story charts.

- *Did you have trouble thinking of an experience to write about?*

- *Have you included all the information you need to start writing?*

PEER CONFERENCE Have children share their story charts with a partner. Have each child explain his or her chart to the partner and then ask if there is anything else that should be included.

CHARACTERS

my hamster, Maggie
my dad

SETTING

my house

PROBLEM

She unlocks cage door.
She gets out and hides.

ENDING

I catch the hamster.
Dad puts a new lock on the door.

Mini Lesson

Organization: Beginning, Middle, End

Introduce Have three children stand up and form a line. Point out that one child is at the beginning, one is in the middle, and one is at the end. Explain that stories have three parts too—beginning, middle, and end. Tell them that a story is like the line of children; if one of the three parts is missing, it's not complete.

Model Tell children that the first part of the story is the beginning. In the beginning, the writer introduces the characters and setting. In the middle, the writer tells about a problem. In the end, the writer tells how the characters fix the problem. Display the story "My Dog" on pages 28–29 of the Big Book. Ask volunteers to point out where the author introduces the characters and setting, describes the problem, and tells how everything works out.

Summarize/Apply Remind children that stories need to have a beginning, a middle, and an end. As children work on their story charts, guide them to include details that tell what happens in the beginning, the middle, and the end of their stories.

WRITER'S BLOCK

Problem	Solution
Children have no personal experience with pets.	Have children look at photos or pictures of animals from books or magazines. Then have them talk to a partner about what could be fun about having that animal as a pet, and how the animal might get into trouble.

ESL STRATEGY

Invite children with varying language proficiencies to draw a picture in each section of the chart. Have them dictate a caption for each picture to you.

HOME-SCHOOL CONNECTION

Encourage children to share their story charts with their families and to ask older family members to share funny stories about pets they had or knew when they were children.

WRITING ACROSS THE CURRICULUM

Social Studies Tell children that they can use story charts to remember things they learn about community workers. For example, they can summarize what they know about firefighters by telling how they solve a particular problem in the community.

<u>CHARACTERS</u> Police officers

<u>SETTING</u>   Our town

<u>PROBLEM</u>   There are too many cars. Children can't cross the street.

<u>ENDING</u>   Police officer stops the cars so children can cross.

Story About a Pet

Drafting

OBJECTIVES

★ RECOGNIZE the characteristics of a story about a pet.

★ RESPOND to a first draft in a shared writing activity.

★ USE a story chart as a plan to write a first draft.

1 Introduce Drafting

Ask children to think of a time when they were listening to a friend tell a story. The story may have been interesting to listen to, but perhaps it was confusing because the friend didn't name the character, left out some important details in the middle, or didn't tell how the story ended. Explain that writers need to include all three parts of a story so it will be clear to the reader.

2 Shared Writing

MODELED WRITING Revisit the story chart you made in prewriting. Copy the model draft from this page onto chart paper or use the write-on pages on pages 53–56 of the Big Book. Explain that the writer used the details from the plan to write this first draft. Read the story with children. Have them identify the characters, setting, problem, and ending.

INTERACTIVE WRITING As children identify the story parts, have volunteers check them off on the chart. Ask children if there is any part of the story they wonder about. Encourage them to suggest what they would add or change and write their ideas at the end of the draft.

3 Independent Writing

Have children reread their own story charts. Suggest that they think of sentences they can write for each of the details they want to include in their stories. After writing a draft, suggest that children think of a title for the story.

EMERGENT WRITERS Suggest that children who need extra support verbalize a summary of the pictures and captions on their prewriting charts. Help children put their words on paper.

TEACHER CONFERENCE You may want to use these questions during your conferences with children.

* *Have you used all the information on the chart?*

* *How did the chart help you with your draft?*

* *How do you feel about your story?*

PEER CONFERENCE Choose pairs of children to read their drafts to each other. Have writers ask their listeners questions such as the following.

* *What do you like about my story?*

* *Is there anything else you want to know?*

Maggie is Missing
by Maria Fernandez

my hamster Maggie is brown and white. She has a pink nose and a tail. Maggie is very smart. One day Maggie got out of her cage. We couldn't find her anywhere Finally she got hungry and came out. I caught her and put her back in the cage. Dad put a new lock on the cage door. Now Maggie stays in her cage.

Mini Lesson

Capitalization at Beginning of Sentence

Introduce Write the following sentences on the board: *this is my dog. he is brown. he wags his tail*. Read the sentences without pausing. Ask children if they think the sentences are hard to read and why. Guide children to see that sentences need to begin with a capital letter. Capital letters make reading easier by signaling the beginning of a new sentence.

Model Call on seven volunteers to each read a sentence in the story "My Dog" and point to the first word in the sentence. Ask children to explain how they knew where to start when it was their turn to read.

Summarize/Apply Remind children that all their sentences should begin with a capital letter. Have children sit in pairs to read their stories aloud. Have them check that all sentences begin with capital letters.

WRITER'S BLOCK

Problem	Solution
Children have trouble maintaining story continuity.	Have children use their charts to tell the story before they begin to write. When they get off track, they can go back and talk through the story again.

ESL STRATEGY

Invite English-language learners to identify the characters and setting and verbalize their stories before writing.

HOME-SCHOOL CONNECTION

Encourage children to share their drafts with family members. Children can ask them to contribute details about a family pet or pet they wish to have. Families might consider providing photos of family pets to personalize children's stories.

WRITING ACROSS THE CURRICULUM

Language Arts Start a card file for books about animals. As children read animal stories, encourage them to add a card to the file by writing the book's title and author and naming the characters and problem. Encourage children to use the card file to find good books to read or ideas for writing.

"Only Joking!" Laughed the Lobster
by Colin West

The lobster scares the other animals when he says a shark is coming. Then a shark really does come.

Story About a Pet

Revising/Editing

OBJECTIVES

★ **RECOGNIZE** that writing can be improved by revising it.

★ **CONTRIBUTE** to the revision of a story about a pet in a shared writing activity.

★ **REVISE** a first draft of a story about a pet.

★ **RECOGNIZE** that a story tells about characters, a setting, a problem, and an ending.

1 Introduce Revising and Editing

Remind children that, like all good writers, they are now ready to read their drafts again to decide if they want to change or add anything and to fix mistakes they find. Reread the Big Book model "My Dog" with children. Ask them if they think the story seems finished or if they would change or add anything. Record children's responses on chart paper.

2 Shared Writing

MODELED WRITING Use the model on this page to make changes to the draft of a story about a pet hamster. Reread the story with children, pointing out changes the writer wanted to make. Talk about the word *tiny* that the writer added. Ask children how this detail tells more about the hamster, Maggie.

Remind children how to use a caret to add words and how to mark a capital letter. Talk about how the writer uses capital letters to write a title. Give each child a copy of the revising and editing marks on page 26 of the Teacher Resource Guide.

INTERACTIVE WRITING Ask volunteers to add the caret and mark for a capital letter. They can also help write the words you will add. As children become more familiar with revising, you may want to present the draft without revisions so that children can suggest changes they would make.

3 Independent Writing

Ask children to quietly reread their stories. Suggest that they ask themselves these questions.

- *Did I tell my story in the right order?*
- *Did I tell how the problem was fixed?*
- *Did I remember to add a title?*

EMERGENT WRITERS Have children who need extra help read their drafts to you. Suggest revisions they might make and guide them in using the correct editing marks to show what they will change.

TEACHER CONFERENCE You may wish to ask the following when children share their revisions.

- *Did you explain the problem and tell how everything works out?*
- *How did you choose your title?*

PEER CONFERENCE Invite children to read their revised stories to partners. Suggest that writers ask listeners the following questions.

- *Are the events in my story clear?*
- *Should I add or change any words?*

Maggie is Missing
by Maria Fernandez

my hamster Maggie is brown and

white. She has a pink nose and a tiny tail.

Maggie is very smart. One day

Maggie got out of her cage. We

couldn't find her anywhere. Finally

she got hungry and came out. I

caught her and put her back in the

cage. Dad put a new lock on the

cage door. Now Maggie stays in

her cage.

Publishing

OBJECTIVE

★ PUBLISH a story about a pet.

Encourage children to use these suggestions to share their stories.

CLASS BOOK OF PETS Bind children's stories together into a class book of pets. Invite children to include pictures and drawings along with their stories. Send the book home with a different child every day, and ask him or her to read stories to family members.

PET PUPPET SHOW Group children according to the kinds of pets they wrote about. Have children make a paper bag pet puppet. Then have the members of each group use their puppets as they read their stories aloud. Invite another class as an audience to share in the fun!

VET VISIT Invite pairs of children to role-play a pet owner and veterinarian. Have the owner read his or her story and the vet offer some advice.

ASSESSMENT OPPORTUNITIES

PORTFOLIO ASSESSMENT If children choose to include their stories in their portfolios, have them also include their prewriting charts and drafts.

TEACHER HOLISTIC ASSESSMENT Use the Teacher Evaluation Checklist on page 37 to evaluate children's stories about a pet.

BENCHMARK PAPERS You may want to use the benchmark papers on pages 38–44 to evaluate children's writing. There is one paper for each level of writing on the Developing Writer's Assessment Continuum.

Meeting Individual Needs

Reader Interest: Write a Strong Conclusion

Introduce Invite children to tell about a TV show or movie with a good ending. Ask whether children would have enjoyed the show as much if they had not seen the ending. Explain that the ending made the show more interesting and that good writers choose an interesting way to end their stories, too.

Model Display the story "My Dog" on pages 28–29 of the Big Book, covering the last two sentences with self-stick notes. Read the story aloud. Point out that something is missing because we don't know what happened. Uncover the two sentences and help children understand that these sentences help them picture Mom sending the unhappy dog outdoors. The ending makes the story funny and interesting and tells how everything works out.

Summarize/Apply Tell children that a good ending is important to a story because your readers will want to know how everything works out. Suggest that they "try out" different endings for their stories by reading them to partners before choosing one.

 WRITER'S BLOCK

Problem	Solution
Children cannot think of interesting titles for their stories.	Suggest that children think about the main idea and look for key words they can use in a title.

ESL STRATEGY
To help children select words to add to their stories, have them say the words in their native languages. Tell them the words in English, and have them read the words with you as you write them.

HOME-SCHOOL CONNECTION
Encourage children to show family members their draft copies and published stories. They can show how much they've learned by explaining how and why they made changes.

WRITING ACROSS THE CURRICULUM
Math Tell children that while drawing pictures adds to a story, pictures can also help them solve math problems. To solve simple addition problems, children can make dots to represent each number and then count them to come up with the sum.

News Story

Introduction

OBJECTIVES

★ RESPOND to a student model of a news story.

★ RECOGNIZE characteristics of a news story.

1 Building Background

To model what a news story is, hold a newspaper and read aloud the following, pretending it's in the paper.

Bedtime Alarm

Wee Willie Winkie was seen running through (your town) in his nightgown. He was rapping at windows and yelling through locks, "Are the children all in bed, for now it's eight o'clock!"

Then discuss who the news story is about, when and where it happened, and why.

2 Meet the Writer

Display "Rain, Rain" on pages 30 and 31 of the Big Book of Writing Models. Point to the title and mention again that a news story's title is called a headline. Then point to the author's name and share that Kristen Galloway is the first-grade "reporter" who wrote the story. You might want to mention that in newspapers, the author's name is called a byline.

3 Respond to a Model

Read the news story aloud. Reinforce that every news story answers five questions: *What happened? Who did it happen to? When did it happen? Where did it happen?* and *Why or how did it happen?* Have children answer these questions as you read the news story again. Make a chart with the questions *Who?, What?, When?, Where?,* and *Why or How?* As children answer the questions, fill in the information on the chart.

Rain, Rain
What? bad storm branch almost fell on cat
Who? people in Houston cat
When? April 3
Where? Houston
Why or How? rained hard lightning

Meeting Individual Needs

LITERATURE CONNECTION

Before your students write their news stories, you may want to introduce them to one or more of these books.

1. *Some Good News* by Cynthia Rylant. Illustrated by Wendy Anderson Halperin. Simon & Schuster, 1999. Three cousins put together a neighborhood newspaper.

2. *The Furry News: How to Make a Newspaper* by Loreen Leedy. Holiday House, 1990. Inside information about how a newspaper is put together.

3. *Mr. Duvall Reports the News* by Jill D. Duvall. Photographs by Lili Duvall. Children's Press, 1997. A TV reporter gathers facts, writes his story, and delivers it on the air.

Mini Lesson

Identifying Form: Real Versus Make-Believe

Introduce Write the following on the board:
After the rain, there were puddles.
Five pigs danced in the puddles.

Have children identify the sentences as telling about something real or make-believe.

Model Explain that for a story to be real, every detail must be true. A story is make-believe if even one part could not really happen. Reread "Rain, Rain," with the children. Stop after each statement and ask if it is real or make-believe. Help children conclude that the news story tells about an event that really happened.

Summarize/Apply Remind children that every sentence in a news story must be true. Tell them that when they write their own news stories, they need to make sure to tell only things that really happened.

News Story

from the

Big Book of Writing Models

pages 30–31

News Story

Prewriting

OBJECTIVES

★ **BRAINSTORM** and **SELECT** a topic for a news story.

★ **RECOGNIZE** the use of a chart for prewriting.

★ **CONTRIBUTE** to a chart in a shared prewriting activity.

★ **MAKE** a chart to identify information to be included in a news story.

1 Introduce Prewriting

With children, look through magazines or newsletters written for children to find headlines and the names of reporters who wrote the articles. Point out the different kinds of stories that appear in a magazine or newspaper and that some stories include photographs.

2 Shared Writing

Tell children that the first step in writing a news story is to find interesting news to share. A good reporter will write a story that tells what readers would like to know about. Ask children to tell the kinds of news stories they would like to read, such as news about important events happening at their school. Tell them that you're going to share a plan with them for a news story about a special school event.

MODELED WRITING Copy the sample chart on this page onto chart paper or use the write-on pages on pages 53–56 of the Big Book. Remind children that before a writer begins to write a news story, a plan is made. Share the chart with the class and discuss how every news story has facts that tell *what, who, when, where,* and *why or how.*

INTERACTIVE WRITING Invite children to ask questions about the information in the chart. Encourage volunteers to suggest other details that might be added to answer each of the questions and have them write their ideas on the chart.

3 Independent Writing

Display the completed chart so children can use it as a model for making their own charts. Suggest that children look at their journals or the class calendar to think of events they might write about. Stress that news stories are about events that really happened.

EMERGENT WRITERS Tell children that some news stories may have more than one author. Allow children who need extra help to work with partners to plan and write their stories. You might also have children draw their details and invite a partner to help label the drawings.

TEACHER CONFERENCE You may want to use the following questions during your conferences with children to discuss their charts.

- *Did you answer the questions* what, who, when, where, *and* why or how?
- *How did you gather your information?*
- *Can you add any more details?*

PEER CONFERENCE Have children share their charts with partners and ask questions such as the following.

- *Which facts are most interesting to you?*
- *Which facts should I leave out?*
- *Does my headline tell what the story will be about?*

Field Day Fun

What?
School Olympics

Who?
students

When?
May 5

Where?
school playground

Why or How?
build school spirit
games, races, contests, prizes

Reader Interest: Writing a Strong Title

Introduce Show children a newspaper or magazine and explain that most readers do not read every article. They look at the titles, or headlines, to find something interesting to read. Share the following headlines with children: "Cool Stuff for Kids," "Road Work Begins," "Water Carnival Opens," "Boo at the Zoo," "Airport Reopens." Ask children which stories they would want to read and why.

Model Reporters who want their stories to be read must choose interesting titles or headlines to catch the readers' attention. Reread the news story in the Big Book. Ask children if they like the headline "Rain, Rain." Ask children to think of other interesting headlines for this story.

Summarize/Apply As soon as children have chosen an idea for a news story, have them make a list of headlines. As they plan their stories, they can add to their lists and then choose their favorite headlines for their published news stories.

WRITER'S BLOCK

Problem	Solution
Children are having trouble gathering information.	Review the three sources of information—reading, watching things happen, and talking to people. Invite children to form teams to research the same event.

ESL STRATEGY

Encourage English-language learners to draw an event. Have them dictate the description of the drawing to you. If details are missing, use questions to help them add details first to the drawing and then to their dictation.

HOME-SCHOOL CONNECTION

Have children tell family members about their topic. Encourage children to talk with their family about what to include in their story. Invite them to add any new details they learn to their webs.

WRITING ACROSS THE CURRICULUM

Social Studies Explain to children that history is news that happened long ago. Have children use a story web to summarize or organize information about historical events they are learning about.

First Thanksgiving Dinner

What?	harvest feast
Who?	Pilgrims Native Americans
When?	fall of 1621
Where?	Plymouth colony
Why or How?	to celebrate and give thanks for their food and their new friends

News Story

Drafting

OBJECTIVES

★ RECOGNIZE the characteristics of a news story.

★ RESPOND to a first draft in a shared writing activity.

★ USE a chart as a plan to write a first draft.

 Introduce Drafting

Ask children what they would want to know if new neighbors were moving in. Discuss how they would ask questions to find out who is moving in, where they are from, when they are coming, how many children there are, and what their names are. Point out that writing a news story is the same. Writers ask many questions and write many drafts of a news story before they are finished.

 Shared Writing

MODELED WRITING Display the chart you made in prewriting and read the facts again with children. Copy the model draft from this page onto chart paper or use the write-on pages on pages 53–56 of the Big Book. Explain that the writer used the details in the chart to write the first draft of the news story. Read the draft with children and discuss how the sentences answer all the questions.

INTERACTIVE WRITING Work together to identify the sentence in the draft that answers each question, and have a volunteer check it off on the chart. Ask children if they would like to change the wording of anything that was written or add details to the story. Invite volunteers to come up and write their ideas at the end of the draft.

3 Independent Writing

Have children use their own charts to write a sentence about each idea in the chart. Start with a sentence that tells what happened. They may want to put a checkmark by each fact as they use it. Remind them that a first draft is the time to get their ideas on paper.

EMERGENT WRITERS Encourage children who need extra support to write one sentence for each question on their chart. Then have them cut the sentences apart and paste them in order.

TEACHER CONFERENCE You may want to use these questions during your conferences with children to discuss their drafts.

* *Did you begin with a sentence that tells the most important idea?*

* *How did your chart help you write your first draft?*

* *Did you answer the questions* what, who, when, where, *and* why or how?

PEER CONFERENCE Pair children and have them take turns reading their stories. Provide tips such as the following.

* *Look at the ideas in your partner's chart.*

* *Listen as your partner reads the news story.*

* *Ask questions if you want to know more.*

Field Day Fun
by Jennifer Marley

The students had a school Olympics on May 5. It was on the school playground. Mr. harvey, our principal, said the Olympics would help build school spirit. There were relay races and a jumping contest. The winners got prizes. Everyone had fun

---

Mini Lesson

Capitalization: Days and Dates

Introduce On the board, list the days of the week. Talk about events that make each day special. Talk about dates that are special too, such as July 4. Then help each child write the date of his or her birthday on the board. Provide a list of months as a model. Ask children what they notice about the names of the days of the week and the months. *(The words begin with a capital letter.)*

Model Remind children that one of the questions news stories answer is *when*, so writers often include the day and date when the event happened. Display "Rain, Rain" for children. Have a volunteer point to and read the date in Kristen's story and name the capital letter that begins the name of the month. Also point out that the name of a special place (*Houston*) also begins with a capital letter.

Summarize/Apply Tell children to make sure they answer the question *when*? with the day and/or date as they write their drafts. Remind them to always begin the names of days and months with a capital letter.

WRITER'S BLOCK

Problem
Children have difficulty organizing their stories.

Solution
Have children number the items on their charts, starting with the most important idea as number 1.

ESL STRATEGY
Have each partner check to see that the questions have all been answered and the author did not leave out any important information.

HOME-SCHOOL CONNECTION
Encourage children to read aloud their news story drafts to family members and ask if they have any questions.

WRITING ACROSS THE CURRICULUM
Music Help children recall the words of a familiar rhyme song or chant, such as "Jack and Jill," by answering as many of the five questions as possible.

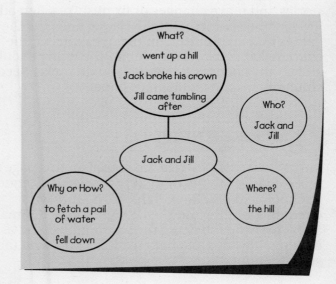

News Story

Revising/Editing

OBJECTIVES

★ RECOGNIZE that writing can be improved by revising it.

★ CONTRIBUTE to the revision of a news story in a shared writing activity.

★ REVISE a first draft of a news story.

★ RECOGNIZE that a news story answers the questions *What? Who? When? Where?* and *Why or How?*

 Introduce Revising and Editing

Remind children that now that they have written their drafts, they are ready to reread their news stories and make changes or fix mistakes. Reread Kristen's news story with the class. Look over the details that answer each of the questions on the chart. Ask if there are any details the writer should add or any changes the writer should make. Record children's responses on chart paper.

 Shared Writing

MODELED WRITING Use the model on this page to make changes to the draft of the news story about a school field day. Reread the news story with children, pointing out the changes the writer made and why. Note the detail the writer added and ask children how this will help readers know who the story is about.

Demonstrate how to use a caret to add words. Also model how to mark a capital letter at the beginning of a person's name and add an exclamation point to the end of a sentence. Give each child a copy of the revising and editing marks on page 26 of the Teacher Resource Guide.

INTERACTIVE WRITING You may want to invite volunteers to come to the chart to add the caret and the exclamation point, and mark the capital letter. As children become more familiar with revising, present the draft without revisions, have children find mistakes, and make changes using revising marks.

3 Independent Writing

Have children quietly reread their drafts and ask themselves these questions to help them see where revisions should be made.

- *Does my news story have an interesting headline?*
- *Have I answered all five questions?*
- *Did I begin and end sentences with capital letters and periods?*

Remind children to look at the model to see changes they might also need to make as they work on their own news stories.

EMERGENT WRITERS For children who need extra support, point out one or two revisions they should make. Provide help as needed.

TEACHER CONFERENCE You may wish to use the following questions when children share their revised drafts with you.

- *Does your first sentence tell the most important idea?*
- *Do you need to add words or fix any mistakes?*

PEER CONFERENCE Invite children to read their revised stories to partners. Suggest that writers ask listeners the following questions.

- *Do you understand what happened?*
- *Is there anything else you want to know?*

Field Day Fun
by Jennifer Marley
at Maple School

The students had a school

Olympics on May 5. It was on the

school playground. Mr. harvey,

our principal, said the Olympics

would help build school spirit.

There were relay races and a

jumping contest. The winners got

prizes. Everyone had fun!

Publishing

OBJECTIVE

★ PUBLISH a news story.

Invite children to use one of these suggestions to share their news stories.

PUBLISH A CLASS NEWSPAPER Ask one or more parent volunteers to type children's stories in newspaper format. Make copies of your class newspaper and give each child two copies—one to keep and one to share with friends or family.

TV NEWSCAST Invite children to sit at a "news desk" and deliver their stories as if they were television reporters. If you have a video camera available, videotape the newscast and invite each child to provide a visual to go with his or her story. Show your newscast to other classes.

RADIO BROADCAST Have children tape-record their news stories. Add appropriate music between stories and play back the tape for the class.

ASSESSMENT OPPORTUNITIES

PORTFOLIO ASSESSMENT If children choose to include their stories in their portfolios, have them also include their prewriting charts and drafts.

TEACHER HOLISTIC ASSESSMENT Use the Teacher Evaluation Checklist on page 37 to evaluate children's news stories.

BENCHMARK PAPERS You may want to use the benchmark papers on pages 38–44 to evaluate children's writing. There is one paper for each level of writing on the Developing Writer's Assessment Continuum.

Meeting Individual Needs

Mini Lesson
Order of Events and Ideas

Introduce Write each sentence from "Rain, Rain," on a sentence strip and display them in random order. Invite children to read the strips with you and then place them in the order they occurred in the story. Point out how the story makes more sense to the reader when the events are in the correct order.

Model Remind children that the events they tell about in their news stories should be in the order in which they happened. Have children look at the draft of the news story you wrote together and check to see that the first sentence tells the reader what the story is about. The remaining details should be in an order that tells what kinds of contests they had, what prizes were awarded, and how everyone felt.

Summarize/Apply Have children look over the facts from their news stories and think about the order in which they happened. Before children write their final copies, they should rearrange details that are out of place to make sure they are in an order that makes sense.

WRITER'S BLOCK

Problem

Children are too shy to share their news stories with the class.

Solution

Invite children to pick a partner to read the story for them. Encourage children to provide positive feedback to each other. These comments will help the shy child be more willing to read aloud.

ESL STRATEGY

Have English-language learners act out their story with partners to be sure that the events in their stories are in an order that makes sense.

HOME-SCHOOL CONNECTION

Ask children to share their published pieces with family members. They can then watch a newscast or read a newspaper story together, pointing out all the parts of a news story.

WRITING ACROSS THE CURRICULUM

Language Arts Suggest that children keep a journal of school or community events that would make good news stories.

Teacher Notes

Imagine That: Writing to Describe

Contents

RESOURCES

TEACHING PLANS

Writing to Describe

Writing to Describe — Unit Planner

WRITING FORM	MINILESSONS				
	Basic Skills/ Writing Process/ Writer's Craft	**Grammar, Usage, Mechanics, Spelling**	**Writing Across the Curriculum**	**Meeting Individual Needs**	**Assessment**
Lesson 1 DESCRIPTION OF A PERSON pp. 110–117 (7–9 days)	• Plan a Composition Using a Story Web, 113 • Use Precise, Vivid Adjectives, 115	• Adjectives, 110 • Declarative Sentences, 117	• Science, 113 • Science, 115 • Health, 117	• Writer's Block, 113, 115, 117 • ESL Strategy, 113, 115, 117 • Home-School Connection, 113, 115, 117	• Teacher Checklist, 99 • Benchmark Papers, 100–106 • Portfolio, 117 • Teacher and Peer Conferencing, 112, 114, 116
Lesson 2 DESCRIPTION OF A PLACE pp. 118–125 (7–9 days)	• Details: Sensory Words, 121	• Nouns, 118 • Period to End a Sentence, 123 • Plural Nouns: Add -s, 125	• Science, 121 • Science, 123 • Science/Language Arts, 125	• Writer's Block, 121, 123, 125 • ESL Strategy, 121, 123, 125 • Home-School Connection, 121, 123, 125	• Teacher Checklist, 99 • Benchmark Papers, 100–106 • Portfolio, 125 • Teacher and Peer Conferencing, 120, 122, 124
Lesson 3 FREE-VERSE POEM pp. 126–133 (7–9 days)	• Rhyme, 126 • Use Precise Action Words, 131 • Publishing: About the Author, 133	• Action Words, 129	• Art, 129 • Science, 131 • Music, 133	• Writer's Block, 129, 131, 133 • ESL Strategy, 129, 131, 133 • Home-School Connection, 129, 131, 133	• Teacher Checklist, 99 • Benchmark Papers, 100–106 • Portfolio, 133 • Teacher and Peer Conferencing, 128, 130, 132
Lesson 4 DESCRIPTION OF A STORY CHARACTER pp. 134–141 (7–9 days)	• Character, 134 • Using a Journal to Get Ideas, 137 • Reader Interest: Write an Attention-Grabbing Beginning, 139	• Capitalization: Proper Names, 141	• Science, 137 • Social Studies, 139 • Language Arts, 141	• Writer's Block, 137, 139, 141 • ESL Strategy, 137, 139, 141 • Home-School Connection, 137, 139, 141	• Teacher Checklist, 99 • Benchmark Papers, 100–106 • Portfolio, 141 • Teacher and Peer Conferencing, 136, 138, 140

Making the Reading-Writing Connection
Writing to Describe

You may want to add the following books to your classroom library. Each category of book represents one form of writing children will be introduced to in *Writing to Describe*. The books serve as models for good writing and are valuable resources to use throughout each lesson. The suggested titles offer opportunities for you to read to the class as well as for children to read themselves.

Use literature to introduce a writing form, to show a model of successful writing, to enhance minilessons, to focus on grammar and usage, or to expand each lesson.

DESCRIPTION OF A PERSON

When Sophie Gets Angry—Really, Really, Angry
by Molly Bang. Scholastic,1999. Sophie learns how to tame her anger and turn it into something positive.

This Quiet Lady
by Charlotte Zolotow. Illustrated by Anita Lobel. Greenwillow, 2000. A little girl learns about her mother through photographs.

What Mommies Do Best/What Daddies Do Best
by Laura Joffe Numeroff. Illustrated by Lynn Munsinger. Simon and Schuster, 1998. These two books (in one) reinforce the best of parent-child relationships.

DESCRIPTION OF A PLACE

Dreaming: A Countdown to Sleep
by Elaine Greenstein. Arthur A. Levine, 2000. Readers will count in this bedtime concept book.

Secret Place
by Eve Bunting. Illustrated by Ted Rand. Clarion, 1996. A sewer drain in the city makes an unlikely place for wild life to call home.

Whose House Is This?
by Wayne Lynch. Whitecap, 2000. Learn about animal habitats all over the world in this photo essay.

FREE-VERSE POEM

Lucky Song
by Vera B. Williams. Greenwillow, 1997. Children will relate to the sing-song quality of Williams's prose.

Sweet Corn: Poems
by James Stevenson. Greenwillow, 1999. Everyday objects and events are elevated to poetry in this collection.

Someone I Like: Poems About People
compiled by Judith Nicholls. Illustrated by Giovanni Manna. Barefoot Books, 2000. Family, friends, and neighbors are the subjects of these poems by a variety of poets.

DESCRIPTION OF A STORY CHARACTER

Leo the Late Bloomer
by Robert Kraus. Illustrated by Jose Aruego. Harpercollins, 1994. Leo learns to do things in his own sweet time.

Imogene's Antlers
by David Small. Crown, 1986. Imogene wakes up to find that she has made an amazing transformation.

The Two Bullies
by Junko Morimoto. Crown, 1999. Two large men display great strength and cleverness in this Japanese folk tale.

The Classroom Writing Center
Writing to Describe

As children begin to engage in different kinds of descriptive writing, you may want to make some additions to your writing center. Here are some ideas.

- ◆ Create a special Word Wall with lists of words that focus on each of the five senses. Children can refer to the word wall when writing.

- ◆ Establish a special Poetry Corner in your classroom library or writing center. Display plenty of poetry books and posters.

- ◆ Invite children to display drawings or photos from home and include a caption they have written to describe what the others see.

Create a Bulletin Board for Writing to Describe

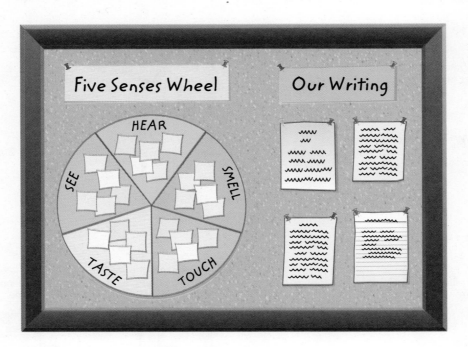

- ◆ Create a board with a five-senses wheel. Label each section of the wheel with one of the senses. Children can help you fill each section with pictures and words. Change the pictures to accommodate the unit's different writing forms.

- ◆ Children can use the display as a resource for writing a description of a person, place, story character, or poem.

- ◆ Provide space on the board to display children's descriptive writing.

Connecting Multiple Intelligences
Writing to Describe

The following activities focus on specific prewriting and publishing ideas for children who demonstrate intelligence in different ways: talent and skill with words (linguistic), with numbers (logical-mathematical), with pictures (spatial), with movement (bodily/kinesthetic), with people (interpersonal), with self (intrapersonal), with music (musical), and/or with nature (environmental or naturalist).

Linguistic
Prewriting — Listen to audio tapes of poetry to learn more about rhythm. Create a list of describing words grouped by sense. Use the list when you write a description or poem.

Logical-Mathematical
Prewriting — Plan to write a counting poem as a free-verse poem. In your description of a place, include things that have shapes of a circle, square, rectangle, and triangle.

Spatial
Prewriting — Look at several pictures of your story character. List words that come to mind.
Publishing — Design a map to show the place you have described in your writing.

Bodily Kinesthetic
Prewriting — Draw a sketch of the person you will describe in writing.
Publishing — Dress like your story character to share your description with a group.

Environmental (Naturalist)
Prewriting — Choose a favorite outdoor spot to write a description of a place. Or plan a free-verse poem to describe weather.
Publishing — Show pictures, photos, or objects as you share a nature poem.

Writing to Describe

Intrapersonal
Prewriting — Spend quiet time in the place you want to describe. Draw pictures and list words to record what you see, hear, feel, and smell.

Interpersonal
Prewriting — Interview classmates who are familiar with your person or story character.
Publishing — Practice reading your poem with two or three classmates. Present your poem as a choral reading to the class.

Musical
Prewriting — Write about a person who loves music or a place where you hear pleasant sounds.
Publishing — Tape-record your poem while playing background music.

Name _____ **Date** _____

Who Am I?

Write about someone you know.

1. _____

2. _____

3. _____

4. _____

5. _____

94

Describe It

Write about what you see, hear, smell, taste, and feel.

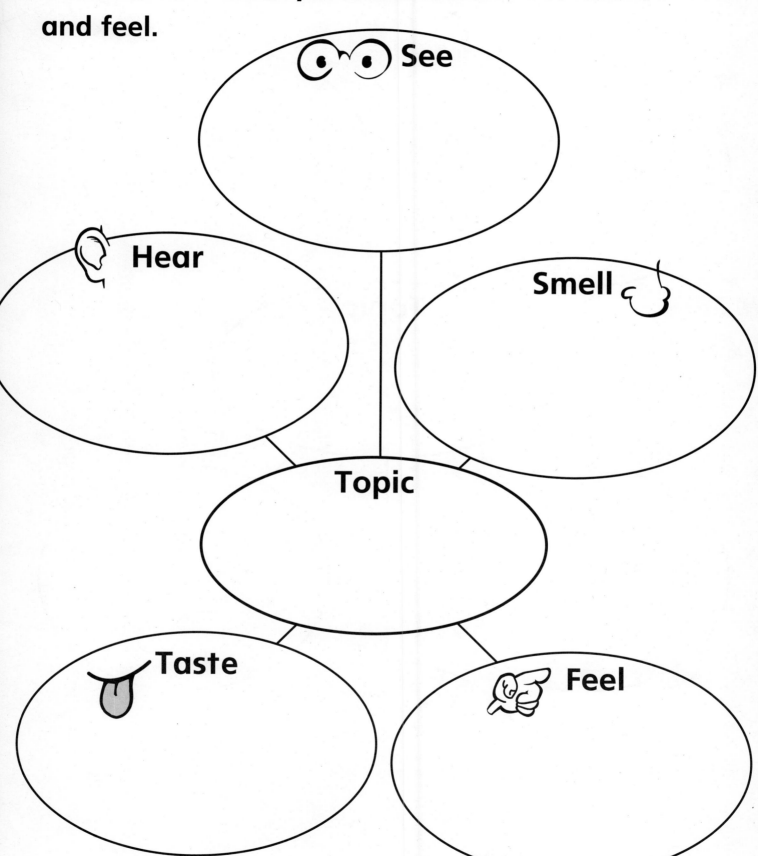

Poetry Web

Write words that tell about your topic.

Topic

Name _____ Date _____

Character Chart

Use this page to write about a story character.

How does the character look?

How does the character act?

How does the character feel?

Evaluating Student Writing
Writing to Describe

The Write Direction offers a variety of assessment options. The following are short descriptions of the assessment opportunities available in this unit. Just select the assessment option that works best for you.

Types of Assessment	Writing Lessons
Benchmark Papers Annotated student writing models are provided as benchmarks for evaluating children's writing. Children's writing can be compared to these models, which represent different developmental stages as specified in the Developing Writer's Assessment Continuum.	Student samples for writing to describe, levels 1–7, pages 100–106
Checklists The Teacher Evaluation Checklist helps track children's progress as their writing skills develop.	• Teacher Evaluation Checklist, page 99
Portfolio Assessment Children's work generated throughout the writing process may be used in creating individual portfolios illustrating children's progress as writers. Suggested pieces for a portfolio include completed works and works-in-progress, graphic organizers, logs, and journals.	• Description of a Person, page 117 • Description of a Place, page 125 • Free-Verse Poem, page 133 • Description of a Story Character, page 141
Teacher and Peer Conferencing Throughout each lesson in this unit, there are opportunities to interact with children, informally questioning them about their progress and concerns. Children also have opportunities to interact with one another to ask questions, share ideas, and react to the partner's writing.	• Description of a Person, pages 114, 116, 118 • Description of a Place, pages 120, 122, 124 • Free-Verse Poem, pages 128, 130, 132 • Description of a Story Character, pages 136, 138, 140

Teacher Evaluation Checklist
Writing to Describe

Name of Writer _____

Date _____

Writing Mode _____

Use this checklist when you are evaluating a child's
- **description of a person**
- **description of a place**
- **free-verse poem**
- **description of a story character**

	YES	NO	Recommendations to Child
Is the topic appropriate for this writing assignment?	❑	❑	
Is the writing focused on the topic?	❑	❑	
Does the writing include details?	❑	❑	
Does the writing include vivid or colorful language?	❑	❑	
Does the writing have a clear structure?	❑	❑	

Does the writer adhere to the conventions of
  grammar?
  usage?
  spelling?
  punctuation?
  capitalization?
	❑
	❑
	❑
	❑
	❑
		❑
		❑
		❑
		❑
		❑	

Is the handwriting legible?	❑	❑	
Was the work done neatly?	❑	❑	

Emerging Writer: Level 1
Writing to Describe

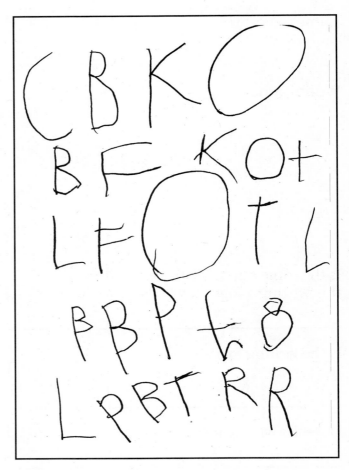

Spider was blue. My other spider is black. They are swinging.

Conventions

Sentence Structure Includes no evidence of intended message.

Directionality, Spacing, and Punctuation Places squiggles, other shapes, letterlike shapes, and/or letters randomly.

Letter Formation and Capitalization Forms squiggles, other shapes, and/or letterlike shapes.

Spelling Represents words using letterlike shapes, and/or letters with no letter-sound correspondence to the intended word; dictation needed to read all words.

Content

Supporting Details Includes no evidence of intended articles or modifiers.

Word Choice Includes no evidence of intended words.

Emerging Writer: Level 2
Writing to Describe

Once a rattlesnake stung me.

Conventions

Sentence Structure Includes 1 intended word or phrase.

Directionality, Spacing, and Punctuation Places letterlike shapes or letters in a left to right direction and may have a space between 2 words.

Letter Formation and Capitalization Forms mostly uppercase letters; may form 1 word using lowercase letters.

Spelling Represents 1–2 words by recording at least 1 dominant sound; may spell 1 word conventionally; dictation needed to read most words.

Content

Supporting Details Includes 1 intended article and/or modifier.

Word Choice Uses 1–3 intended high-frequency routine words.

Writing to Describe

Title **LION K** (king)

One DaY The LION NR ot (run) (to)

The ZOO

One day the lion ran to the zoo.

Conventions

Sentence Structure Includes 1 intended simple sentence.

Directionality, Spacing, and Punctuation Places letters and/or words in a left to right direction and leaves spaces between 3 or more words; may attempt punctuation.

Letter Formation and Capitalization Forms 2 or more words using lowercase letters.

Spelling Represents most words by recording 1 or more dominant sounds; may spell 2–3 different words conventionally; dictation needed to read some words.

Content

Supporting Details Includes 2 intended modifiers.

Word Choice Uses 4 or more intended high-frequency routine words.

Early Writer: Level 4
Writing to Describe

Title The Sek [snake]

The Sek is eten. [snake eating]

The Sek is glon to The wrd [snake going water]

The Sek is in The wrd [snake water]

Conventions

Sentence Structure Includes 2–4 simple sentences and/or 1 compound or complex sentence.

Sentence Variation Begins all sentences with the same word.

Punctuation Ends 1 sentence or the story with a period.

Capitalization Capitalizes first word in 1 sentence; other letters may be inappropriately capitalized.

Spelling Spells 4–8 different words conventionally; dictation needed to read a few words.

Content

Opening Begins with an action or a fact in the first of 2–3 related thoughts or sentences.

Transitions Uses 1 transitional word or phrase to connect thoughts. (Note: No transitional word or phrase is scored level 3.)

Development of Ideas Uses a glimmer of at least 1 strategy to develop an idea.

Supporting Details Includes 3–4 different modifiers.

Word Choice Uses 1 precise word that is more exact in meaning.

Closing Stops with no ending after 2 or more related thoughts or sentences.

Early Writer: Level 5
Writing to Describe

Title: Dashom

Dashom is My Special friend.

because Dashom is fun

Dashom is Neis. *(nice)*

Dashom is prete. *(pretty)*

I like Dashom.

Conventions

Sentence Structure Includes at least 5 simple sentences and/or 2 compound or complex sentences.

Sentence Variation Varies the way 2–3 sentences begin.

Punctuation Ends 2 to 4 sentences with periods; may use other forms of punctuation appropriately at times.

Capitalization Capitalizes first word in 2–4 sentences; may use other forms of capitalization appropriately at times.

Spelling Spells 9 or more different one-syllable words conventionally.

Content

Opening Begins with an action or a fact in the first of 4 or more related sentences.

Transitions Uses 2 different transitional words or phrases to connect thoughts or ideas.

Development of Ideas Uses 1 strategy somewhat effectively to develop an idea.

Supporting Details Includes 5 or more different modifiers.

Word Choice Uses 2 precise words that are more exact in meaning.

Closing Signals ending with "The End."

Early Writer: Level 6
Writing to Describe

> Going to my room.
>
> A speacil place to me is my Bed room because me and it has shard a lot of memeries togeather. And that's were I do all of my home work I keep my room clean every day. Sometimes when I'm filling down my bed room help's me get over my sadnies. Me and my room are like Brother and sister he alway's help's me when I'm down and I help hem when hes filling down. I just have to say me and me room has shard a lot of mimories and are very klass Friends.

Conventions

Sentence Structure   Includes 3 compound and/or complex sentences.

Sentence Variation   Varies the way 4–5 sentences begin.

Punctuation   Ends at least 5 sentences with periods; may use other forms of punctuation appropriately at times.

Capitalization   Capitalizes first word in at least 5 sentences; may use other forms of capitalization appropriately at times.

Spelling   Spells 3–5 different two-syllable words conventionally.

Content

Opening   Creates a brief context or introduction with 1 opening sentence.

Transitions   Uses 3 different transitional words or phrases to connect thoughts or ideas.

Development of Ideas   Uses 1 strategy somewhat effectively and at least a glimmer of 1 other strategy to develop ideas.

Supporting Details   Supports 1 idea with details in at least 3 sentences.

Word Choice   Uses 3–4 precise words that are more exact in meaning.

Closing   Creates a logical ending or resolves the problem in at least 1 sentence; may include "The End."

Transitional Writer: Level 7
Writing to Describe

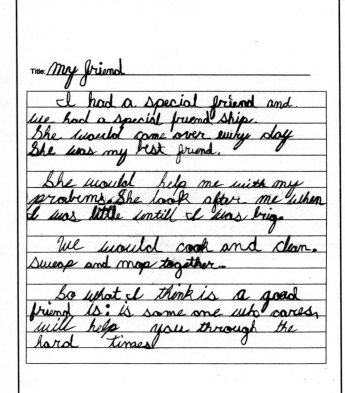

Title: My friend

I had a special friend and we had a special friend ship. She would come over every day She was my best friend.

She would help me with my probems. She look after me when I was little intill I was big.

We would cook and clean. Sweep and mop together.

So what I think is a good friend is: is some one who cares, will help you through the hard times.

a friend is not bossy, is nice, not a bully.

Friends some one you can open up to. They will pick you up when your down.

does not matter if they are fat or thin smart or dume. its whats on the inside that counts.

my friend is true blue.

BY Lindsay Fehr

Conventions

Sentence Structure Includes 4–6 compound and/or complex sentences.

Sentence Variation Varies the way 6–7 sentences begin.

Punctuation Ends at least 6 sentences with periods and uses 2 other forms of punctuation appropriately most of the time.

Capitalization Capitalizes first word in at least 6 sentences and uses 1 other form of capitalization appropriately most of the time.

Spelling Spells 6 to 8 different two-syllable words conventionally.

Content

Opening Creates a context or introduction somewhat effectively with 2 opening sentences.

Transitions Uses 4–5 different transitional words, phrases, and/or clauses to connect thoughts or ideas.

Development of Ideas Uses at least 2 strategies somewhat effectively to develop ideas.

Supporting Details Supports 2 ideas with details in at least 3 sentences; may be paragraphed.

Word Choice Uses 5–6 precise words or phrases that are more exact in meaning.

Closing Creates a brief closing (wrap-up, summary, conclusion) with at least 1 sentence; may include "The End."

Home Letter

Dear Family,

Your child is learning about writing to describe. Our class of writers will be using their five senses to discover words that can be used to tell about a familiar person, to describe a place, and to tell others about a story character. Your child will also become a poet! Watch for descriptions and poems your child will bring home to share with you.

Try these activities that call for using words to describe things.

1 Play games with your child that involve describing things, such as "I Spy" or "Twenty Questions."

2 As you read books together, pause before turning the page and have your child describe what he or she sees in the illustrations.

3 Read poetry and recite action rhymes with your child. How about reciting jingles as you jump rope together?

4 Look for books in the library that contain descriptive writing. These books are worth looking for.
- *Animal Trunk: Silly Poems to Read Aloud* by Charles Ghigna. Harry N. Abrams, 1999. The 15 playful poems about all kinds of animals are great fun for reading aloud.
- *Mouse Views: What the Class Pet Saw* by Bruce McMillan. Holiday House, 1993. The items from a classroom are described from the perspective of a small mouse.
- *Seven Blind Mice* by Ed Young. Putnam, 1992. Each of seven blind mice are able to describe only one part of an elephant. Based on limited information, they describe the animal incorrectly.
- *Tuesday* by David Wiesner. Houghton Mifflin, 1991. Frogs flying on lily pads invade the village during the night. Investigators find no evidence except lily pads all over the place.

Sincerely,

Carta para el hogar

Estimada familia,

Su hijo/a está estudiando la escritura para describir. Nuestra clase de redacción se valdrá de sus cinco sentidos para descubrir palabras que sirven para contar algo acerca de una persona conocida, para describir un lugar o para relatarle a los demás cómo es un personaje de un cuento. Su hijo también ¡se convertirá en poeta! Estén atentos a las descripciones y poemas que su hijo/a traerá a casa para compartirlos con ustedes.

Prueben estas actividades que requieren el uso de palabras para describir.

1 Hagan juegos que requieran que se describan cosas, tales como "Soy espía" o "20 preguntas".

2 Mientras lean los libros juntos, deténganse antes de cambiar de página y pídanle a su hijo/a que describa lo que él o ella ve en las ilustraciones.

3 Lean poesías y reciten rimas de acción con su hijo/a. ¿Y por qué no dicen estribillos mientras saltan la cuerda juntos?

4 Busquen libros en la biblioteca que contengan escritura descriptiva. Los siguientes libros son buenos ejemplos:

◆ ***Animal Trunk: Silly Poems to Read Aloud*** por Charles Ghigna. Harry N. Abrams, 1999. Los 15 poemas lúdicos acerca de todo tipo de animales son muy divertidos de leer en voz alta.

◆ ***Mouse Views: What the Class Pet Saw*** por Bruce McMillan, Holiday House, 1993. Los artículos de un salón de clases son vistos desde la perspectiva de un ratoncito.

◆ ***Seven Blind Mice*** por Ed Young. Putnam, 1992. Cada uno de los siete ratoncitos ciegos sólo pueden describir una parte de un elefante. Basados en la información tan limitada, describen el animal incorrectamente.

Sinceramente,

Teacher Notes

Description of a Person

Introduction

OBJECTIVES

★ **RESPOND** to a description of a person.

★ **RECOGNIZE** the characteristics of a description of a person.

1 Building Background

Describe a child in the room without naming him or her. Use precise words to describe hair color, eye color, clothes, behavior, likes and dislikes, and so on. (Be sure that all of the descriptions are positive.) Invite children to guess whom you are describing. Continue with more descriptions.

2 Meet the Writer

Ask children what words come to their minds when they hear the word *grandmother*. Tell children you are going to read a description of a grandmother. Display pages 32–33 of the Big Book of Writing Models and point to the name Becky Ray McCain. Tell children that she is the author of the book *Grandmother's Dreamcatcher*, which is about a girl who goes to stay with her grandmother while her parents are away. Explain that you are reading only the part of the book where the little girl describes her grandmother.

3 Respond to a Model

Encourage children to close their eyes and picture the grandmother in their minds as they listen to you read. Once you have finished, make an outlined drawing of a body on the chalkboard. Label it Grandmother. Ask children what words describe the grandmother in the story. Volunteers can copy words from the Big Book text to write inside the drawing.

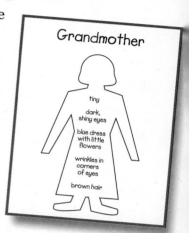

Meeting Individual Needs

LITERATURE CONNECTION

Children may enjoy hearing one or more of these wonderfully descriptive stories. The stories may spark children's ideas as they write their own descriptions.

1. *When Sophie Gets Angry—Really, Really, Angry* by Molly Bang. Scholastic, 1999. Sophie learns how to tame her anger and turn it into something positive.

2. *This Quiet Lady* by Charlotte Zolotow. Illustrated by Anita Lobel. Greenwillow, 1992. A little girl learns about her mother through photographs.

3. *What Mommies Do Best/What Daddies Do Best* by Laura Joffe Numeroff. Illustrated by Lynn Munsinger. Simon and Schuster, 1998. These two books (in one) reinforce the best of parent-child relationships.

Mini Lesson

Describing Words

Introduce To introduce the idea of describing words, give children clues and have them identify an object from your description. For example, *I'm thinking of something that is cold, sweet, and orange. What is it?* (orange juice)

Ask children to name the words that let them know what the object is. Explain that these are describing words that tell how someone or something looks, sounds, feels, or smells.

Model Reread the description of Grandmother on pages 32–33 of the Big Book. Invite volunteers to name a describing word that is used to tell about the following things and person: *dress* (blue, cotton), *flowers* (little), *Grandmother* (Chippewa, tiny, brown), *eyes* (dark, shiny). Have children circle the words inside the drawing of the grandmother you made earlier.

Summarize/Apply Help children understand that describing words help the reader to see what the writer sees.

110

Description of a Person

from the

Big Book of Writing Models

pages 32–33

Description of a Person

Prewriting

OBJECTIVES

★ RECOGNIZE the use of a list for prewriting.

★ SELECT describing words that can be used to tell about a person.

★ CONTRIBUTE to a list in a shared prewriting activity.

★ MAKE a list to plan writing.

 Introduce Prewriting

Have children pretend a family member has come to visit the class. Ask children to think of words they could use to describe this person. Invite volunteers to role-play introducing the family member to the group. Point out that when we introduce someone we know well to others, we use describing words to tell something about them.

2 Shared Writing

Explain that when you write a description of a person, you will want to choose a person you know. Ask children if they think they know the workers in the school well enough to describe them. Tell children that you will share one writer's plan with them for a description of a school principal.

MODELED WRITING Copy the sample list from this page onto chart paper or use the list on page 49 of the Big Book. Remind children that good writers make a plan before they begin writing so they can think about ideas they want to include. Share the list with children and discuss what the words tell about the principal.

INTERACTIVE WRITING Invite children to ask questions or suggest other information that can be added to the list. Invite volunteers to circle describing words the writer has used in the plan and then add ideas of their own.

3 Independent Writing

Have children think of someone they can write about. This person might be a friend, a family member, a neighbor, or someone else they know well. Make copies of the blackline master on page 94 for children to use to plan a description about a person. Encourage them to use the plan you made as a guide.

EMERGENT WRITERS To help children get started, prompt them to think about words that tell about the person they want to write about. Have them finish oral sentences such as *I am writing about (name of person). He/she looks like _____. His/her favorite thing is _____. He/she likes to _____.*

TEACHER CONFERENCE As children share their lists with you, consider asking these questions.

- *Why did you choose this person to write about?*

- *Have you used enough describing words?*

- *Is there anything else you want your readers to know about this person?*

PEER CONFERENCE Pair children and invite them to read each other's lists. Encourage partners to ask questions and make comments to help one another decide if any new words can be added or if some words do not fit.

Our Principal

friendly

students like him

tall

brown hair

wears glasses

likes baseball

Plan a Composition Using a Web

Introduce As an alternative to the list used in prewriting, brainstorm describing words by making a web. Display a blank web, such as the one on page 50 of the Big Book. Talk about how children have used webs before and why the webs were helpful to them.

Model Write *Our Principal* in the middle circle of the web. On the lines surrounding the web, write the adjectives used to describe the principal. Children may want to volunteer additional words and phrases.

Summarize/Apply Review with children that they can organize their ideas before they write in many different ways, such as lists, drawings, webs, and maps. Encourage them to decide which writing plan they like best.

WRITER'S BLOCK

Problem	Solution
Children are having difficulty describing the person.	Suggest that children draw a picture of themselves with this person. Help children write one or two words to tell how the person looks, acts, and sounds.

ESL STRATEGY

To foster an understanding of planning a description, have children describe a favorite food or a stuffed toy before trying to describe a classmate.

HOME-SCHOOL CONNECTION

Invite children to share their lists with their families, who may be able to suggest other words to add. Remind children to explain that they will be writing a description of this person.

WRITING ACROSS THE CURRICULUM

Science Children can use labeled drawings to describe the characteristics of animals they are studying. Help them draw the outline of an animal, label it, and write describing words inside the shape.

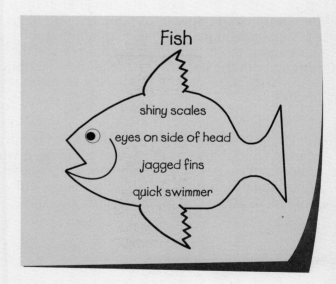

Fish
shiny scales
eyes on side of head
jagged fins
quick swimmer

Drafting

OBJECTIVES

★ RECOGNIZE the characteristics of a description of a person.

★ RESPOND to a first draft in a shared writing activity.

★ USE a list as a plan to write a first draft.

1 Introduce Drafting

Show children a blank sheet of art paper. Have them imagine they are going to paint a picture. Ask them what they do before beginning to paint. Just as they picture in their minds what to paint and which colors they will use, a writer uses a plan to decide what ideas to include in a description.

2 Shared Writing

MODELED WRITING Copy the model draft from this page onto chart paper or use the write-on pages in the Big Book on pages 53–56. Explain that the writer used the details from the list to write the sentences in the description. Read the description with children. Talk about describing words that are used.

INTERACTIVE WRITING Have children help you match details from the plan with those in the draft, putting checkmarks by those that are used. Invite children to suggest anything they would change or add to the description. They can come up and write ideas at the end of the description.

3 Independent Writing

Just as the writer did, have children follow their plans to write their own descriptions. They can put a checkmark by each detail as they include it in a sentence. Remind them that a good way to begin is to name the person they are writing about and tell something interesting about the person.

EMERGENT WRITERS Consider having emergent writers write one sentence that names the person they are describing and two descriptive sentences. If necessary, provide a sentence frame children can complete with words from their chart. They can copy the sentences you provide.

TEACHER CONFERENCE During your drafting conference, you may want to ask children these questions.

- *Do you start by telling whom you are describing?*
- *Did you use words that help the reader "see" this person?*
- *Is there anything else you want to say?*

PEER CONFERENCE Invite partners to read their descriptions to one another. Suggest that the writer ask the following questions.

- *If you close your eyes, can you "see" the person?*
- *Is there anything missing from my description?*

My Principal
by Lee Cheng

My school principal, Mr.

Harvey, is a great guy! He has

brown hair and wears glasses.

he is tall. He likes to play

baseball. He is frendley to all

of his students. I like

Mr. Harvey.

Use Precise/Vivid Adjectives

Introduce On the board write adjectives such as *long, wiggly, furry, tall, loud, funny,* and *brown*. As you point to each word, invite children to name nouns that can be described by each of the words: for example, *long (worm, snake, river, hair, ride, football field, feet, tail).*

Model Write these two sentences on the board:

The worm lives in the dirt.

The long wiggly worm lives in the damp brown dirt.

Discuss how the sentences are different. Help children understand that, although both sentences are about the worm, the sentence with adjectives helps you picture exactly what the worm and dirt are like.

Summarize/Apply Remind children to use adjectives in their own writing. They should ask themselves what words will help readers make pictures in their minds of the person, place, or thing being described.

WRITER'S BLOCK

Problem	Solution
Children use a limited vocabulary to describe size, shape, color, and other qualities.	Build word banks or lists of descriptive words with children.

ESL STRATEGY

Have children read aloud their drafts. A classmate who is more proficient in English can ask questions and help choose and write additional adjectives.

HOME-SCHOOL CONNECTION

Encourage students to read their drafts to their families. Have family members ask questions about the person being described that might suggest details to be added.

WRITING ACROSS THE CURRICULUM

Science As children learn more about using adjectives in their writing, they will be able to write sentences to describe science topics, such as weather, animals and animal habitats, and rules for good health.

The sun hides behind white puffy clouds. The sky turns dark gray. The wind blows the tall trees. Heavy rain starts to fall.

Revising/Editing

OBJECTIVES

★ **RECOGNIZE** that a description of a person can be improved by revising it.

★ **CONTRIBUTE** to the revision of a description of a person in a shared writing activity.

★ **REVISE** a first draft of a description of a person.

★ **RECOGNIZE** the use of the words *he/she* in a description of a person.

1 Introduce Revising and Editing

Revisit Big Book pages 32–33 and reread the description. Ask children if there is anything more they would like to know about Grandmother. What ideas do they think the writer could add? Record their ideas on chart paper.

2 Shared Writing

MODELED WRITING Use the model on this page to make changes to the draft of the description of a school principal. As you reread the description with children, point out how the writer made changes to add more details and vary the beginning of a sentence. Point out the use of the pronoun *he* to refer to Mr. Harvey.

Remind children that a caret is used to add words and a misspelled word is circled with the correct spelling written above. Give each child a copy of the revising and editing marks on page 26 of the Teacher Resource Guide.

INTERACTIVE WRITING Choose volunteers to help you mark changes by inserting the caret or circling the misspelled word. As children become more skilled in revising, you may want to present the draft and have them find and mark the changes for missing punctuation, capital letters, and misspellings.

3 Independent Writing

As children begin revising their drafts, suggest they ask themselves these questions.

- *What words can I change to make my description better?*

- *Have I used a capital letter and a period to begin and end each sentence?*

EMERGENT WRITERS Select one sentence where a describing word could be added to give more detail.

TEACHER CONFERENCE When children share their revised drafts with you, you may wish to ask them these questions.

- *What is the most important thing you want your readers to know?*

- *Do you give many examples that describe the most important thing?*

- *Have you started sentences with different words?*

PEER CONFERENCE Pair children of varying abilities. Have them share their descriptions. Invite them to react to their classmates' writing by answering the following questions.

- *What do you like best about the description?*

- *Is there anything you would change?*

My Principal
by Lee Cheng

My school principal, Mr.

Harvey, is a great guy! He has ^curly

brown hair and wears glasses.

he is tall. ~~He~~ ^Mr. Harvey likes to play

baseball. He is (frendley) friendly to all

of his students. I like

Mr. Harvey.

Publishing

OBJECTIVE

★ **PUBLISH a description of a person.**

Children can share their descriptions in a number of ways. Here are a few suggestions.

PEOPLE POSTERS Have children write a clean copy of their descriptions. Then have them mount the description along with the list created in prewriting on a sheet of posterboard or construction paper. Add a drawing of the person.

MAIL-A-DESCRIPTION Suggest that children make a clean copy of their descriptions on stationery that they have decorated. Then with the help of a family member, they can mail their description to the person they have written about.

AUTHOR'S CHAIR Invite each child to read his or her description from the classroom Author's Chair. Include a drawing or photograph of the person being described.

ASSESSMENT OPPORTUNITIES

PORTFOLIO ASSESSMENT If children choose to include their descriptions in their portfolios, have them also include their prewriting charts and drafts.

TEACHER HOLISTIC ASSESSMENT Use the Teacher Evaluation Checklist on page 99 to evaluate children's descriptions.

BENCHMARK PAPERS You may want to use the benchmark papers on pages 100–106 to evaluate children's writing. There is one paper for each level of writing on the Developing Writer's Assessment Continuum.

Meeting Individual Needs

Mini Lesson — Declarative Sentences

Introduce Teach children this rhyming chant: *Some sentences tell. They don't ask or yell. When you write a sentence that tells, my friend, Use a period at the end.* Explain to children that a declarative (or telling) sentence tells about someone or something. It begins with a capital letter and ends with a period.

Model Write these sentences on the board.

that girl has long black hair

my neighbor loves to play soccer

my friend is very shy

Invite children to read the sentences aloud. Volunteers can insert capital letters and write periods at the ends of the sentences. After each sentence is written correctly, repeat the chant together.

Summarize/Apply Ask children to count the number of declarative sentences they wrote in their descriptions. Remind them to check that each sentence begins with a capital letter and ends with a period.

WRITER'S BLOCK

Problem	Solution
Children repeat the same spelling errors again and again.	Encourage children to write words they have trouble remembering in their picture dictionaries.

ESL STRATEGY

Give children index cards on which you have written sample sentences, highlighting the capital letters and end marks. Children can use the cards as models as they revise their own work.

HOME-SCHOOL CONNECTION

Invite children to take home their descriptions. Family members can discuss what they like best about them.

WRITING ACROSS THE CURRICULUM

Health Encourage children to use adjectives as they write about health topics, such as a healthful meal.

> **A Healthy Breakfast**
>
> a glass of <u>cold</u> <u>orange</u> juice
>
> a <u>large</u> bowl of <u>crunchy</u> cereal

Description of a Place

Introduction

OBJECTIVES

★ RESPOND to a student model of a description of a place.

★ RECOGNIZE the characteristics of a description of a place.

1 Building Background

Take children on an imaginary walk through a place such as a zoo, woods, neighborhood, or school. Encourage children to participate by asking questions using each of the five senses. *What colors do you see? What do you smell? What sounds do you hear?*

2 Meet the Writer

Display the description "The Zoo" on pages 34–35 of the Big Book of Writing Models. Point to the writer's name. Explain that Joseph Astudillo is in first grade, and he wrote this description to tell others about a favorite place he visited. Read the title "The Zoo." Talk about why Joseph wrote about the zoo.

3 Respond to a Model

Read Joseph's description aloud to children. As you read each page, ask children to notice the details that Joseph includes and the senses he uses in his description and in his drawings. When you finish reading, encourage children to contribute things you would smell, taste, see, hear, and feel at the zoo. Record children's responses in a chart.

The Zoo				
See	Hear	Smell	Taste	Feel
trees	loud noise			
elephant	whistle			
lion				
brown fur				

Meeting Individual Needs

LITERATURE CONNECTION

Before children write their descriptions, you may want to introduce them to one or more of these books.

1. *Dreaming: A Countdown to Sleep* by Elaine Greenstein. Arthur A. Levine, 2000. Readers will count in this bedtime concept book.

2. *Secret Place* by Eve Bunting. Illustrated by Ted Rand. Clarion, 1996. A sewer drain in the city makes an unlikely place for wildlife to call home.

3. *Whose House Is This?* by Wayne Lynch. Whitecap, 2000. Learn about animal habitats all over the world in this photo essay.

Mini Lesson: Nouns

Introduce Invite children to help you name things found at a zoo, such as a bear, zookeeper, and restaurant. Record children's responses on the board in a chart under the headings *Person, Place,* or *Thing*. Explain that words that name people, places, or things are called nouns. Write *Nouns* at the top of the chart.

Model Have children look at the story "The Zoo" on pages 34–35 of the Big Book. Ask children to pick out nouns in the description. Guide volunteers to write each word in the correct column on the board.

Summarize/Apply Remind children that nouns are words that name people, places, and things and that when children are describing a person, place, or thing they are writing about nouns.

Description of a Place
from the
Big Book of Writing Models
pages 34–35

Description of a Place

Prewriting

OBJECTIVES

★ **BRAINSTORM** and **SELECT** a topic for a description of a place.

★ **RECOGNIZE** the use of a chart for prewriting.

★ **CONTRIBUTE** to a chart in a shared prewriting activity.

★ **MAKE** a chart to identify information to be included in a description of a place.

 Introduce Prewriting

Talk with children about how they use each of the five senses: touch, taste, smell, sight, and sound. Reread "The Zoo" on pages 34–35 of the Big Book of Writing Models. Discuss how Joseph may have planned his writing by thinking about how he used each of his five senses to enjoy the zoo.

 Shared Writing

Point out that in the description children just read, Joseph tells what he saw on a visit to a favorite place. Ask children to volunteer the names of some of their favorite places, listing their ideas on the board. Tell children that you are going to share one writer's plan with them for a description of a classroom.

MODELED WRITING Reproduce on chart paper the sample chart from this page. Remind children that good writers think about the details they want to include before they begin writing. Share the chart with the class and talk about how the writer uses the five senses to plan details for a description of a place.

INTERACTIVE WRITING Invite children to ask questions or suggest details they know about a classroom that they can come up and add to the chart. Point out that writers include many details in a planning chart but use only the best ideas when they write.

3 Independent Writing

Have children look again at the list of the names of favorite places on the board and choose one place to write about. Make copies of the blackline master on page 95 for children to use in planning their descriptions. Display the chart you made as a model.

EMERGENT WRITERS Suggest that children draw pictures on their charts and tell the words they want to use. Help children label the pictures by slowly saying the words as they write. Read the words together.

TEACHER CONFERENCE Discuss children's charts in individual conferences. You might use these questions to guide you.

- *What place did you choose?*
- *What do you see in this place? What do you hear (smell, taste, feel)?*
- *What else do you remember about this place?*

PEER CONFERENCE Select pairs of children to sit together and discuss their favorite places by sharing their charts. Tell children what is expected.

- *Talk about why you think the place is special.*
- *Ask if there is anything else you should include.*

Our Classroom

See	Hear	Smell	Taste	Feel
desks flag chalk- board poster	children talking squeaky chalk bell	flowers	juice crackers	smooth paper hard book

Mini Lesson

Details: Sensory Words

Introduce Ask children to close their eyes and picture the classroom door. What color is it? What shape is it? What does it feel like? How does it sound when it closes? Explain that writers can ask themselves questions using their five senses to think of interesting words that help describe things. Give an example: *Our door is metal; Our red metal door squeaks when you close it.* Ask the children which sentence gives a better description of the door.

Model Have children look again at the chart you made during shared writing. Ask yourself questions about the five senses aloud to demonstrate how you can think of sensory words to add to the ideas listed in your chart. Invite children to offer and add sensory words to your chart as well.

Summarize/Apply Remind children that using words about color, shape, size, smell, taste, and touch can help them write better descriptions and create "pictures" for their readers.

WRITER'S BLOCK

Problem	Solution
Children don't remember details about a place they visited.	Have children look at pictures of similar places or discuss the place with a classmate who has been there.

ESL STRATEGY

Provide paper with drawings that show the five senses—eye (See), ear (Hear), nose (Smell), mouth (Taste), hand (Feel). Help children draw and then list ideas for as many of the senses as possible. Focus on only sight and sound if children seem overwhelmed.

HOME-SCHOOL CONNECTION

Children can visit or discuss their favorite place with family members and have them suggest details and descriptive information that can be added to the chart.

WRITING ACROSS THE CURRICULUM

Science Children can answer questions using their senses to make observations and record data as they study changing outdoor habitats or indoor experiments.

Rock Creek

April 9

What do I see? – birds, lizards, beetles

What do I hear? – birds, frogs, water

What do I smell? – grass, moss

What do I feel? – mist, squishy mud

Drafting

OBJECTIVES

★ **RECOGNIZE** the characteristics of a description of a place.

★ **RESPOND** to a first draft in a shared writing activity.

★ **USE** a chart as a plan to write a first draft.

1 Introduce Drafting

Ask children if they and their families like to visit certain places year after year, such as a state fair, an amusement park, or a circus. Discuss how each year the rides and acts get bigger and better for the visitors who come. Point out how writing is the same. Writers keep thinking of ways to make their drafts better before sharing with their readers.

2 Shared Writing

MODELED WRITING Display the five senses chart you made in prewriting. Copy the model draft from this page onto chart paper or use the write-on pages in the Big Book on pages 53–56. Read the description with children and have them give examples of how the writer used the details from the chart to write the first draft. Discuss which details tell what they see, hear, smell, taste, and feel in the classroom being described.

INTERACTIVE WRITING Volunteers can circle details from the planning chart as you talk about them. Ask children if they would change or add to the description. Encourage them to come up and write their ideas at the end of the draft.

3 Independent Writing

Encourage children to begin choosing the details from their charts that they want to include in their descriptions. They can circle details as they use them in sentences to describe a favorite place. Remind children that the purpose of this draft is to get ideas on paper.

EMERGENT WRITERS Suggest that children draw a picture of the place they're writing about and then write about what they see.

TEACHER CONFERENCE You may want to conference with children to discuss their drafts. Questions such as the following can guide your discussion.

- *How did you choose what to describe?*
- *How is your chart helpful to you?*
- *Are there other details you think you should include?*

PEER CONFERENCE Pairs of children can read their descriptions to each other. Remind them to listen quietly and to tell what details they like about their partners' descriptions.

Our Classroom
by Maria Vega

In the morning, our classroom is a nice place to be. I smell the flowers on the table. Our pictures hang on the walls. Then I hear the bell ring The chalk squeaks on the board. Everyone is working.

Using a Period at End of Sentence

Introduce Explain that all sentences tell a complete thought. Some sentences are telling sentences. A telling sentence ends in a period. Write the following sentences on the chalkboard:

The hippo swims.

The bears sleep in trees.

Read each sentence. Ask children what each sentence tells about. Point out the period at the end of each sentence.

Model Read sentences from Joseph's story on pages 34–35 of the Big Book. Take turns with volunteers to point to the periods in "The Zoo." Explain that each period signals that a telling sentence is finished.

Summarize/Apply Remind children that when they write, they need to remember to end each sentence with the correct punctuation mark. Encourage children to check their writing to be sure that they have placed a period at the end of each telling sentence.

WRITER'S BLOCK

Problem	Solution
Children do not know how to begin their first drafts.	Suggest that children begin by naming the place they are going to describe. For example, _____ is my favorite place to be.

ESL STRATEGY

Provide children with unfinished sentences to complete their draft. These sentences might include *My favorite place is _____. When I'm there, I see _____. I hear _____. I like this place because _____.*

HOME-SCHOOL CONNECTION

Have family members help children compare their prewriting charts with their drafts to see if there are other good details to include. Let family members know that the draft of the description is not meant to be perfect.

WRITING ACROSS THE CURRICULUM

Social Studies When children visit places in the community, they can use descriptive words to write about what they've seen.

The huge red fire engines roared down the street. Six firefighters in helmets and tall boots held onto the sides.

Revising/Editing

OBJECTIVES

★ **RECOGNIZE** that writing can be improved by revising it.

★ **CONTRIBUTE** to the revision of a description in a shared writing activity.

★ **REVISE** a first draft of a description of a place.

★ **RECOGNIZE** the use of words that add details about color, sounds, and textures.

 Introduce Revising and Editing

Remind children that this is the time for them to go back and make changes to the drafts they have written. Reread Joseph's description of the zoo. Ask children what details Joseph might have added to help readers picture the zoo even more clearly. Remind children of their five senses—what other senses could Joseph have used in his writing?

 Shared Writing

MODELED WRITING Use the model on this page to make changes to the draft of a description of a place. As you reread the description with children, pause to talk about each change the writer made. Ask children if they can think of other words the writer could have used to describe the flowers, pictures, and the classroom.

Review how to use a caret to add a word and draw a line through words you want to change or take out. Model how to look back at your chart to see if there are some details you have not used.

INTERACTIVE WRITING You may wish to have volunteers come up to insert carets, draw a line through a word to delete it, and add a period. You may also decide that children are ready to make changes and to find and correct mistakes on their own.

3 Independent Writing

Have children look at their charts and find details they have not circled. They may want to add one or two of those details. Remind children that they will want to describe a place so that readers can see it when they close their eyes.

EMERGENT WRITERS Have children who need extra support read their drafts to you. Have them use a caret to add one color, sound, or texture word to a detail in their description. You might suggest a place where a detail could be added.

TEACHER CONFERENCE You may wish to use the following questions when children share their revised drafts with you.

• *Have you checked your paper for capital letters and periods?*

• *Are there any details from your chart that you would like to add?*

PEER CONFERENCE Have children take turns reading their drafts to partners. Suggest that writers ask listeners the following questions.

• *Do my words tell you what my favorite place is like?*

• *Should I add anything?*

Our Classroom
by Maria Vega

In the morning, our classroom is a
~~special~~ ^ ~~nice~~ place to be. I smell the ^yellow flowers
on the table. Our ^colorful pictures hang on
the walls. Then I hear the bell ring ⊙

The chalk squeaks on the board.

Everyone is working.

Publishing

OBJECTIVE

★ PUBLISH a description of a place.

Children can use the ideas below to share their descriptions of places with family and classmates.

GIANT POSTCARDS Have children draw pictures on tagboard of the places they described. Then they can turn over the drawing and copy their descriptions on the back.

TRAVEL LOG Children can share their descriptions of favorite places by giving oral presentations. Have each child create a travel poster showing his or her place to display during the reading. You may wish to videotape the presentations to share during family night at school.

ROAD MAP Children can copy their place descriptions onto large index cards. Create a bulletin-board display, connecting the cards with red, blue, and black yarn to resemble a road map.

ASSESSMENT OPPORTUNITIES

PORTFOLIO ASSESSMENT If children choose to include their descriptions in their portfolios, have them also include their prewriting charts and drafts.

TEACHER HOLISTIC ASSESSMENT Use the Teacher Evaluation Checklist on page 99 to evaluate children's descriptions.

BENCHMARK PAPERS You may want to use the benchmark papers on pages 100–106 to evaluate children's writing. There is one paper for each level of writing on the Developing Writer's Assessment Continuum.

Meeting Individual Needs

Mini Lesson — Plural Nouns

Introduce Remind children that nouns are words that name people, places, or things. Point to one child and say, *I see one student.* Point to two children and say, *I see two students.* Identify the word *student* as a noun in each sentence. Explain that *-s* can be added to some nouns when you are talking about more than one.

Model Write the following on the board:

1 lion	2 lion___
1 zoo	3 zoo___
1 zookeeper	4 zookeeper___
1 cart	3 cart___

Complete the first example by identifying the noun (*lion*); telling whether it's a person, place, or thing (*thing*); and adding an *-s* to the end of *2 lion___ (lions)*. Then invite volunteers to come to the board and repeat with the rest of the words.

Summarize/Apply Remind children that an *-s* can be added to some words to mean "more than one." With the class, check your shared writing draft to be sure you added *-s* to any plural nouns that needed it.

WRITER'S BLOCK

Problem	Solution
Children are having trouble revising their drafts.	Suggest that children look at their descriptions and try to add words that name a color, a sound, and a texture.

ESL STRATEGY

Have children talk about their descriptions with a partner. Suggest that children work together to add describing words.

HOME-SCHOOL CONNECTION

Encourage children to work with family members to find photographs or postcards of the places they have written about or of other favorite places.

WRITING ACROSS THE CURRICULUM

Science/Language Arts Children can use sensory details to compare two different places where animals live and record their observations in a chart.

Free-Verse Poem

Introduction

OBJECTIVES

★ RESPOND to a model of a free-verse poem written by a published author.

★ RECOGNIZE the characteristics of a free-verse poem.

1 Building Background

Recite with children familiar poems or rhymes. Invite them to tell what they know about poems. List their responses on chart paper. Add to the chart as their knowledge grows. Help children understand that poems use words in a special way to describe something or tell how the writer feels. Poems may or may not rhyme, but they have a rhythm.

2 Meet the Writer

Display page 36 of the Big Book of Writing Models. Read the author's name. Tell children that Lindamichelle Baron writes poetry for adults and children. She began writing poetry when she was about six years old and hasn't stopped since. She uses her poetry to teach reading and writing. This poem tells about how good it feels to laugh.

3 Respond to a Model

Introduce "When My Brother Laughs" as a free-verse poem, and read it aloud. Point to each word as you say it, especially the words on the last line. Help children show what they have learned about the writer's brother in an idea web, such as the one shown. Then ask the children:

- *Does the poem make you feel good? Why?*
- *Why do you think the poet wrote the last line the way she did?*
- *How does the shape of the words help you see what the writer means?*

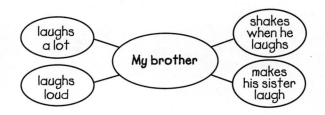

Meeting Individual Needs

LITERATURE CONNECTION

Before your students write their own poems, you may want to introduce them to one of these books.

1. *Lucky Song* by Vera B. Williams. Greenwillow, 1997. Children will relate to the sing-song quality of Williams's prose.

2. *Sweet Corn: Poems by James Stevenson.* Greenwillow, 1995. Everyday objects and events are elevated to poetry in this collection.

3. *Someone I Like: Poems About People* compiled by Judith Nicholls. Illustrated by Giovanni Manna. Barefoot Books, 2000. Family, friends, and neighbors are the subjects of these poems by a variety of poets.

Mini Lesson
Rhyme

Introduce Tell children that *pig* and *big* are rhyming words because they end with the same sound. Say real or nonsense words that rhyme with children's names. After you say each word, have children whose names rhyme with the word stand up.

Model Write *belly* on the board and read the word. Erase initial *b*, replace it with *j*, and read *jelly*. Then use both words in a short rhyme, such as *My brother's belly shakes like jelly.* Write other words from "When My Brother Laughs," and have volunteers change the first letter to make a rhyming word. Work with children to use the word pairs in short rhymes.

Summarize/Apply Remind children that words that end the same way are rhyming words. Tell children that when they write poetry, they might use rhyming words. Stress that poems, especially free-verse poems, do not have to have rhymes.

Free-Verse Poem

from the

Big Book of Writing Models

page 36

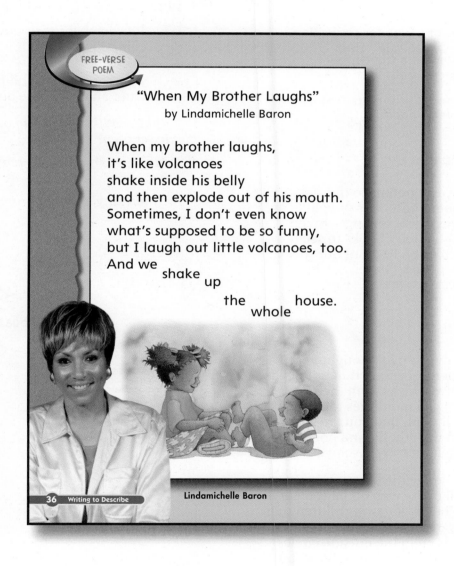

FREE-VERSE POEM

"When My Brother Laughs"
by Lindamichelle Baron

When my brother laughs,
it's like volcanoes
shake inside his belly
and then explode out of his mouth.
Sometimes, I don't even know
what's supposed to be so funny,
but I laugh out little volcanoes, too.
And we
shake up

the whole house.

36 Writing to Describe

Lindamichelle Baron

Prewriting

OBJECTIVES

★ BRAINSTORM and SELECT a topic for a free-verse poem.

★ RECOGNIZE the use of a web for prewriting.

★ CONTRIBUTE to a web in a shared prewriting activity.

★ MAKE a web to identify information to be included in a free-verse poem.

 Introduce Prewriting

Read a few short free-verse poems to the class. Talk about whether each poem describes people, places, or things, or tells about feelings. Invite children to look through poetry books to see how the poems look. Ask children to point out special things they notice about each poem. Ask how children think the poets got their ideas.

 Shared Writing

Ask children to name things they thought about as they listened to the poems. Explain that writers use ideas from their own lives, ideas from their journals, photos, or special memories to choose a subject for a poem. Tell them that you are going to share one writer's plan with them for a poem about something they know about too—a school bus.

MODELED WRITING Use the information in the web on this page to fill in the web on page 50 of the Big Book of Writing Models. Remind children that the main idea or topic of the poem goes in the center circle and details go in the outside circles. Talk about the different kinds of ideas the writer may include in a poem about a school bus.

INTERACTIVE WRITING Invite children to ask questions about the web or contribute ideas that can be added. Remind children that the purpose of making a web is to think of as many ideas as they can. Have volunteers come up and add details to tell how a school bus looks, how it makes them feel, how it sounds, or what it does.

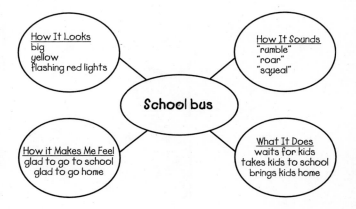

3 Independent Writing

Encourage children to think of special things in their own lives to determine an idea for a poem. Make copies of the blackline master on page 96 for children to use to plan what they will write. Display the web you made as a model.

EMERGENT WRITERS Help children get started by guiding them to write their topic in the center circle. Ask questions to help them think of details and word choices to build the web.

TEACHER CONFERENCE You may want to use the following questions during your conferences with children to discuss their webs.

- *What are you going to write about?*
- *Why did you choose this idea?*
- *Can you think of any more ideas to add?*

PEER CONFERENCE Have children share their web with a partner and ask these questions.

- *Would you like to read a poem about the idea I have chosen?*
- *Do the ideas on my web remind you of other ideas?*
- *Are there any ideas that don't seem to belong?*

Action Verbs

Introduce Invite children to play a simple one-word version of the game Charades. Children take turns pantomiming an action, such as *jump, jog, climb,* or *sweep.* The others guess by naming the word as you write it on the board. Read together your list of words. Explain that the words are action words, or verbs, because they tell what someone or something does.

Model Reread "When My Brother Laughs," pointing to each word. Invite children to find action words *(laughs, shake, explode).* As each word is identified, have children perform the action.

Summarize/Apply Remind children to use verbs as they write their free-verse poems. Verbs will tell readers what the subject of the poem is doing.

 WRITER'S BLOCK

Problem
Children cannot think of a topic.

Solution
Share a few poems with children that have a familiar theme, such as family, friends, pets, or a trip. Ask children what the poem reminds them of and use this idea to write a poem of their own.

ESL STRATEGY
Invite English-language learners to draw pictures about their topic for the web. Partners can help write captions for the web as they talk about the pictures.

HOME-SCHOOL CONNECTION
Invite children to share their writing ideas with a family member. As children talk with family members about their topics, they may think of more ideas for their web.

WRITING ACROSS THE CURRICULUM
Art Tell children that they can use a web to plan ideas for pictures they will draw and color or paint in art class. Suggest that children plan their next picture by using a web to organize details.

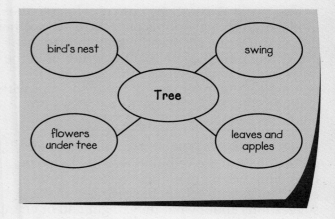

Free-Verse Poem

Drafting

OBJECTIVES

★ **RECOGNIZE** the characteristics of a free-verse poem.

★ **RESPOND** to a first draft in a shared writing activity.

★ **USE** a web as a plan to write a first draft.

 Introduce Drafting

Initiate a discussion about putting together a puzzle and how some pieces fit together easily, while others take several tries. Lead children to see that writing is like putting together a puzzle. Some parts will be easy for them to write, while other parts will take several tries before they find the right words.

2 Shared Writing

MODELED WRITING Copy onto chart paper the model draft shown on this page. Skip every other line as you write. Display the draft next to the prewriting web. Explain that the writer used the ideas from the web to write this first draft of a poem. Read the poem about the school bus with children. Talk about words the writer uses to describe the bus.

INTERACTIVE WRITING Invite children to check off the ideas in the web that were included in the poem. Ask them to think about their own experiences with school buses and to make suggestions about what they might add or change. Children can write their ideas on the chart paper at the end of the poem.

3 Independent Writing

Tell children to use their webs to decide what ideas to include in their poems. Encourage them to write freely and to think about how their topic makes them feel and what it reminds them of.

EMERGENT WRITERS Have children say their poem into a tape recorder so that the teacher can help them write the poem by sounding out words.

TEACHER CONFERENCE You may want to use these questions during your conference with children to discuss their drafts.

* *How are you doing with your poem?*
* *This is a great topic! Can you say anything more about it?*
* *How did you use your web as you were writing your draft?*

PEER CONFERENCE Pair children and remind them how to work together in a peer conference.

* *Try to picture your partner's poem in your head.*
* *Tell what you like about the poem.*
* *Make comments and suggestions.*

School Bus
by Thomas Borden

Big yelow bus rolls into the yard,

rumbling, squealing,

making noise.

It comes to a stop,

red lights on,

watching for kids.

Let's go!

Glad you're here

Mini Lesson

Use Precise/Vivid Verbs

Introduce Write *move* on the board. Ask a volunteer to move. Explain that *move* is an action verb, but it does not tell exactly how to move. Ask volunteers to skip, crawl, and hop. Write the words on the board and ask children to name other words that paint pictures in their mind of different ways to move.

Model Write *come* on a self-stick note and cover the word *explode* in the first verse of "When My Brother Laughs." Read the new version. Take off the note, and read the published poem. Ask what children see in their minds when they read the word *explode*. Ask why the word *explode* is a better word than *come*.

Summarize/Apply Remind children that poems say a lot in a few words. When children write poems, explain that they can say more if they choose words that tell their readers exactly what they want them to see in their minds.

WRITER'S BLOCK

Problem	Solution
Children have trouble choosing just the right words.	Help children review their webs to choose the most important ideas. Ask them to think of how they can share these ideas using words that readers will be able to picture in their minds.

ESL STRATEGY

If children are having difficulty thinking of words to use in their poems, have them draw a picture of their topic and work with a partner who can help them think of adjectives and action verbs.

HOME-SCHOOL CONNECTION

Send home a note asking family members to review the first draft for ideas and content rather than form or spelling. Remind them to first tell what they like about the writing and then ask questions.

WRITING ACROSS THE CURRICULUM

Science When children record science observations in a learning log, invite them to use just the right action verbs to explain what they see.

First, the egg <u>cracked</u> in one tiny place. Then, a beak <u>poked</u> through to make a small hole. The chick <u>pecked</u> until he <u>squeezed</u> himself out of the shell.

Revising/Editing

OBJECTIVES

★ **RECOGNIZE** that writing can be improved by revising it.

★ **CONTRIBUTE** to the revision of a free-verse poem in a shared writing activity.

★ **REVISE** a first draft of a free-verse poem.

★ **RECOGNIZE** the use of precise/vivid words.

 Introduce Revising and Editing

Remind children that all good writers go over their writing to fix mistakes and to make changes. This is what children will do in the revising/editing stage. Reread "When My Brother Laughs" on page 36 of the Big Book and talk about how the author uses just the right words to tell about her brother. Ask children what they like best about the poem and if there is anything they would change.

 Shared Writing

MODELED WRITING Reread the draft of the poem about the school bus. Use the model on this page to show changes the writer made to the poem. Think aloud as you circle and rewrite a misspelled word, circle a sentence and draw an arrow to show where it will be moved, and add an exclamation point.

Ask children what they think of the change the writer made by changing the word *on* to a more exact word and by changing the order of the final two sentences. Does the poem sound better?

INTERACTIVE WRITING You may want to ask children to check the draft for spelling and punctuation errors and invite volunteers to make changes using revising marks they have already learned.

3 Independent Writing

Have children reread their own drafts and ask themselves these questions.

- *Have I chosen the best words to say exactly what I mean?*

- *How does my poem sound when I read it aloud?*

Remind children to check for spelling, capitalization, and punctuation as they edit.

EMERGENT WRITERS Let children copy their drafts on the computer and use the word-processing program to help them experiment with placing line breaks in different places.

TEACHER CONFERENCE You may wish to ask the following questions when children share their revised drafts with you.

- *What words will help your reader picture just what you are describing?*

- *Have you used action words to tell about your topic?*

PEER CONFERENCE Invite children to read their revised poems to their partners. Suggest that the writer ask the listener the following questions.

- *What do you see in your mind when you hear my poem?*

- *Are there any words I should change?*

School Bus
by Thomas Borden

Big ~~yelow~~ *yellow* bus rolls into the yard,

rumbling, squealing,

making noise.

It comes to a stop,

red lights ~~on,~~ *flashing*

watching for kids.

Let's go!

Glad you're here!

Publishing

OBJECTIVE

★ PUBLISH a free-verse poem.

Children can use one of these suggestions to share their poems.

POETRY FESTIVAL Set up an Author's Chair with a sign that says "Poetry Reading Today." Have children take turns reading their poems aloud.

"FIRST POEMS" ANTHOLOGY Tell children that collections of stories and poems are called anthologies. Have children illustrate their poems. Then bind them together to make their own class anthology.

POETS AND ARTISTS Pair children. Have them read each other's poems and think about what picture the poem paints. Then have children use their ideas to illustrate their partner's poem.

ASSESSMENT OPPORTUNITIES

PORTFOLIO ASSESSMENT If children choose to include their poems in their portfolios, have them also include their prewriting webs and drafts.

TEACHER HOLISTIC ASSESSMENT Use the Teacher Evaluation Checklist on page 99 to evaluate children's poems.

BENCHMARK PAPERS You may want to use the benchmark papers on pages 100–106 to evaluate children's writing. There is one paper for each level of writing on the Developing Writer's Assessment Continuum.

Meeting Individual Needs

Publishing: About the Author

Introduce Show picture books that have author notes. Display an About the Author section from a book jacket, show the picture if available, and read the information aloud.

Model Review the Meet the Author information about Lindamichelle Baron that you shared at the beginning of this lesson. Ask children what other things they would like to know about the poet. List on chart paper the kinds of information children would include in an About the Author section.

Summarize/Apply Tell children that reading about an author can help them know the author and understand how and why he or she got ideas for writing. Ask children to write their own About the Author paragraph to go with their poems.

WRITER'S BLOCK

Problem	Solution
Children are frustrated by making mistakes as they copy their final drafts.	Have children hold a paper strip or ruler under the line they are copying to keep their place.

ESL STRATEGY

Read children's poems into a tape recorder, pausing between words and lines to create a rhythm. Have children listen to the tape and copy your rhythm as they repeat each line after you.

HOME-SCHOOL CONNECTION

Tell children to share both their draft and their published poem with family members and show how they improved their poem by revising and editing.

WRITING ACROSS THE CURRICULUM

Music After children engage in a musical activity, invite them to express what they felt or experienced by writing a free-verse poem.

Description of a Character

Introduction

OBJECTIVES

★ **RESPOND** to a student model of a description of a story character.

★ **RECOGNIZE** the characteristics of a description of a story character.

1 Building Background

Introduce a description of a story character by reading a story about a favorite character as children listen. Then ask children to think of words to describe this character, including how the character looks, acts, and feels and how children feel about the character. List the words in a chart as children say them.

2 Meet the Writer

Direct children's attention to the character description "The Cat in the Hat" on page 37 of the Big Book of Writing Models. Explain that the writer, Betty Maya Foott, is in first grade. She wrote a description of her favorite book character, The Cat in the Hat. Ask children what they already know about the cat in this story.

3 Respond to a Model

As you read aloud Betty Maya's description, draw attention to words the writer uses to describe the character. Pause periodically to ask *What new information does Betty Maya share about The Cat in the Hat?* Then have children tell in their own words what they learned about the cat from the description. Record children's responses in a chart.

The Cat in the Hat

How the character looks
red tie
striped hat

How the character acts
like a know-it-all
fixes his mistakes

How the character feels
happy

Meeting Individual Needs

LITERATURE CONNECTION

Before students write their character descriptions, introduce them to memorable characters in books such as the following.

1. *Leo the Late Bloomer* by Robert Kraus. Illustrated by Jose Aruego. Harpercollins, 1987. Leo learns to do things in his own sweet time.

2. *Imogene's Antlers* by David Small. Crown, 1985. Imogene wakes up to find that she has made an amazing transformation.

3. *The Two Bullies* by Junko Morimoto. Crown, 1999. Two large men display amazing strength and cleverness in this Japanese folk tale.

Mini Lesson
Character

Introduce Have children share their favorite story characters. Discuss which of these characters are people and which are animals. Then have children identify which characters seem real and which are make-believe.

Model Show children an illustration from *The Cat in the Hat*. Explain that the illustrations and the words in a story can give clues about how a character looks, acts, and feels. For example, you can tell by The Cat's hat and his expression that he might act silly. Read aloud sections of the book to children and talk about ideas children learn about The Cat from the author's words.

Summarize/Apply Remind children that words and story pictures give clues to what a character is like. Have children think about the characters they will describe in their writing.

Description of a Story Character
from the
Big Book of Writing Models
page 37

Prewriting

OBJECTIVES

★ BRAINSTORM and SELECT a character for a description of a story character.

★ RECOGNIZE the use of a chart for prewriting.

★ CONTRIBUTE to a chart in a shared prewriting activity.

★ MAKE a chart to list ideas that can be included in a description of a character.

1 Introduce Prewriting

Look at the chart that children helped to make about The Cat in the Hat. Ask children how such a chart may have helped Betty Maya to plan and write her description. Point out that planning ahead helps writers remember the important ideas they want to include in their writing.

2 Shared Writing

Ask children to name favorite story characters. List them on chart paper. Prompt, if necessary, by reminding children of stories they are reading or have read. Tell them that you're going to share a plan for a description of a story character whose name is Little Critter.

MODELED WRITING Use the details from the sample chart on this page to make your own character chart. Remind children that making a chart like this one will help them plan what they want to say about the character before they begin to write. As you share the chart with children, point out details that tell how the character looks, acts, and feels.

INTERACTIVE WRITING Invite children to ask questions or suggest other ideas to add to the character chart. You might encourage them to think about how other characters relate to Little Critter or additional words that can be used to tell how Little Critter looks. Remind children to include as many ideas as they can.

3 Independent Writing

Invite children to look at the brainstorming list of characters, books in the classroom, and literature logs to choose a character to describe. Make copies of the blackline master on page 97 for children to use in planning their descriptions. Encourage children to refer to the books as they make their character charts, using words to tell about how their characters look, act, and feel.

EMERGENT WRITERS Children needing extra support might reread the book with a partner and then complete the chart together.

TEACHER CONFERENCE Conference with children to talk about the character charts they have made. Use questions like the following as a starting point.

- *What do you like most about this character?*
- *What does the character like to do?*
- *What words did you put in your chart to tell how the character looks, acts, and feels?*

PEER CONFERENCE Have children get together with partners to share their charts. Provide the following questions for children to ask one another.

- *What character did you pick?*
- *Read the words in your chart to tell me about your character.*
- *Why do you like this character?*

Little Critter

How does the character look?
green pants
bare feet

How does the character act?
gets in trouble
pouts
changes his mind

How does the character feel?
mad
happy

Using a Journal to Get Ideas

Introduce Tell children that when they are trying to think of an idea to write about, they should think about ideas they know or experiences they have had. One great place to look for ideas to write a character description is in their journals or literature logs.

Model As you look once again at Betty Maya's character description from the Big Book of Writing Models, talk about how after reading the book the writer may have written notes or made drawings about The Cat in the Hat in her journal or literature log. Explain that the writer could then use these notes for ideas to write about the character.

Summarize/Apply Encourage children to review journal or log entries they may have previously written about a story character. They can use their entries to help them write about their favorite characters.

WRITER'S BLOCK

Problem	Solution
Children cannot think of character traits to write in their charts.	Have children look at illustrations to tell how the character looks. Prompt them with sentences such as: *The character must feel _____ because* (include story detail).

ESL STRATEGY

Children can express character traits by using facial expressions or pantomime. As children reveal traits, partners can write them down. Model the process to prompt children's thinking.

HOME-SCHOOL CONNECTION

Encourage children to acquaint family members with their favorite characters by reading stories aloud at home. After reading, families can discuss characters and their traits.

WRITING ACROSS THE CURRICULUM

Science Once children are comfortable creating character charts for writing, use the same process to have children record details about wildlife.

White-tailed Deer

How does the animal look?
tan coat
fawn has spots

How does the animal act?
lifts tail when in danger
comes out mostly at night

How does the animal feel?
safe in forests and farmland
afraid of people

Description of a Character

Drafting

OBJECTIVES

★ **RECOGNIZE** the characteristics of a description of a story character.

★ **RESPOND** to a first draft in a shared writing activity.

★ **USE** a chart as a plan to write a first draft.

 Introduce Drafting

Tell children that they are ready to write descriptions to tell others about favorite story characters. Ask children to demonstrate how they would introduce a friend to their parents. In the same way, remind children to include enough details in their descriptions so that their readers will get to know their characters and why they like them.

 Shared Writing

MODELED WRITING Display the character chart you made in prewriting. Copy the model draft from this page onto chart paper or use the write-on pages on pages 53–56 of the Big Book of Writing Models. Show how the writer uses the details from the chart to write the description. Read the description with children, pointing out details that tell how the character looks, acts, and feels.

INTERACTIVE WRITING As you talk about the details that tell about Little Critter, invite volunteers to check them off on the chart. Encourage children to contribute ideas by telling what they would add or change. Have children come up and write their ideas as sentences at the end of the description.

3 **Independent Writing**

Encourage children to circle the details in their character charts that they think are important to include in their descriptions. They might want to check off each detail as they include it in the draft.

EMERGENT WRITERS Have children verbalize sentences to tell who the character is and what the character acts and feels like. Then help children write sentences that they can later read.

TEACHER CONFERENCE The following questions can be used as you conference with children about their drafts.

- *How can I help with your description?*
- *Which ideas from your character chart have you used?*
- *Is there another idea from your chart that you can use in a telling sentence?*

PEER CONFERENCE Pairs of children can read their descriptions to each other. Remind them how to behave as they listen.

- *Pay attention as your partner reads. Ask any questions that you have about the character.*
- *Tell what you like about the story character.*

Little Critter
by Christa Neale

Little Critter is an animal in a story.

He wears green pants but has bare feet. He keeps doing things that get him in trouble. He gets mad

He changes his mind.

I like Little critter because he is like me.

Mini Lesson

Reader Interest: Write an Attention-Grabbing Beginning

Introduce Ask children what makes them want to read a book. Talk about how they might look for an interesting title, glance through a book to look at the pictures, or read the first page. Lead children to suggest that an exciting beginning will get them interested in a story and make them want to read more.

Model Read aloud the first sentence of Betty Maya's description of The Cat in the Hat on page 37 of the Big Book. Discuss how this sentence is interesting and makes readers want to find out more. Compare it to the opening sentence *The Cat in the Hat is a story character*. Encourage children to share ideas about writing opening sentences for descriptions of their favorite characters.

Summarize/Apply Tell children to take some extra time to write their opening sentence. Getting their writing off to a strong start will make it more interesting and will get their readers' attention. Children might read their opening sentences aloud and take suggestions from classmates to make their beginnings stronger.

WRITER'S BLOCK

Problem	Solution
Children are having trouble thinking of words to describe their characters.	Have children discuss their characters with other children who are familiar with the story. Encourage children to brainstorm describing words that tell about the character.

ESL STRATEGY

Create a simple form for children to fill out. A sample form could begin *My favorite character is _____. This character looks like _____. I like this character because _____.*

HOME-SCHOOL CONNECTION

Inform family members that the purpose of the draft is to write down ideas. Family members can help children by recalling or rereading parts of a story that feature the special character.

WRITING ACROSS THE CURRICULUM

Social Studies Encourage children to describe people they read about in social studies. Remind them to think about how the people look, act, and feel.

Abraham Lincoln

Abraham Lincoln was very tall. He wore a big black hat, and he had a beard. He loved to learn. When he grew up, he acted strong and brave. He believed that all people should be free.

Revising/Editing

OBJECTIVES

★ **RECOGNIZE** that writing can be improved by revising it.

★ **CONTRIBUTE** to the revision of a description of a story character in a shared writing activity.

★ **REVISE** a first draft of a description of a story character.

★ **RECOGNIZE** the use of vivid words to add details.

1 Introduce Revising and Editing

Explain that once a draft is written, a good writer goes back to make changes or fix mistakes. Reread Betty Maya's description of The Cat in the Hat. Ask children if they can think of any words Betty Maya could have added to give readers a better idea of what The Cat is like. Record their ideas on chart paper.

2 Shared Writing

MODELED WRITING Use the model on this page to make changes to the draft of a character description. Then reread the description with children, talking about each change. Have children look back at the character chart to see the details the writer decides to add. Ask children how these changes make the description clearer.

Review how to insert a word by using a caret and writing the change above the line. Draw three lines under letters that should be capitalized and add a period if one is missing. Give each child a copy of the revising and editing marks on page 26 of the Teacher Resource Guide.

INTERACTIVE WRITING You may want to present the draft without revisions to determine if children will notice the need for a capital letter in a name and a period to end a sentence. Invite volunteers to draw carets and add new words as revisions are discussed.

3 Independent Writing

Have children reread their first drafts and ask themselves the following questions.

- *Do I tell who I am describing?*
- *Have I told how my character looks, acts, and feels?*
- *Is there anything I should add?*

Remind children that it is part of revising to mark up their first drafts and change their original ideas.

EMERGENT WRITERS Read children's descriptions with them. Pause after each sentence to ask if there are any words to add or change. Help children check spelling and punctuation.

TEACHER CONFERENCE You may wish to use the following questions when children share their revised drafts with you.

- *Can you add any details to help your reader think your story character is funny, interesting, or special?*
- *Did you use your picture dictionary to help with your spelling?*

PEER CONFERENCE Have children take turns reading their drafts to partners. Suggest that writers ask listeners the following questions.

- *How do you like my favorite story character?*
- *Is there anything else you would like to know?*

Little Critter
by Christa Neale

Little Critter is an animal in a story.

He wears green pants but has bare feet. He keeps doing things that get
and pouts.
him in trouble. He gets mad.
and then he is happy
He changes his mind.

I like Little critter because he is

like me.

Publishing

OBJECTIVE

★ PUBLISH a description of a story character.

The ideas below will help children share their story character descriptions with family and classmates.

BOOK JACKET Have children create book jackets. On the covers, they can write the characters' names and their own names. Then they can copy their character descriptions on the inside flap of the jacket. Display the book jackets in the classroom.

MEET MY FRIEND Have children make simple stick puppets of their story characters and then share their character descriptions by reading them aloud. Children can manipulate their puppets as though they are introducing a new friend to the class.

PHOTO ALBUM Have students draw pictures of their favorite characters. The pictures can be mounted in a book, one picture per page, with the character descriptions included.

ASSESSMENT OPPORTUNITIES

PORTFOLIO ASSESSMENT If children choose to include their descriptions in their portfolios, have them also include their prewriting charts and drafts.

TEACHER HOLISTIC ASSESSMENT Use the Teacher Evaluation Checklist on page 99 to evaluate children's descriptions.

BENCHMARK PAPERS You may want to use the benchmark papers on pages 100–106 to evaluate children's writing. There is one paper for each level of writing on the Developing Writer's Assessment Continuum.

Meeting Individual Needs

Capitalization: Proper Nouns

Introduce Remind children that nouns are words that name people, places, or things. Explain that proper nouns name a special person, place, or thing. Write your full name on the chalkboard. Underline each capital letter. Explain that a capital letter signals a proper noun.

Model Invite children to write the names of their favorite characters on the board. Point out that the character's names begin with capital letters. Repeat the activity with the names of specific settings from children's stories, such as *The Hundred-Acre Wood, Mulberry Street,* or *Paris.*

Summarize/Apply Remind children that a capital letter is used to signal a proper noun—a word that names a particular person, place, or thing. Invite children to review their drafts for specific names of characters, settings, or any other proper noun that may need to begin with a capital letter.

WRITER'S BLOCK

Problem	Solution
Children are having trouble thinking of a way to end their descriptions.	Suggest that they end by telling the one thing they like best about their characters.

ESL STRATEGY

Children can make lists of words that describe how their characters act: *happy, friendly, silly, brave.* Consider pairing children for this activity.

HOME-SCHOOL CONNECTION

Encourage children to bring in books from home to share in a display. Children can use the books to introduce memorable characters.

WRITING ACROSS THE CURRICULUM

Language Arts Children can use story character descriptions when they write book reports.

Teacher Notes

Just the Facts: Writing to Inform

Contents

RESOURCES

TEACHING PLANS

Writing to Inform
Unit Planner

MINILESSONS

WRITING FORM	Basic Skills/ Writing Process/ Writer's Craft	Grammar, Usage, Mechanics, Spelling	Writing Across the Curriculum	Meeting Individual Needs	Assessment
Lesson 1 **BOOK REPORT** pp. 164–171 (7–9 days)	• Identify Main Idea, 164 • Plan a Composition Using Character/ Setting Chart, 167	• Capitalization: Titles of Books, 169 • Checking Spelling, 171	• Science, 167 • Language Arts, 169 • Math, 171	• Writer's Block, 167, 169, 171 • ESL Strategy, 167, 169, 171 • Home-School Connection, 167, 169, 171	• Teacher Checklist, 153 • Benchmark Papers, 154–160 • Portfolio, 171 • Teacher and Peer Conferencing, 166, 168, 170
Lesson 2 **THANK-YOU NOTE** pp. 172–179 (7–9 days)	• Sentences: Expanding by Adding Details, 177 • Replace Overused Words, 179	• Comma in Letter Parts, 172 • Capitalization in Letter Parts, 175	• Science, 175 • Social Studies, 177 • Social Studies, 179	• Writer's Block, 175, 177, 179 • ESL Strategy, 175, 177, 179 • Home-School Connection, 175, 177, 179	• Teacher Checklist, 153 • Benchmark Papers, 154–160 • Portfolio, 179 • Teacher and Peer Conferencing, 174, 176, 178
Lesson 3 **REPORT** pp. 180–187 (7–9 days)	• Make and Record Observations, 180 • Add Facts and Reasons to Support Main Idea, 185 • Publishing: Using Illustrations or Diagrams, 187	• Use Complete Sentences, 183	• Science/Social Studies, 183 • Science, 185 • Science, 187	• Writer's Block, 183, 185, 187 • ESL Strategy, 183, 185, 187 • Home-School Connection, 183, 185, 187	• Teacher Checklist, 153 • Benchmark Papers, 154–160 • Portfolio, 187 • Teacher and Peer Conferencing, 182, 184, 186
Lesson 4 **DIRECTIONS** pp. 188–195 (7–9 days)	• Use Time-Order Words, 188 • Plan a Composition by Using a List, 191 • Top-to-Bottom Progression, 193 • Sentence Variety— Beginnings, 195		• Science, 191 • Math, 193 • Art, 195	• Writer's Block, 191, 193, 195 • ESL Strategy, 191, 193, 195 • Home-School Connection, 191, 193, 195	• Teacher Checklist, 153 • Benchmark Papers, 154–160 • Portfolio, 195 • Teacher and Peer Conferencing, 190, 192, 194

Making the Reading-Writing Connection
Writing to Inform

You may want to add the following books to your classroom library. Each category of book represents one form of writing children will be introduced to in *Writing to Inform*. The books serve as models for good writing and are valuable resources to use throughout each lesson. The suggested titles offer opportunities for you to read to the class as well as for children to read themselves.

Use literature to introduce a writing form, to show a model of successful writing, to enhance minilessons, to focus on grammar and usage, or to expand each lesson.

BOOK REPORT

The Library Dragon
by Carmen Agra Deedy. Illustrated by Michael White. Peachtree, 1994. Miss Lotta Scales, the dragon/librarian at Sunrise School, is determined to protect the books from the children.

A Bedtime Story
by Mem Fox. Illustrated by Elivia Savadier. Mondo Publishing, 1996. Polly, Mom, and Dad share the joy of reading together.

Edward and the Pirates
by David McPhail. Little Brown, 1997. Edward's adventure shows that, with a little imagination, books can come to life.

THANK-YOU NOTE

The Gardener
by Sarah Stewart. Illustrated by David Small. Farrar, Straus & Giroux, 1997. Lydia Grace's humble letters home during the Depression show what happiness a child can bring.

Clever Letters: Fun Ways to Wiggle Your Words
by Laura Allen. Illustrated by Valerie Coursen. Pleasant Co., 1997. Lots of creative ideas for writing and presentation.

Letter Writer Starter Set
by Nancy Cobb. Illustrated by Laura Cornell. Reader's Digest, 1999. More ideas for writers.

REPORT

Red-Eyed Tree Frog
by Joy Cowley. Photographs by Nic Bishop. Scholastic, 1999. Learn about this particular frog's fascinating behavior.

Open Wide: Tooth School Inside
by Laurie Keller. Henry Holt, 2000. This humorous tale on oral hygiene provides lots of information about teeth and dentistry.

Look What Came From China
by Miles Harvey. Franklin Watts, 1999. Photographs and text about inventions, discoveries, and famous people in Chinese history.

DIRECTIONS

Seeds Grow
by Angela Shelf Medearis. Illustrated by Jill Dubin. Cartwheel Books, 2000. The steps involved in planting and growing seeds are explained in this simple text.

Pete's a Pizza
by William Steig. Harpercollins, 1998. Just how does Pete become a pizza? His father knows the secret recipe.

A Drop of Water: A Book of Science and Wonder
by Walter Wick. Scholastic, 1997. Follow a drop of water on a journey.

The Classroom Writing Center
Writing to Inform

You can enhance your classroom writing center to focus on *Writing to Inform*. Here are some suggestions to consider.

◆ Create a class message board where children can write and post messages to name and tell about favorite books they have read.

◆ Supply extra-special stationery for children to write thank-you notes.

◆ Include software at your computer station that allows children to make greeting cards. Drawing software that includes stamps will allow children to stamp a picture or place a graphic on the screen and type information for a report.

Create a Bulletin Board for **Writing to Inform**

◆ Set up a class "Know-It-All" board. Divide your board into three areas. In each section, place a write-on white board with dry-erase markers. (If you use white mural paper for children to write on, it will have to be changed daily).

◆ Children can take turns using one section to write about a good book they have read. The board in another section can be used for writing a thank-you message. The third section can be used to share directions telling how to do something.

◆ Post a sign-up sheet for each section so that each child has a turn to write.

Monday	Kiyo	Marcus	Maria
Tuesday			
Wednesday			

Connecting Multiple Intelligences
Writing to Inform

The following activities focus on specific prewriting, drafting, and publishing ideas for children who demonstrate intelligence in different ways: talent and skill with words (linguistic), with numbers (logical-mathematical), with pictures (spatial), with movement (bodily/kinesthetic), with people (interpersonal), with self (intrapersonal), with music (musical), and/or with nature (environmental or naturalist).

Linguistic
Drafting — Tape-record your report draft. Listen to it and then decide what to add or change.
Publishing — Give a presentation of your directions or report with props.

Logical-Mathematical
Prewriting — Order three books from most to least favorite. Use your favorite to write your book report.
Drafting — Write directions for a counting or adding game.

Spatial
Publishing — Turn your report or directions into a multi-page booklet with drawings.
Use drawings, photos, or a model to make your report come alive.

Bodily Kinesthetic
Prewriting/Drafting — Practice the steps of your directions before and as you write them.
Publishing — Make a bulletin-board display of your report.

Writing to Inform

Environmental (Naturalist)
Prewriting — Plan to write a report about a nature theme you are interested in.
Drafting — Write directions for planting a garden or making crafts using natural materials.

Intrapersonal
Prewriting — Look in your literature log to find a favorite book to write about.
Publishing — Personalize your thank-you letters by drawing a picture of yourself with what you are thankful for.

Interpersonal
Prewriting — Work with a partner to plan and find information about a shared idea for a report.
Publishing — Read aloud your thank-you letter to the person for whom it was intended.

Musical
Prewriting — Plan to write directions that will teach others the steps of a dance or how to play a musical game.
Publishing — Make up a song to add to your report.

Thank-You Note

Write a note to say "thank you."

Date _____

Dear _____,

Thank you for _____

_____

_____

_____

_____

_____

 **Love,**

_____

Name _____ Date _____

Book Report

Use this page to write about a book you've read.

Title _____

_____

Author _____

Characters _____

_____

Setting _____

_____

The book is about _____

_____

_____

_____

Web

Write facts about your topic in the circles.

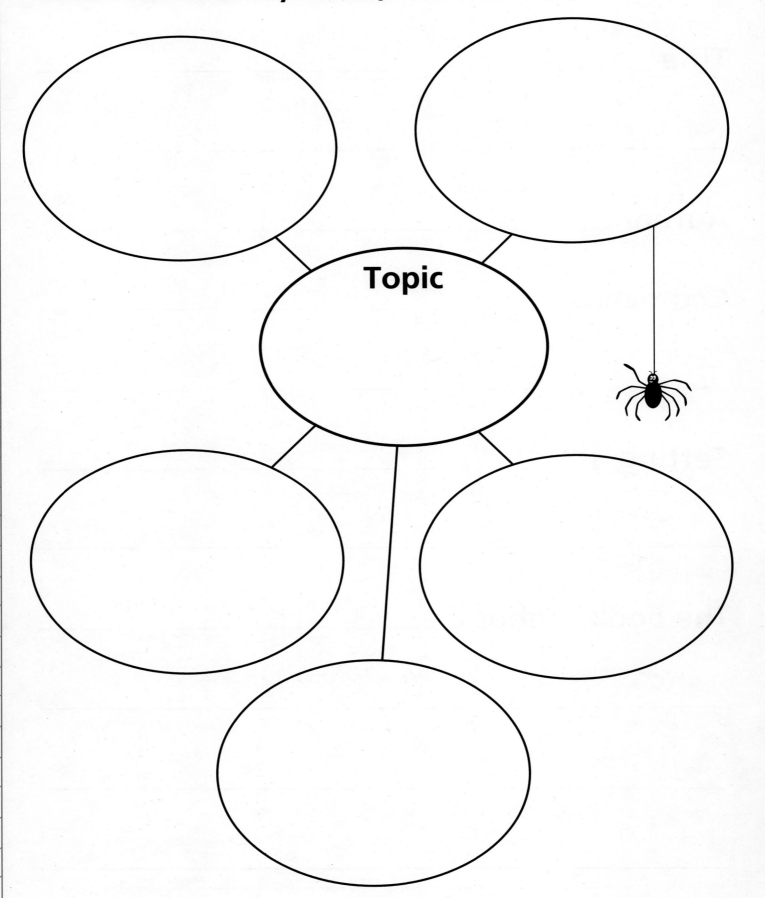

Topic

Name _____   **Date** _____

What Comes Next?

Write sentences in the boxes. Cut the boxes apart. Put the sentences in order.

First, _____

_____

Next, _____

_____

Then, _____

_____

Last, _____

_____

Evaluating Student Writing
Writing to Inform

The Write Direction offers a variety of assessment options. The following are short descriptions of the assessment opportunities available in this unit. Just select the assessment option that works best for you.

Types of Assessment	Writing Lessons
Benchmark Papers Annotated student writing models are provided as benchmarks for evaluating children's writing. Children's writing can be compared to these models, which represent different developmental stages as specified in the Developing Writer's Assessment Continuum.	Student samples for writing to inform, levels 1–7, pages 154–160
Checklists The Teacher Evaluation Checklist helps track children's progress as their writing skills develop.	• Teacher Evaluation Checklist, page 153
Portfolio Assessment Children's work generated throughout the writing process may be used in creating individual portfolios illustrating children's progress as writers. Suggested pieces for a portfolio include completed works and works-in-progress, graphic organizers, logs, and journals.	• Book Report, page 171 • Thank-You Note, page 179 • Report, page 187 • Directions, page 195
Teacher and Peer Conferencing Throughout each lesson in this unit, there are opportunities to interact with children, informally questioning them about their progress and concerns. Children also have opportunities to interact with one another to ask questions, share ideas, and react to the partner's writing.	• Book Report, pages 166, 168, 170 • Thank-You Note, pages 174, 176, 178 • Report, pages 182, 184, 186 • Directions, pages 190, 192, 194

Teacher Evaluation Checklist
Writing to Inform

Name of Writer _____

Date _____

Writing Mode _____

Use this checklist when you are evaluating a child's
- **book report**
- **thank-you note**
- **report**
- **directions**

	YES	NO	Recommendations to Child
Is the topic appropriate for this writing assignment?	❏	❏	
Is the writing focused on the topic?	❏	❏	
Does the writing include facts and details that support the focus?	❏	❏	
Is the information well organized?	❏	❏	
Does the writing have a clear structure?	❏	❏	
Does the writer adhere to the conventions of grammar? usage? spelling? punctuation? capitalization?	❏ ❏ ❏ ❏ ❏	❏ ❏ ❏ ❏ ❏	
Is the handwriting legible?	❏	❏	
Was the work done neatly?	❏	❏	

153

Emerging Writer: Level 1
Writing to Inform

Dictated message: Stegosaurus. Tree There's grass. The purple things are bubbles. Skies

Conventions

Sentence Structure Includes no evidence of intended message.

Directionality, Spacing, and Punctuation Places squiggles, other shapes, letterlike shapes, and/or letters randomly.

Letter Formation and Capitalization: Forms squiggles, other shapes, and/or letterlike shapes.

Spelling Represents words using letterlike shapes, and/or letters with no letter-sound correspondence to the intended word; dictation needed to read all words.

Content

Supporting Details Includes no evidence of intended articles or modifiers.

Word Choice Includes no evidence of intended words.

Writing to Inform

Conventions

Sentence Structure Includes 1 intended word or phrase.

Directionality, Spacing, and Punctuation Places letterlike shapes or letters in a left to right direction and may have a space between 2 words.

Letter Formation and Capitalization Forms mostly uppercase letters; may form 1 word using lowercase letters.

Spelling Represents 1–2 words by recording at least 1 dominant sound; may spell 1 word conventionally; dictation needed to read most words.

Content

Supporting Details Includes 1 intended article and/or modifier.

Word Choice Uses 1–3 intended high-frequency routine words.

Writing to Inform

Title _Sakx_ [Snakes]

Sakx kn l lV ln the zoo. [Snakes]

Snakes can live in the zoo.

Conventions

Sentence Structure Includes 1 intended simple sentence.

Directionality, Spacing, and Punctuation Places letters and/or words in a left to right direction and leaves spaces between 3 or more words; may attempt punctuation.

Letter Formation and Capitalization Forms 2 or more words using lowercase letters.

Spelling Represents most words by recording 1 or more dominant sounds; may spell 2–3 different words conventionally; dictation needed to read some words.

Content

Supporting Details Includes 2 intended modifiers.

Word Choice Uses 4 or more intended high-frequency routine words.

Early Writer: Level 4
Writing to Inform

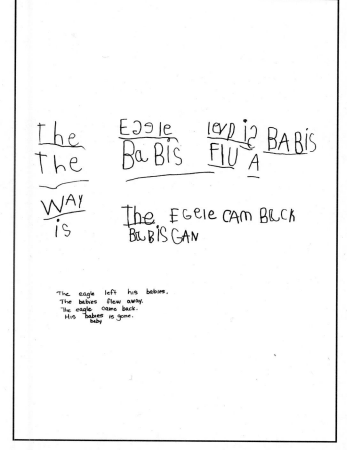

The eagle left his babies. The babies flew away.

The eagle came back. His babies/baby is gone.

Conventions

Sentence Structure Includes 2–3 simple sentences and/or 1 compound or complex sentence.

Sentence Variation Begins all sentences with the same word.

Punctuation Ends 1 sentence or the story with a period.

Capitalization Capitalizes first word in 1 sentence; capitalize other letters may be inappropriately.

Spelling Spells 4–8 different words conventionally; dictation needed to read a few words.

Content

Opening Begins with an action or a fact in the first of 2–3 related thoughts or sentences.

Transitions Uses 1 transitional word or phrase to connect thoughts. (Note: No transitional word or phrase is scored level 3.)

Development of Ideas Uses a glimmer of at least 1 strategy to develop an idea.

Supporting Details Includes 3–4 different modifiers.

Word Choice Uses 1 precise word that is more exact in meaning.

Closing Stops with no ending after 2 or more related thoughts or sentences.

Early Writer: Level 5
Writing to Inform

Title: _Dear grandpa,_

I am so happy that you help me every
word in chines book, and you read alot storys,
and you had teach me about news, you are
such a good man!

Conventions

Sentence Structure Includes at least 5 simple sentences and/or 2 compound or complex sentences.

Sentence Variation Varies the way 2–3 sentences begin.

Punctuation Ends 2 to 4 sentences with periods; may use other forms of punctuation appropriately at times.

Capitalization Capitalizes first word in 2–4 sentences; may use other forms of capitalization appropriately at times.

Spelling Spells 9 or more different one-syllable words conventionally.

Content

Opening Begins with an action or a fact in the first of 4 or more related sentences.

Transitions Uses 2 different transitional words or phrases to connect thoughts or ideas.

Development of Ideas Uses 1 strategy somewhat effectively to develop an idea.

Supporting Details Includes 5 or more different modifiers.

Word Choice Uses 2 precise words that are more exact in meaning.

Closing Signals ending with "The End."

Early Writer: Level 6
Writing to Inform

Title: MY Speacal People

MY Speacal People are my grandma and grandpa becuse there always there when I Ill or Just blue. My grandpa is the Trick Player and my grandma is The sweet one there both Funny I can't have any thing to drink with out laghting. Thay can cher you up in a minite. becuse there so funny and cher ful.
That's why there my speacal people.

Conventions

Sentence Structure Includes 3 compound and/or complex sentences.

Sentence Variation Varies the way 4–5 sentences begin.

Punctuation Ends at least 5 sentences with periods; may use other forms of punctuation appropriately at times.

Capitalization Capitalizes first word in at least 5 sentences; may use other forms of capitalization appropriately at times.

Spelling Spells 3–5 different two-syllable words conventionally.

Content

Opening Creates a brief context or introduction with 1 opening sentence.

Transitions Uses 3 different transitional words or phrases to connect thoughts or ideas.

Development of Ideas Uses 1 strategy somewhat effectively and at least a glimmer of 1 other strategy to develop ideas.

Supporting Details Supports 1 idea with details in at least 3 sentences.

Word Choice Uses 3–4 precise words that are more exact in meaning.

Closing Creates a logical ending or resolves the problem in at least 1 sentence; may include "The End."

Transitional Writer: Level 7
Writing to Inform

Manatees

    Manatees are gentle creatures.
Manatees can be really long. Also manatees
are warm-blooded and they are mammals.
A baby manatee drinks milk under its
mother's flap. Manatees go up to the
surface to breathe air every 3 or 5 minutes.
A female manatee would weigh about 2000
pounds and a male weighs about 1000 pounds.
    Manatees are in danger of
extinction. They are endangered because
some motor boats are speeding and
hurting the manatees. Some people
are polluting the water and some

people are putting fishing nets in the
manatees food which is seaweed.
    There are sevaral things we
could do to help manatees. We can stop
putting fishing nets in the manatees
food. We can leave the manatees in their
own habitats.

Conventions

Sentence Structure Includes 4–6 compound and/or complex sentences.

Sentence Variation Varies the way 6–7 sentences begin.

Punctuation Ends at least 6 sentences with periods and uses 2 other forms of punctuation appropriately most of the time.

Capitalization Capitalizes first word in at least 6 sentences and uses 1 other form of capitalization appropriately most of the time.

Spelling Spells 6–8 different two-syllable words conventionally.

Content

Opening Creates a context or introduction somewhat effectively with 2 opening sentences.

Transitions Uses 4–5 different transitional words, phrases, and/or clauses to connect thoughts or ideas.

Development of Ideas Uses at least 2 strategies somewhat effectively to develop ideas.

Supporting Details Supports 2 ideas with details in at least 3 sentences; may be paragraphed.

Word Choice Uses 5–6 precise words or phrases that are more exact in meaning.

Closing Creates a brief closing (wrap-up, summary, conclusion) with at least 1 sentence; may include "The End."

Home Letter

Dear Family,

Do you read book reviews before buying a book? Do you write a thank-you note to express appreciation? Perhaps you jot down the directions for making a favorite recipe to share with a friend. These are all examples of writing to inform.

Your child will be learning how to write thank-you notes, directions, and a report too. You can help at home by allowing your child to watch and listen as you write notes and directions. Also show your child how you use resources to do writing for your job, such as using a dictionary or the spell-check on your computer as you write a report or send E-mail.

Here are some other ways to help your child use writing to inform.

1 Create a family message board. Write notes to one another.

2 Help your child communicate using E-mail. Sending a thank-you note or an invitation through electronic mail is fun and provides lots of writing practice.

3 Follow directions for making a recipe or a craft. Your child can send E-mail to share directions with a friend.

4 Discover books you can read together that give information. Here are a few books to look for.
- ◆ *How to Make an Apple Pie and See the World* by Marjorie Priceman. Random House, 1994. Your child will embark on a trip around the world to collect the ingredients for an apple pie.
- ◆ *Cactus Hotel* by Brenda Z. Guiberson. Holt, 1991. Your child can observe the life cycle of a giant cactus and all the animals that call it "home."
- ◆ *First-Time Writer's Guide to Book Reports and Other Writing Projects* by Dana Voth. Lowell House, 2000. Tips and guidelines to help your child with writing projects.

Sincerely,

Carta para el hogar

Estimada familia,

¿Leen ustedes reseñas de libros antes de comprarlos? ¿Escriben notas de agradecimiento para expresar gratitud? Quizás anotan las instrucciones de una receta favorita para compartirla con amistades. Éstos son ejemplos de escritura para informar.

Su hijo/a aprenderá a escribir notas de agradecimiento, instrucciones y también un informe. Ustedes pueden serle de ayuda permitiéndole que les escuche y vea escribir notas e instrucciones. También muéstrenle a su hijo/a cómo se usan diccionarios y programas de ortografía en la computadora para escribir informes y correspondencia electrónica en el trabajo.

A continuación se presentan otras maneras de ayudar a su hijo/a a escribir para informar.

1 Creen un tablero de avisos familiar. Escríbanse notas mutuamente.

2 Ayuden a su hijo/a a usar el correo electrónico para comunicarse. Resulta divertido enviar notas de agradecimiento o una invitación por correo electrónico y ofrece abundante práctica de escritura.

3 Sigan las instrucciones para una receta o una artesanía. Su hijo/a puede enviar correo electrónico para compartir instrucciones con un amigo.

4 Descubran libros informativos que pueden leer juntos. Los siguientes libros resultan de utilidad:
- *How to Make an Apple Pie and See the World* por Marjorie Priceman. Random House, 1994. Su hijo/a participará en un viaje alrededor del mundo en busca de los ingredientes para un pastel de manzana.
- *Cactus Hotel* por Brenda Z Guiberson. Holt, 1991. Su hijo/a puede observar el ciclo vital de un cacto gigante y de todos los animales que lo consideran su "hogar."

Sinceramente,

Teacher Notes

Book Report

Introduction

OBJECTIVES

★ RESPOND to a student model of a book report.

★ RECOGNIZE the characteristics of a book report.

1 Building Background

To introduce the idea of writing a book report, invite children to name a favorite book and briefly tell why they think other children should read it. Explain that writing a book report is one way to share favorite books. The purpose of the book report is to tell someone who has not read the book a little bit about it.

2 Meet the Writer

Direct children's attention to the book report "Winnie the Pooh and Tigger Too" on pages 38–39 of the Big Book of Writing Models. Ask a volunteer to point to the name of the writer, Angel Velez. Explain that Angel is a first grader who wrote this report to tell about a favorite book.

3 Respond to a Model

Read aloud the book report about *Winnie the Pooh and Tigger Too.* After you read, ask children what they learned about the book. As children discuss the book, have them help you fill in a story chart that names the book, the author, the characters, the setting, and the main idea of the book. If necessary, review literary terms: *A character is an animal or person in a story; the setting is where and when a story takes place.*

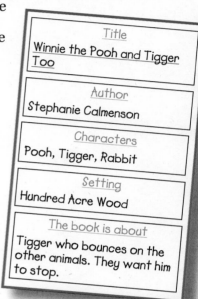

Title
Winnie the Pooh and Tigger Too
Author
Stephanie Calmenson
Characters
Pooh, Tigger, Rabbit
Setting
Hundred Acre Wood
The book is about
Tigger who bounces on the other animals. They want him to stop.

Meeting Individual Needs

LITERATURE CONNECTION

Before beginning their reports, children may enjoy one or more of these books.

1. *The Library Dragon* by Carmen Agra Deedy. Illustrated by Michael P. White. Peachtree Publishers, 1994. Miss Lotta Scales, the dragon librarian at Sunrise School, is determined to protect the books from the children.

2. *A Bedtime Story* by Mem Fox. Illustrated by Elivia Savadier. Mondo Publishing, 1996. Polly, Mom, and Dad share the joy of reading together.

3. *Edward and the Pirates* by David McPhail. Little, Brown, and Company, 1997. Edward's adventure shows that, with a little imagination, books can come to life.

Mini Lesson

Identifying Main Idea

Introduce Display a familiar book with a simple story line. Can children tell you in one sentence what the book is about? Help them agree on a sentence for you to write on the board. Explain that this sentence tells the main idea, or most important idea, of the book.

Model Return to the Big Book of Writing Models and reread the report about Winnie the Pooh. Have children decide on a main idea for the book, prompting and modeling as necessary. *(Two animal friends try to teach a friend a lesson.)*

Summarize/Apply Explain that being able to tell the main idea of a story is an important part of planning a book report because you will want the readers to know what the book is about. Remind children that to find the main idea they can ask themselves *What is this story about?*

Book Report

from the

Big Book of Writing Models

pages 38–39

Prewriting

OBJECTIVES

★ BRAINSTORM and SELECT a topic for a book report.

★ RECOGNIZE the use of a story chart for prewriting.

★ CONTRIBUTE to a story chart in a shared prewriting activity.

★ MAKE a story chart to record information to be included in a book report.

1 Introduce Prewriting

Initiate a discussion with children about charts. What charts do children use at home? at school? Children may name chore charts, classroom helper charts, and so on. Point out a chart in your classroom, emphasizing how the chart organizes and keeps track of information. Tell children that writers can use charts to organize information for reports.

2 Shared Writing

Explain that writers need to choose topics for their work before they begin to write. Ask children what books they have enjoyed reading in class and at home. What books would they like to tell others about? Tell children that you are going to share a plan for a book report about an adventure story called *The Reluctant Dragon*. Read the story with the class if they are not familiar with it.

MODELED WRITING Use the information in the sample chart on this page to create a chart similar to the one children created for "Winnie the Pooh and Tigger Too." Remind children that good writers think about what to write before they begin and that all of the parts on this chart are important to include in a book report.

INTERACTIVE WRITING Invite children to ask questions about the chart or to make suggestions. Volunteers can come up and write their ideas on the chart.

3 Independent Writing

Encourage children to look at their literature logs, leaf through the classroom library, or brainstorm with each other to select books for their reports. Make copies of the blackline master on page 149 for children to use as they plan their book reports. Encourage them to use the chart you made as a guide.

EMERGENT WRITERS Children who need extra support can draw pictures to show what the book is about. Then as children explain their drawings to you, help them write words or captions.

TEACHER CONFERENCE Conference with children to discuss their book reports. You might use the following questions to prompt discussion about the work.

- *Are you having trouble filling in any of the details? How can you find the information you need?*

- *Did you tell why you liked the story?*

- *Is there any more information you want to add?*

PEER CONFERENCE Organize children into small groups. Have them show and read their story charts to one another. Suggest these tips for listeners.

- *Listen to what each writer has to say.*

- *Ask questions if you don't understand.*

- *Tell whether or not you think you would like to read this book.*

Title
The Reluctant Dragon
Author
Kenneth Grahame

Characters
a boy
a dragon
St. George

Setting
at the dragon's cave

This Book Is About
The people in the village are afraid of the dragon.
St. George comes to kill the dragon.
A boy wants to stop him.

Why You Like It
The ending surprised me.
I liked the dragon because he was not like other dragons.
The ending made me feel good.

Mini Lesson

Planning a Report Using a Story Chart

Introduce Ask children how a road map could help them plan a trip. Lead children to suggest that maps help people plan ahead so that they don't become lost. Explain that using a story chart to plan what they will write is like using a road map. If they follow their charts, they won't become "lost" when they write.

Model Display the chart that you made in the Shared Writing activity. Show children how the information on the chart will help you write a book report. Think aloud as you point to each section of the chart and say how you will include the information in your report, beginning with the title and author. Looking at each section of the chart will remind you what to include in your report.

Summarize/Apply Reinforce how children can use their story charts like a road map as they write. As they include the information from each box on the chart, they can put a checkmark by it.

WRITER'S BLOCK

Problem	Solution
Children list too many events as they tell what the book is about.	Read through each of the events with children and ask *Is this part important to understanding the story?* You might suggest that children tell just two or three main events.

ESL STRATEGY

Have children with varying language proficiencies work with a partner to read a book and plan a report. Children can record information such as title, author, and character names.

HOME-SCHOOL CONNECTION

Encourage children to share books at home with their family members. Family members can discuss what they like best about the books they read.

WRITING ACROSS THE CURRICULUM

Science Children can use charts similar to a story chart to record information and observations about animals.

Animal
   Squirrel
Where it lives
   woods, backyards
What it looks like
   gray or brown fur
   bushy tail
What it eats
   nuts
   berries

Drafting

OBJECTIVES

★ **RECOGNIZE** the characteristics of a book report.

★ **RESPOND** to a first draft in a shared writing activity.

★ **USE** a story chart as a plan to write a first draft.

1 Introduce Drafting

Ask if anyone has ever used a recipe to bake a cake. Compare the recipe to a writing plan. You have to follow the plan to make a cake. Following a plan also makes a better book report. Beginning cooks may try several times before they make a perfect cake. Writers may write several drafts before their reports are ready to publish.

2 Shared Writing

MODELED WRITING Display the story chart that you made during prewriting and reread it with the class. Copy the model draft on this page onto chart paper, skipping every other line. Explain that the writer used the chart to write the first draft of the book report. Discuss the parts of the book that are explained in the report.

INTERACTIVE WRITING As you identify the parts of the book that are included in the report, have volunteers check them off on the chart. Ask children if there is anything they would like to change or add to the report. Encourage them to add their own ideas.

3 Independent Writing

Provide help as needed as children use their own charts to write their first drafts. Have children follow the model in the Big Book or use the blackline master on page 149 to make copies of a book report form for them to use.

EMERGENT WRITERS Provide children with a simple book report form. Help them write the title and author. Then talk about the characters and setting and what happened in the story. Have them write one sentence about each one.

TEACHER CONFERENCE Discuss drafts with children. You might want to use these questions.

- *How did you begin your report?*
- *Show me in your report where you write about characters and the setting and tell what the book is about.*
- *Is there any more information you could add?*

PEER CONFERENCE Let pairs of children read their book reports to one another. Remind listeners of the following guidelines.

- *Listen quietly to the other person's book report.*
- *Tell what you like about the book report.*

The Reluctant dragon
Written by Kenneth Grahame

This story is about a dragon. The people in the village are afraid of him. They want St. George to kill the dragon. one day a boy visits the dragon. The boy finds out that the dragon is kind. How can the boy save the dragon You will have to read the book to find out. I liked this book because the ending surprized me. It made me feel good.

Capitalizing Book Titles

Introduce Explain that there are two rules for writing book titles correctly. One is to always capitalize the first word in a title. The second is to capitalize every important word in a title. Discuss which words in titles are not important.

Model Look at the title in the Big Book—"Winnie the Pooh and Tigger Too." Ask children to tell why some of the words begin with capital letters. Then find books in the classroom library with titles written in uppercase and lowercase letters. Help children read the titles. Prompt children to tell why certain words are capitalized and others are not.

Summarize/Apply Have children look at the book title you have written on the planning chart and explain why certain words begin with capital letters. Repeat the exercise with titles they have written. Have they correctly capitalized words in the titles?

WRITER'S BLOCK

Problem	Solution
Children have trouble identifying a main idea to write about.	Suggest that they choose a partner and tell them about the book first.

ESL STRATEGY

If children are working in pairs, suggest that each partner tries to write one or two sentences for the report. An English-proficient classmate can copy the sentences into one report for the pair.

HOME-SCHOOL CONNECTION

Encourage children to take their drafts home to discuss with their families. Send a note reminding their families that right now children are just trying to get their ideas on paper. Family members can tell what they like about the reports and ask questions about parts they don't understand.

WRITING ACROSS THE CURRICULUM

Language Arts As children write in their literature logs the names of books they have read, encourage them to double-check titles to make sure they have used capital letters correctly. Remind them to capitalize the first and last names of the authors and illustrators, too.

Books I Like

Albert's Ballgame by Leslie Tryon

Take Me Out to the Ballgame by Alec Gillman

Cat Is Back at Bat by John Stadler

Revising/Editing

OBJECTIVES

★ **RECOGNIZE** that writing can be improved by revising it.

★ **CONTRIBUTE** to the revision of a book report in a shared writing activity.

★ **REVISE** a first draft of a book report.

★ **RECOGNIZE** that a book report tells about the characters, setting, and main events of a story.

1 Introduce Revising and Editing

Remind children that good writers always look again at their writing to think about changes they want to make. Reread "Winnie the Pooh and Tigger Too" with the class. Ask if they have more questions about the story. What kinds of changes would they make to this report? Record children's ideas on chart paper.

2 Shared Writing

MODELED WRITING Use the model on this page to make changes to the draft of the report on *The Reluctant Dragon.* Reread the report with children. Point out the changes that the writer made. Do they think the report makes sense? Does it make them want to read the book?

Show how to draw three lines under a letter that should be capitalized. Also model how to circle a misspelled word and write the correct spelling above it. Point out the insertion of a question mark at the end of a question. Give each child a copy of the revising and editing marks on page 26 of the Teacher Resource Guide.

INTERACTIVE WRITING As children become more familiar with revising, you may want to present the draft without the revisions. Children can find the mistakes and make changes using the revising marks they have learned.

3 Independent Writing

Have children silently reread their first drafts. Encourage them to ask themselves these questions.

- *Do I want to say any more about the book?*
- *Are there any words I want to add or change?*
- *Did I capitalize words in the title?*

EMERGENT WRITERS Have children who need extra support read their drafts to you. Help them revise one or two errors.

TEACHER CONFERENCE You may wish to use the following questions when children share their revised drafts with you.

- *Have you said everything you want to say about the book?*
- *Is there anything you want to change or add?*

PEER CONFERENCE Pair children and have them read their drafts to one another. Suggest that partners ask the following questions.

- *Is there anything else you want to know?*
- *Do you see any corrections I should make?*

The Reluctant dragon
Written by Kenneth Grahame

fierce

This story is about a dragon. The

people in the village are afraid of

him. They want St. George to kill the

dragon. one day a boy visits the

dragon. The boy finds out that the

dragon is kind. How can the boy

save the dragon You will have to

read the book to find out. I liked

this book because the ending

surprised

surprized me. It made me feel good.

Publishing

OBJECTIVE

★ PUBLISH a book report.

Children can use some or all of these ideas to share their book reports with their friends and families.

READING BINDER Have children illustrate their reports. Then collect them and save them in a binder in the classroom library.

BUY MY BOOK Invite children to create "television commercials" about the books they read. They can read their reports to classmates and add props such as posters or costumes.

BOOK JACKETS Children can use folded pieces of construction paper to create jackets for the books they read. They can draw their favorite scenes and include the names of the author and illustrator.

ASSESSMENT OPPORTUNITIES

PORTFOLIO ASSESSMENT If children choose to include their book reports in their portfolios, have them also include their prewriting charts and drafts.

TEACHER HOLISTIC ASSESSMENT Use the Teacher Evaluation Checklist on page 153 to evaluate children's book reports.

BENCHMARK PAPERS You may want to use the benchmark papers on pages 154–160 to evaluate children's writing. There is one paper for each level of writing on the Developing Writer's Assessment Continuum.

Meeting Individual Needs

Mini Lesson

Checking Spelling

Introduce Display the copy of the book report marked for revising and remind children that you had to correct a spelling mistake before writing the final copy. Have them identify the mistake.

Model Prompt children to suggest strategies they can use to spell words and correct spelling errors.

- *Sound out the word when you spell it to make sure you are not forgetting any letter sounds.*
- *Find the word in the book you read, in a dictionary, or perhaps on a word wall.*
- *Ask for help spelling it.*
- *Use spell-check on a computer.*

Summarize/Apply Remind children that whenever good writers are not positive they have spelled a word correctly, they double-check its spelling.

WRITER'S BLOCK

Problem	Solution
Children miss obvious spelling errors when they revise.	Help children sound out the word. Have them add it to their picture dictionaries.

ESL STRATEGY

Make a cumulative list of frequently used words that the children are learning to understand, read, and spell. Review the list each time you add a word. Post the words on a word wall.

HOME-SCHOOL CONNECTION

Encourage children to go to libraries with their families to select books. Then invite children to tell the class about the books they enjoyed at home.

WRITING ACROSS THE CURRICULUM

Math As children learn about different topics, suggest that they add a page to their picture dictionaries of subject-related words they are learning to read and spell.

Thank-You Note

Introduction

OBJECTIVES

★ **RESPOND** to a model of a thank-you note.

★ **RECOGNIZE** the characteristics of a thank-you note.

1 Building Background

To introduce the idea of writing a thank-you note, have children draw pictures that show special things that others did for them or gave them. Then have children show their pictures. Prompt children to discuss how they could say "thank you." Display their pictures in the classroom to inspire ideas.

2 Meet the Writer

Direct children's attention to the thank-you note on page 40 of the Big Book of Writing Models and explain that this letter is from a book called *Manners*. The author, Aliki, is an adult who wrote the book to teach children about good manners. Ask children why a thank-you note is included in a book about good manners.

3 Respond to a Model

Read the thank-you note aloud to the class. Ask children who the writer is and how they know. Ask the name of the person who will be receiving the letter. Have a volunteer point to the person's name. Talk about why the letter was written. Make a list of ideas as children name them. Review all the parts of a letter. Write the words *date, greeting, message, closing,* and *name of the writer* on self-stick notes. As you review the parts of a letter, have a volunteer attach the labels to the Big Book page.

> My Letter to Grammy
> Thank you for the cap.
> It is beautiful.
> It is warm.
> I love you.

Meeting Individual Needs

LITERATURE CONNECTION

Before children write their thank-you notes, you may want to introduce them to one of these books.

1. *The Gardener* by Sarah Stewart. Illustrated by David Small. Farrar, Straus & Giroux, 1999. Lydia Grace's humble letters home during the Depression show what happiness a child brings.

2. *Clever Letters* by Laura Allen. Illustrated by Valerie Coursen. Pleasant Co., 1999. Lots of creative ideas for writing and presentation.

3. *Letter Writer Starter Set* by Nancy Cobb. Illustrated by Laura Cornell. Reader's Digest, 1999. More ideas for writers.

Mini Lesson

Using Commas in Letter Parts

Introduce Display the thank-you note on page 40 of the Big Book of Writing Models. Point out and identify the commas after the greeting and closing.

Model Let children take turns coming forward to trace the commas with their fingers while reading aloud the greeting and closing of the note. Show the children several different thank-you notes or letters and have them point out the commas after the greeting and closing.

Summarize/Apply Remind children to properly punctuate the greetings and closings in their own letters. You might have children copy the greetings and closings from the board to use as references as they write.

Thank-You Note
from the
Big Book of Writing Models
page 40

Thank-You Note

Prewriting

OBJECTIVES

★ BRAINSTORM and SELECT a topic for a thank-you note.

★ RECOGNIZE the use of a list for prewriting.

★ CONTRIBUTE to a list in a shared prewriting activity.

★ MAKE a list to identify information to be included in a thank-you note.

1 Introduce Prewriting

Ask children to name reasons for which people use lists. Prompt them to include ideas such as grocery lists, things to pack for a trip, and chore lists. Point out that lists help people remember things and organize their thoughts. Tell children that writers often use lists to jot down ideas they want to include in their writing.

2 Shared Writing

Remind children that they should choose their topics before they begin writing. Have children talk about people who did nice things for them. Who has helped them at school? Who has given them special gifts? What would children say to these people if they were going to write to them? Tell children that you are going to share a plan with them for a thank-you note to a school librarian.

MODELED WRITING Use the information on the sample list shown here to fill in the list on page 49 of the Big Book of Writing Models. Remind children that creating lists is a good way to think of ideas they want to include in their writing. Share the list with children, pointing out that each idea belongs in the message part of the letter.

INTERACTIVE WRITING Invite children to help you make the list more complete. Use prompting questions to get them talking about their own experiences with helpful people at school. Then allow time for volunteers to add their own ideas to the list.

3 Independent Writing

Encourage children to decide whom they will thank. Make copies of the blackline master on page 6 so that children can create their own lists of what they wish to say in their letters. Remind them to tell what they are thankful for and why.

EMERGENT WRITERS Children can dictate their ideas to you. You might ask questions to get them started, such as *Who will receive your letter? What did this person do for you? What made it so special?* List their ideas as they discuss them with you.

TEACHER CONFERENCE Take time to meet individually with children. You might ask questions like the following.

- *Have you thought about how to begin and end your note?*

- *Did you remember to say why you are writing?*

- *Is there anything else you would like to say to this person?*

PEER CONFERENCE Children can work in pairs to read one another's lists. Writers can ask listeners questions such as these.

- *Do you understand what I am saying thank you for?*

- *What information do you think I should add?*

My Letter to Ms. Verdugo

1. Thanks for your help at the library.

2. You showed me where to find things.

3. I liked the story you read.

4. I know where things are.

5. I can find books at the library.

Capitalization in Letter Parts

Introduce Ask a volunteer to point to a lowercase letter and a capital letter on an alphabet chart in the room. Discuss when capital letters are used in writing (names of people, days, months, first words of sentences).

Model Remind children that, in friendly letters, they need to use capital letters for people's names, the month, the first word of the greeting and closing, and in the beginnings of sentences. Write several lowercase examples of dates, greetings, and closings on the board. Invite volunteers to change letters that should be capitalized.

Summarize/Apply Remind children to use the rules listed above for capitalizing letters in their own thank-you notes.

WRITER'S BLOCK

Problem	Solution
Children have not included reasons for appreciating the gift or favor.	Encourage children to meet with partners and tell them the names of the people they wish to thank and why. Model using the words *I want to thank (name of person) because* _____.

ESL STRATEGY

If children have difficulty creating a list like the prewriting model, invite them to draw pictures showing what was received or done for them and how they looked. Then ask children to tell more about their drawings.

HOME-SCHOOL CONNECTION

Encourage children to share their lists with family members. Family members can suggest other ideas that might be included.

WRITING ACROSS THE CURRICULUM

Science Children can make lists to keep track of ideas in science. Remind them to give their lists titles and to be sure that everything on a particular list belongs with that title.

Animals We Saw on Our Hike
1. spider
2. ant
3. ladybug
4. blue jay
5. squirrel

Thank-You Note

Drafting

OBJECTIVES

★ **RECOGNIZE** the characteristics of a thank-you note.

★ **RESPOND** to a first draft in a shared writing activity.

★ **USE** a list as a plan to write a first draft.

1 Introduce Drafting

Ask children if anyone in the class plays a musical instrument. Discuss how playing an instrument takes a lot of practice—it is difficult at first! Writing is often the same. It takes hard work to make the draft "finished." Children may need to write their notes several times to be sure that they sound right.

2 Shared Writing

MODELED WRITING Display the list you made in prewriting and reread it with children. Then copy the model draft shown on this page onto chart paper or use the write-on pages on pages 53–56 of the Big Book. Explain that the writer used ideas from the list to write his note. Read the note aloud with children. Discuss what the writer was thankful for and how he showed his appreciation.

INTERACTIVE WRITING As you read the letter, ask volunteers to check off the items on the list that were included. Would children like to add or change anything in the note? Invite them to come up to include their ideas.

3 Independent Writing

Have children follow the model in the Big Book for the form of a thank-you note or make copies of the blackline master on page 148 for them to use. They may want to cross ideas off the list as they include them in their letters. Remind children that, in the first draft stage, their goal is to get their ideas on paper.

EMERGENT WRITERS Provide children with a thank-you note form to use or take these writers through the process step by step.

TEACHER CONFERENCE As children write their notes, take the time to conference with them about their writing. You might ask questions such as these.

- *Have you included the date and a greeting?*
- *Show me where you name the person you are writing to.*
- *Did you tell why you are saying thank you?*
- *Have you included a closing and your name?*

PEER CONFERENCE Pair up children so they can read their thank-you notes to each other. Remind them of these conferencing guidelines.

- *Listen quietly while another person reads.*
- *Tell what you like about your partner's note.*
- *Ask questions about something that's not clear.*

April 8, 2002

dear Ms. Verdugo

Thank you for your help at the library. I know where everything is now. I liked the story you read! It made me laugh. I want to come back to get more books like that.

your friend,

Jason

Mini Lesson

Expanding Sentences by Adding Details

Introduce Tell children that when writers revise, they may decide to add words to make their writing more interesting or to tell their readers more.

Model Display the thank-you note in the Big Book. Show children that Lisa used the word *beautiful* to tell her Grammy what she thinks about the hat. Can children find the words that tell when the hat will keep her warm? (*all winter*) Discuss how those words make the letter clearer and more interesting.

Summarize/Apply Have children reread their drafts and think of details they can add. Demonstrate how to use a caret mark to insert new words.

WRITER'S BLOCK

Problem	Solution
Children are having difficulty organizing the sentences in their drafts.	Suggest a "formula," such as *Sentence 1: what you are saying thank you for* *Sentence 2: why you like it* *Sentence 3: how it makes you feel.*

ESL STRATEGY

Have children look again at the picture they drew of what they are saying thank you for. Prompt them to dictate simple sentences as you write. Encourage them to copy these sentences onto their papers and then read them to you.

HOME-SCHOOL CONNECTION

Encourage families to help their children suggest ideas for thank-you letters to other relatives. Adults or older siblings can work with the children to write drafts of these letters.

WRITING ACROSS THE CURRICULUM

Language Arts Suggest that children draft thank-you notes to parents or community members following a memorable field trip. Encourage them to use computers to write so that they can add capital letters, punctuation, and more details as they are needed.

February 14, 2002

Dear Mr. Garrow,

We had fun at the museum. Thank you for showing us the dinosaur bones. They were awesome! It was fun to hear about how you dug up the bones.

Your friend,

Alexis

Thank-You Note

Revising/Editing

OBJECTIVES

★ RECOGNIZE that writing can be improved by revising it.

★ CONTRIBUTE to the revision of a thank-you note in a shared writing activity.

★ REVISE a first draft of a thank-you note.

★ RECOGNIZE that a thank-you note has a date, a greeting, a message, a closing, and the name of the writer.

1 Introduce Revising and Editing

Remind children that revising is the last step before they publish their work. Reread the model thank-you note. Can children think of other details that could be added? Could the letter be more interesting? Record children's ideas for additions or changes to the letter on chart paper.

2 Shared Writing

MODELED WRITING Make changes to the thank-you note you wrote with the class. Use the model and reread the note, pointing out the changes the writer made as you go. Do children think the changes make the note better? Why do they think so?

Model how to fix the greeting of the note by adding a capital letter and the appropriate punctuation. Give each child a copy of the revising and editing marks on page 26 of the Teacher Resource Guide.

INTERACTIVE WRITING Consider presenting the draft without revisions if children are proficient at revising. Children can use the revising marks they have learned to fix the mistakes they find.

3 Independent Writing

As children quietly review their first drafts, suggest they ask themselves these questions.

- *Have I put in all the capital letters and commas that are found in a letter?*

- *Have I left out or misspelled any words?*

- *Are there any words I want to change?*

Remind them to use a caret to add words and to draw a line through words they want to change. You might also model how to mark letters that should be capitalized and how to circle punctuation marks that need to be added to final drafts.

EMERGENT WRITERS Have children who need extra support use their fingers to follow the words in their drafts as they read them aloud. Have them compare their drafts to the model to find capitalization and punctuation mistakes.

TEACHER CONFERENCE You may wish to use the following questions when children share their revised drafts with you.

- *Is there more you want to say to this person?*

- *In what ways does your letter look like the letter in the Big Book?*

PEER CONFERENCE Pair children of varying abilities and have them read their drafts to one another. Suggest that the writer ask the listener the following questions.

- *Will you help me check for all the letter parts?*

- *Is there anything you think I should add?*

April 8, 2002

dear Ms. Verdugo,

Thank you for your help at the
last week
library. I know where everything is
animal
now. I liked the story you read! It

made me laugh. I want to come back

to get more books like that.

your friend,

Jason

Publishing

OBJECTIVE

★ PUBLISH a thank-you note.

Here are ideas children can use to share their thank-you notes with family and classmates.

CREATING ENVELOPES Children may enjoy making envelopes for their letters. They can fold and tape construction paper to form envelopes, decorating the envelopes if they wish. Children can mail or hand-deliver notes to their recipients.

PERSONAL TOUCHES Consider having children use print shop programs to create their notes. They can add borders, pictures, decorative fonts, and so on.

TALKING TELEGRAMS Invite each child to choose a partner. One partner dresses up as a telegram delivery person. Have the delivery person read aloud his or her thank-you note to the partner. Ask partners to switch roles and repeat.

ASSESSMENT OPPORTUNITIES

PORTFOLIO ASSESSMENT If children choose to include their notes in their portfolios, have them also include their prewriting charts and drafts.

TEACHER HOLISTIC ASSESSMENT Use the Teacher Evaluation Checklist on page 153 to evaluate children's thank-you notes.

BENCHMARK PAPERS You may want to use the benchmark papers on pages 154–160 to evaluate children's writing. There is one paper for each level of writing on the Developing Writer's Assessment Continuum.

Meeting Individual Needs

Mini Lesson: Replacing an Overused Word

Introduce Write the following sentence on the board: *The cap is very nice.* Ask whether *nice* tells them very much about the cap or why you like it. Point out that words like *nice* are used often and really don't say much. Other words give more information.

Model Ask children what kinds of words they could use to tell how you feel about the cap. Write their suggestions on the board; for example:

The cap is beautiful.

The cap looks like a rainbow.

The cap is warm.

The cap is soft and pretty.

Summarize/Apply Emphasize that good writers ask themselves whether any of their words are used so often that they don't mean much. If the answer is yes, suggest that they use words that give the reader a better picture instead.

WRITER'S BLOCK

Problem	Solution
Children may be concerned about spelling and form.	Encourage children to use invented spelling, pictures, or blank space that can be filled in later with help.

ESL STRATEGY

Children with limited proficiency in English may rely more on pictures than on words to convey their messages. Consider allowing them to create "word stories" or drawings to show their thanks.

HOME-SCHOOL CONNECTION

Encourage children to take their final copies of thank-you notes home so their families can help them mail the notes to their intended recipients.

WRITING ACROSS THE CURRICULUM

Social Studies As children write names of places in their learning logs, encourage them to use commas and capital letters correctly in writing place names, just as they do when addressing an envelope.

Introduction

OBJECTIVES

★ RESPOND to a student model of a report.

★ RECOGNIZE the characteristics of a report.

1 Building Background

To introduce report writing, read aloud a short nonfiction book about an animal. Explain to children that the book will tell facts or true things about the animal. Talk about some things children might want to know about an animal, such as where it lives, what it looks like, what it eats, and what may be unusual about it. Ask children to listen carefully as you read. Then invite them to share information they learned.

2 Meet the Writer

Open the Big Book of Writing Models to page 41 and display the report "Butterflies." Introduce the writer, Spencer Chasteen. Tell children that Spencer is in first grade. Invite volunteers to point to the title and the author's name as you read them aloud. Let children know that the purpose of the report is to give the reader information about butterflies.

3 Respond to a Model

Read "Butterflies" aloud, focusing children's attention on the pictures and text. After reading the report, invite children to tell what they learned about butterflies. Create an idea web and label it with the word "Butterflies" in the center circle of the web. List facts about butterflies in smaller circles around the web. Draw lines to join each fact to the title.

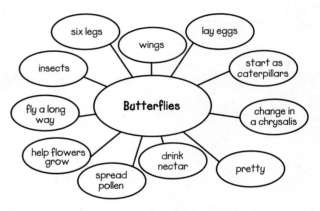

Meeting Individual Needs

LITERATURE CONNECTION

Before children write their report, you may want to introduce them to these nonfiction books.

1. *Red-Eyed Tree Frog* by Joy Cowley. Photographs by Nic Bishop. Scholastic, 1999. Learn about this particular frog's fascinating behavior.

2. *Open Wide: Tooth School Inside* by Laurie Keller. Henry Holt, 2000. This humorous tale on oral hygiene provides lots of information about teeth and dentistry.

3. *Look What Came From China* by Miles Harvey. Franklin Watts, 1998. Photographs and text about inventions, discoveries, and famous people in Chinese history.

Mini Lesson

Make and Record Observations

Introduce Take children on a walk outside. Ask them to make observations: *look* with their eyes, *listen* with their ears, *touch* with their hands, and *smell* with their noses. When you get back to the room, ask children what they observed on the walk. Record their observations on the board and discuss them.

Model Direct children to pages 41–47 of the Big Book. Invite children to study the illustrations as you reread "Butterflies." Ask what the author, Spencer Chasteen, might have observed before he wrote his report.

Summarize/Apply Tell children that observing and recording information will help them prepare for their writing. It is important to write down your observations so you will remember them when it is time to write.

Report

from the

Big Book of Writing Models

pages 41–47

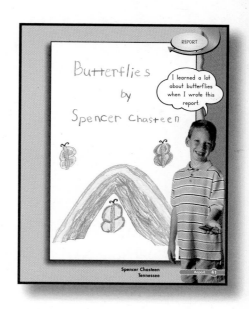

Butterflies are insects. They have six legs. They have wings. They lay eggs.

First, the mother butterfly lays eggs. The eggs hatch. Out come caterpillars.

The caterpillar eats and eats. Then it makes a chrysalis. The caterpillar stays in the chrysalis for two weeks. When it comes out, it is a butterfly.

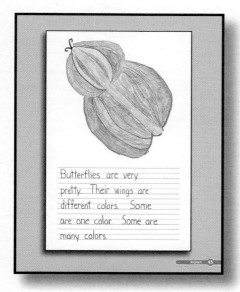

Butterflies are very pretty. Their wings are different colors. Some are one color. Some are many colors.

Butterflies like flowers. They drink the nectar. They spread pollen from flower to flower. This helps more flowers grow.

Butterflies have strong wings. They can fly a long way. Some butterflies can fly across the ocean.

Prewriting

OBJECTIVES

★ BRAINSTORM and SELECT a topic for a report.

★ RECOGNIZE the use of an idea web for prewriting.

★ CONTRIBUTE to an idea web in a shared prewriting activity.

★ MAKE an idea web to identify information to be included in a report.

1 Introduce Prewriting

Discuss with children different things they can do to remember information. Children might mention writing lists, making up rhymes or other mnemonic devices, and so on. Revisit the web about butterflies with children. Ask them how a web like this could help them remember things.

2 Shared Writing

Explain that a writer must choose a topic before beginning to write. Ask children to name some animals that they like or that they would like to know more about. Prompt by mentioning different categories of animals, such as jungle animals, water animals, and household pets. Tell children you are going to share a plan for a report about elephants.

MODELED WRITING Use the information in the sample web to fill in the web on page 52 of the Big Book of Writing Models. Point out that a web is a good way to remember information. Discuss the web with children, showing how each of the lines that connects to *Elephants* includes a fact about elephants. (Add additional circles if necessary.)

INTERACTIVE WRITING Invite children to add to the web, explaining that writers sometimes talk with others to get ideas for their work. You might model how to check children's ideas in simple reference works before you add the facts to the web. Point out that you might not use every fact in your report.

3 Independent Writing

Encourage children to use reference sources such as classroom books, CD-ROM encyclopedias, and websites to find out more about the animals they chose. Make copies of the blackline master on page 150 for a web children can use to collect ideas for their reports.

EMERGENT WRITERS If children have trouble getting started, start a discussion about an animal and record their ideas on the board. Use their ideas to create a web that children can later read on their own.

TEACHER CONFERENCE Discuss the children's webs with questions such as the following.

- *Tell me about the animal you're writing about.*
- *Where did you get your information?*
- *What other questions might you want to ask about your animal?*

PEER CONFERENCE Pair children of varying abilities and encourage them to share their animal webs with one another. Have the writer ask the listener the following questions.

- *Have I told you enough about my animal?*
- *Is there anything else I should add about my animal?*
- *Did you learn anything new about my animal?*

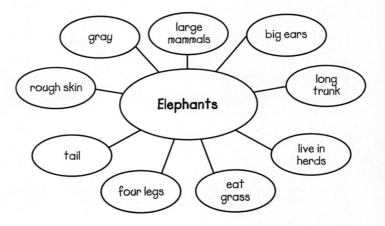

Using Complete Sentences

Introduce Write the following on the board:

a dog

Ask children what the words tell them. Then explain that this is not a complete sentence. It does not tell the reader anything. Have children suggest words that could be added to make the group of words a complete sentence. Use several of the words to write complete sentences. Point out that the sentences start with capital letters and end with periods.

Model Display pages 41–47 of the Big Book. Invite volunteers to point to sentences in the student model as you read them aloud. Encourage them to identify the capital letters and periods of each complete sentence.

Summarize/Apply Remind children that a sentence should make sense to them and tell them something. Encourage them to check their writing for complete sentences.

 WRITER'S BLOCK

Problem
Children write too few items on their webs.

Solution
Encourage them to choose a book about their animal and discuss it with a classmate.

ESL STRATEGY
Have children create picture webs by drawing the traits of their animals rather than using words to describe them. English-proficient partners can help label the pictures.

HOME-SCHOOL CONNECTION
Have children share their webs with family members and ask them to suggest other information or details that could be added.

WRITING ACROSS THE CURRICULUM
Science/Social Studies As children learn about topics in other subject areas, encourage them to make webs to summarize what they have learned. For example, following a unit of study about shelters, children can create webs to record various kinds.

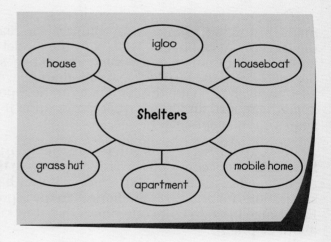

Drafting

OBJECTIVES

★ RECOGNIZE the characteristics of a report.

★ RESPOND to a first draft in a shared writing activity.

★ USE a web as a plan to write a first draft.

1 Introduce Drafting

Tell children that when they learn a lot about an interesting subject, they can either tell classmates or family members about it or they can write about it in a report. Point out that they already have a lot of great ideas in the webs they made. Now they need to put some of these ideas in sentence form to include them in reports.

2 Shared Writing

MODELED WRITING Display the web that you made during prewriting. Invite volunteers to read the facts about elephants. Then copy the model report on chart paper, or use the write-on pages on pages 53–56 of the Big Book. Explain that the writer used the web to create the sentences in the report. Read the report, discussing what information it shares about elephants.

INTERACTIVE WRITING As you reread the report, have volunteers check off the facts on the web that are detailed in the report. Ask children if they have suggestions for additions or changes to the report. Encourage them to write other facts that they know about elephants.

3 Independent Writing

Have children use their webs to write reports of their own. They might cross off or put a checkmark next to each piece of information they use. Remind them that they do not need to include all the ideas from their webs.

EMERGENT WRITERS Suggest that children choose one or two ideas from the web to use in sentences. Guide them as they write each word of the sentence, providing help as needed.

TEACHER CONFERENCE Consider using these or similar questions during your conference with children to discuss their drafts.

• *How is your report coming along?*

• *Which items from your web did you decide to include?*

• *What part of writing your report has been the most difficult?*

PEER CONFERENCE Pair children of varying abilities and have them read their reports to one another. Have the writer ask the listener the following questions.

• *How do you like my report?*

• *Did I leave anything out?*

Elephants
by Ann Johnson

Elephants are large mammals.

these gray animals eat grass.

They use their big ears and tail to

keep cool. Elephants use their

trunks to put food and water in

their mouths. Elephants are amazing

Mini Lesson

Add Facts and Reasons to Support Main Idea

Introduce Tell children that reports should contain facts—details that are true. These facts and reasons should support their topics and help readers better understand the points they are trying to make.

Model Refer children to the Big Book, pages 41–47, and reread the report "Butterflies." The main idea, that butterflies are insects, is supported by many facts and details. Lead children to understand how those details show that butterflies are insects.

Summarize/Apply Have children check their own drafts to confirm that their main ideas are supported by facts and reasons. Provide nonfiction books and encyclopedias to assist children in finding "facts" about their topics.

WRITER'S BLOCK

Problem	Solution
Children are having trouble knowing how to start their reports.	Encourage children to write an opening sentence that introduces, or names, the animal in the report.

ESL STRATEGY

Make a class word wall by posting words children might need to write their reports. You might include high-frequency words as well as general animal terms (*animal, color, food, lives*).

HOME-SCHOOL CONNECTION

Ask children to share the first drafts of their reports with family members. Remind family members that this is a draft and that changes and corrections will be made later.

WRITING ACROSS THE CURRICULUM

Science As children write reports in science, encourage them to first record important words they want to remember and then to include these words in sentences.

> Words to remember:
> seeds
> light
> soil
> sunflower
> What did I do with a sunflower seed?
> I planted it in some soil. I watered it every day. I made sure it got plenty of light. It grew into a beautiful sunflower.

Report

Revising/Editing

OBJECTIVES

★ RECOGNIZE that writing can be improved by revising it.

★ CONTRIBUTE to the revision of a report in a shared writing activity.

★ REVISE a first draft of a report.

★ RECOGNIZE that reports contain facts and details.

 ## Introduce Revising and Editing

Remind children that good writers reread their drafts and go back to make changes or corrections. Writers revise reports so that the information they include is accurate and makes sense to their readers. Reread "Butterflies" with the class. Do children still have questions about butterflies? What information would they add to the report?

 ## Shared Writing

MODELED WRITING Use the model on this page to make changes to the draft of the report about elephants. As you reread the report with children, point out the changes the writer made. Note the information the writer added. How does the information help them picture elephants more clearly as they read?

Demonstrate how to draw three lines under letters to show that they should be capitalized. You might also model using a caret to add a word or words to the draft. Give each child a copy of the revising and editing marks on page 26 of the Teacher Resource Guide.

INTERACTIVE WRITING Consider presenting the draft without revisions if children are proficient at revising. Children can find the mistakes and make changes using the revising marks they've learned.

3 Independent Writing

Ask children to reread their first drafts. Encourage them to ask themselves these questions.

- *Have I given enough information about the animal?*

- *Is there anything I want to add or take out?*

- *Did I start sentences with capital letters and end them with periods?*

Remind children to draw a line through words they want to change. Encourage them to use the model you revised in Shared Writing as a resource.

EMERGENT WRITERS Invite emergent writers to read their drafts to you. As children pause at the end of each sentence, ask them to check for an ending mark. Help children add appropriate end marks for each of their sentences. Talk about whether they should add words to make their ideas clearer.

TEACHER CONFERENCE As children share their revised drafts with you, consider asking them the following questions.

- *What do you think your readers will learn about the animal?*

- *How do you feel about this animal?*

- *Are there facts you want to change or add?*

PEER CONFERENCE Have pairs of children read their drafts to one another. Invite the writer to ask the listener questions such as the following.

- *Does my report make sense to you?*

- *Is there anything else you want to know?*

Elephants
by Ann Johnson

Elephants are large mammals.

these gray animals eat grass.

They use their ~~big~~ huge ears ~~and tail~~ to

keep cool. Elephants use their long

trunks to put food and water in

their mouths. Elephants are amazing!

Publishing

OBJECTIVE

★ PUBLISH a report.

Explain to children that it's time to make neat copies of their reports to share. Here are ways children can share their reports with family and classmates.

ZOO DISPLAY Decorate your classroom door to resemble the entrance of a zoo. Post the words *It's a Zoo in Here!* Inside your room, display the animal reports on a bulletin board for all to enjoy.

ORAL PRESENTATION Some children may want to present their reports orally by telling important facts and the animals. Invite children to make and wear animal masks or display photographs or pictures that show the animals.

ANIMAL ENCYCLOPEDIA Bind the reports alphabetically by animal into a class book. Create a cover for this animal encyclopedia.

ASSESSMENT OPPORTUNITIES

PORTFOLIO ASSESSMENT If children choose to include their reports in their portfolios, have them also include their prewriting web and drafts.

TEACHER HOLISTIC ASSESSMENT Use the Teacher Evaluation Checklist on page 153 to evaluate children's reports.

BENCHMARK PAPERS You may want to use the benchmark papers on pages 154–160 to evaluate children's writing. There is one paper for each level of writing on the Developing Writer's Assessment Continuum.

Meeting Individual Needs

Mini Lesson — Publishing— Using Illustrations or Diagrams

Introduce Show children the illustrations in several picture books. Initiate a discussion on how the illustrations make the stories more interesting and easier to understand.

Model Show children the butterfly illustrations Spencer Chasteen drew on Big Book page 41. Ask children leading questions, such as *How do the illustrations tell you more about butterflies? What details are easy to see in the pictures?*

Summarize/Apply Invite children to draw illustrations of the animals they wrote about in their reports. Ask them to show their illustrations to the class. Invite classmates to tell how those illustrations help them better understand the animals pictured.

WRITER'S BLOCK

Problem	Solution
Children include information in their reports that is not accurate.	Put a question mark near any facts that you think are not true. Help children use simple reference sources to check their facts.

ESL STRATEGY
Have students practice reading their report into a tape recorder until they feel comfortable reading it aloud to the class.

HOME-SCHOOL CONNECTION
Encourage children to share their finished report with their family. Ask family members to discuss characteristics of their favorite animals.

WRITING ACROSS THE CURRICULUM
Science When children go on field trips for science, encourage them to look and listen carefully and to list what they see and hear. They can use their lists to create reports about the field trip.

187

Directions

Introduction

OBJECTIVES

★ **RESPOND** to a student model of directions.

★ **RECOGNIZE** the characteristics of directions.

1 Building Background

Introduce the idea that directions belong in sequential order. Choose a familiar task, such as making a sandwich or feeding a classroom pet. Invite one volunteer to pantomime the steps, one at a time. Discuss the steps with children as you record them on the board. Reread the complete list, encouraging children to read along and pantomime the actions.

2 Meet the Writer

Point to and read aloud the title on page 48 of the Big Book of Writing Models. Read the name of the author of the directions "How to Make Chocolate Milk." Share with children that Jay Bennington is a first-grade writer. He wrote the directions to tell the steps, in order, for making chocolate milk.

3 Respond to a Model

Read aloud Jay's directions. Encourage children to read along with you, picturing the steps in their minds. Invite children to act out each step as you read the directions a second time. Discuss the order of the steps and the words the writer used to show the order. List the words on the board.

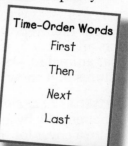

Time-Order Words

First

Then

Next

Last

Meeting Individual Needs

LITERATURE CONNECTION

Before children write their own sets of directions, you may want to introduce them to one or more of these books.

1. *Seeds Grow* by Angela Shelf Medearis. Illustrated by Jill Dubin. Cartwheel Books, 2000. The steps involved in planting and growing seeds are explained in this simple text.

2. *Pete's a Pizza* by William Steig. Harper, 1998. Just how does Pete become a pizza? His father knows the secret recipe.

3. *A Drop of Water* by Walter Wick. Scholastic, 1997. Follow a drop of water on its journey.

★Mini Lesson★ Using Time-Order Words

Introduce Discuss the events of the previous day using the time-order words *first, next,* and *last.* For example: *First, we had math. Next, we played kickball. Last, we went to lunch.*

Write *first, next,* and *last* on the board. Tell children that these are time-order words. They tell the order in which things happen.

Model Direct children to page 48 of the Big Book. Reread "How to Make Chocolate Milk" and invite children to raise their hands every time you read a time-order word.

Summarize/Apply Have small groups of children work together to create lists of other words that tell order. Children can copy their lists into their journals and use the words in their writing.

Directions

from the

Big Book of Writing Models

page 48

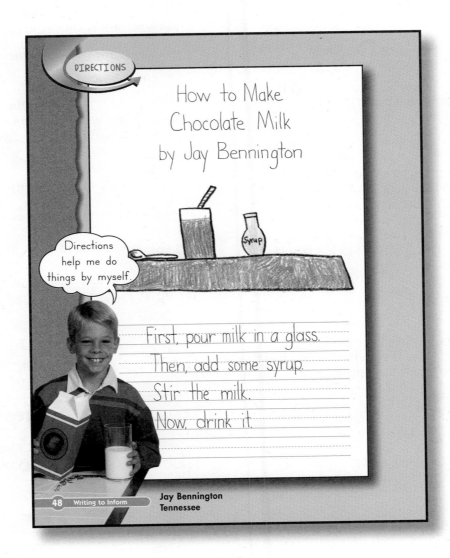

Directions

Prewriting

OBJECTIVES

★ BRAINSTORM and SELECT a topic for a set of directions.

★ RECOGNIZE the use of a chart for prewriting.

★ CONTRIBUTE to a chart in a shared prewriting activity.

★ MAKE a chart to identify information to be included in a set of directions.

1 Introduce Prewriting

Bring in some directions to share with children, such as cooking directions on a box of pasta or directions for a simple board game. Read the directions aloud and point out that the directions are in order. Remind children that following directions is useful in real life—it helps you learn how to do something correctly.

2 Shared Writing

Remind children that before they begin to write, they must choose a topic. Have children suggest simple tasks that require following directions or a series of steps, such as making a sandwich, sharpening a pencil, or planting a seed. Tell them that you are going to share a plan for directions that explain the steps in brushing teeth.

MODELED WRITING Use the information on the sample chart on this page to create a chart on the board or on chart paper. Remind children that good writers plan their writing so that it makes sense. Share the chart with the class and discuss the words that are used to keep the steps in order.

INTERACTIVE WRITING Invite children to discuss their ideas about the chart. Do they think any steps are missing or out of order? Have volunteers come up and write their ideas on the chart. Point out that the steps need to have enough information so that they are easy to follow.

3 Independent Writing

Encourage children to select topics for their own sets of directions. Remind them of the ideas they suggested in the beginning of the shared writing activity. Make copies of the blackline master on page 151 for sentence strips that children can cut apart and arrange in order to plan their directions.

EMERGENT WRITERS Have children draw a series of four pictures to show the steps of their process. Work with children or have them work with partners to create simple captions for each picture.

TEACHER CONFERENCE As you conference with children, you might use the following questions to discuss their flowcharts.

- *Why did you choose this topic for writing?*

- *What did you do to think about each step?*

- *Do you need help explaining any step?*

PEER CONFERENCE Encourage children to share their charts with partners. Provide questions such as the following to help children.

- *What am I giving directions for?*

- *Do you understand my steps?*

Directions for Brushing Teeth

First, put toothpaste on your toothbrush.

↓

Next, put water on your toothbrush.

↓

Then, brush your teeth.

↓

Last, rinse your mouth.

Planning a Composition by Using a List

Introduce Show children a list you have made, such as a grocery list or a "to do" list. Ask children why people make lists. Lead them to realize that lists can help people organize information and important facts.

Model Reread "How to Make Chocolate Milk" on page 48 of the Big Book. Ask children to help create a list of things needed to make chocolate milk. Tell children if they are writing recipes, they may wish to include lists of ingredients. Children may also want to list the steps in a process before they write as an alternative to creating a chart.

Summarize/Apply Be sure that children recognize that lists can help them remember and organize ideas they want to include in their writing. Encourage them to use lists in other subject areas (such as lists of items needed for a science experiment or lists of equipment needed for a game).

WRITER'S BLOCK

Problem
Children have selected topics that require too many steps.

Solution
Help children narrow their original choices by selecting only portions of the processes. Limit the number of steps to four.

ESL STRATEGY
Encourage children to pantomime the steps in the processes they chose. Partners who are English-proficient can record the steps based on the pantomiming. Then partners can read the steps together.

HOME-SCHOOL CONNECTION
Have children share their charts with families. Family members can act out the steps so that children can see if any steps are missing or unclear.

WRITING ACROSS THE CURRICULUM
Science Encourage children to use charts and order words as they write in their science logs.

Science Experiment

First, add two drops of red food coloring to a glass of water.

Then, place the stem of a white carnation in the red water.

Last, watch as the white carnation turns pink.

Drafting

OBJECTIVES

★ RECOGNIZE the characteristics of a set of directions.

★ RESPOND to a first draft in a shared writing activity.

★ USE a chart as a plan to write a first draft.

1 Introduce Drafting

Ask children what happened the first time they ever tried to tie their shoes. Were they successful on the first attempt? Explain that just as it takes practice to tie shoes correctly, it takes practice to be a good writer. Writers often create several drafts before their work is finished and ready to publish.

2 Shared Writing

MODELED WRITING Display the chart you made during prewriting and reread it with children. Copy the model draft on this page onto chart paper or use the write-on pages on pages 53–56 of the Big Book. Skip every other line to leave room for revisions. Explain that the writer used the chart to create the directions. Discuss the order of the steps and the words used to show that order.

INTERACTIVE WRITING As you identify each of the steps included in the directions, have children check them off on the chart. Ask children if there is anything they would like to add to make the directions clearer and easier to understand. Have them write their ideas on the paper.

3 Independent Writing

Encourage children to use their charts as they write their first drafts. Remind them that the goals for writing the draft are to put the steps in order and to use words that make the directions easy to follow.

EMERGENT WRITERS Consider having emergent writers copy the picture captions from their flowcharts without elaboration. They can focus on including all of the steps in correct order.

TEACHER CONFERENCE Use these questions as you conference with children to discuss their first drafts.

- *How did you decide to start your directions?*
- *Did you include each step from your chart?*
- *Did you use words that make your directions easy to understand?*

PEER CONFERENCE Pair children and have them read their directions to each other. Encourage listeners to try to picture or pantomime the steps. Writers can ask these questions.

- *Do my directions make sense?*
- *Can you follow my directions? Should I add anything?*

Brushing Teeth

by Thomas Borden

First, put toothpaste on your toothbrush.

put water on your toothbrush.

Then, brush your top and bottom teeth.

Last, rinse your mouth.

Top-to-Bottom Progression

Introduce Bring a stepladder into the room, or draw one on the board. Place a stuffed animal or a picture of one on the top rung. Ask children where the animal is. *(top)* Slowly move the animal down the ladder to the bottom rung. Ask children where the animal is now. *(bottom)*

Model Display the chart you created to help illustrate the directions for brushing teeth. Select one volunteer to point to the top of the chart and another volunteer to point to the bottom of the chart.

Summarize/Apply Invite children to point to the tops of their charts and read each sentence as they go from top to bottom.

WRITER'S BLOCK

Problem
Children are having difficulty writing their directions in the correct order.

Solution
Suggest that children number the steps on their charts and in their drafts rather than use order words.

ESL STRATEGY
Assist children by writing order words or numerals on each line of a sheet of paper. Hold up one finger and say *first* or *number one*. The child can dictate what happens first as you write. Continue for the other steps. Read the steps together.

HOME-SCHOOL CONNECTION
Encourage children to take their directions home and read them aloud, one step at a time. Can family members follow their directions?

WRITING ACROSS THE CURRICULUM
Mathematics Children can use their knowledge of sequencing events to explain how to solve math problems.

Solving a Subtraction Problem

1. First, collect 13 red chips.
2. Then, take away 7 chips.
3. Next, count the chips that are left.
4. Finally, you will know the answer to 13 − 7.

Revising/Editing

OBJECTIVES

★ RECOGNIZE that writing can be improved by revising it.

★ CONTRIBUTE to the revision of a set of directions in a shared writing activity.

★ REVISE a first draft of a set of directions.

★ RECOGNIZE the use of time-order words in directions.

1 Introduce Revising and Editing

Remind children that good writers usually reread first drafts to make changes or fix mistakes. Reread "How to Make Chocolate Milk" with children. Ask if they have any ideas for making the directions clearer. Could they successfully make a glass of chocolate milk by using these directions? What might they change? Record children's responses on chart paper.

2 Shared Writing

MODELED WRITING Use the model on this page to make changes to the draft of the directions for brushing teeth. Reread the directions with children, noting the changes the writer made as you go. Point out the words the writer added. Do they help make the directions easier to understand?

Demonstrate how to use a caret to add words to the draft. Also model how to add punctuation, circling it so that it is easy to see the change. Give each child a copy of the revising and editing marks on page 26 of the Teacher Resource Guide.

INTERACTIVE WRITING If children are familiar with revising, consider presenting the draft without revisions. Children can find the mistakes and make changes using the revision marks they've learned.

3 Independent Writing

Invite children to reread their first drafts and encourage them to think about these questions.

- *Are my directions in the correct order?*
- *Should I add anything?*
- *Are my directions easy to understand?*

Remind children that they can use a caret to add words. Suggest that they check for capital letters and ending marks in every sentence.

EMERGENT WRITERS Help emergent writers by using one color crayon to highlight letters that need to be capitalized and another color crayon for places where ending marks should be.

TEACHER CONFERENCE When children share their revised drafts with you, consider asking these questions.

- *Is there anything you want to add or change?*
- *Do you think your directions are easy to understand? Why or why not?*
- *Do you have capital letters and ending marks where they need to be?*

PEER CONFERENCE As children conference with partners, they may wish to ask each other these questions.

- *Do my directions make sense to you?*
- *What else do you need to know to follow these directions?*

Brushing Teeth

by Thomas Borden

a little

First, put toothpaste on your

toothbrush.

Next,

put water on your toothbrush.

Then, brush your top and bottom

teeth ⊙

with water

Last, rinse your mouth.

Publishing

OBJECTIVE

★ PUBLISH a set of directions.

Here are a few ways children can share their directions with family and classmates.

CLASS HOW-TO HANDBOOK Compile the final drafts of the directions in a book entitled "Our Class How-To Handbook." Children can add other directions for projects, science labs, art activities, or games.

INFOMERCIALS Videotape children reading and performing their directions. Add music and share the finished video with other classes.

TRY-IT DAY Choose children's directions that can be followed by pantomiming or using simple props. Display directions with props at various stations in the classroom. Allow children ample opportunity to visit each station and read and act out the directions.

ASSESSMENT OPPORTUNITIES

PORTFOLIO ASSESSMENT If children choose to include their directions in their portfolios, have them also include their prewriting charts and drafts.

TEACHER HOLISTIC ASSESSMENT Use the Teacher Evaluation Checklist on page 153 to evaluate children's directions.

BENCHMARK PAPERS You may want to use the benchmark papers on pages 154–160 to evaluate children's writing. There is one paper for each level of writing on the Developing Writer's Assessment Continuum.

Meeting Individual Needs

Mini Lesson

Sentence Variety— Beginnings

Introduce Ask children what they ate for dinner the night before. How would they feel if they had to eat the same meal every night? *(It would become boring.)* Tell children that writers use different kinds of sentences for the same reason—they don't want their readers to become bored. Using different kinds of sentences keeps writing exciting.

Model Write the following sentences on the board and read them aloud.

Bobby drank a glass of chocolate milk.

Bobby brushed his teeth.

Bobby got ready for bed.

Discuss with children how they can change the sentences so they all do not start the same way. Record children's suggestions.

Summarize/Apply Remind children to vary the beginnings of their sentences when they write. Encourage them to review their sets of directions and check the beginnings of their sentences.

WRITER'S BLOCK

Problem

Children don't elaborate on the steps in their directions.

Solution

Copy children's drafts and place write-on lines where children could add descriptive or time-order words. Invite them to "fill in the blanks" to make the directions easier to understand.

ESL STRATEGY

Offer a comic strip as an alternate publishing idea. Children can draw the steps in four separate panels, writing words in captions or speech bubbles.

HOME-SCHOOL CONNECTION

Encourage children to work with family members to use sets of directions at home. They could learn how to make recipes, assemble toys, or play a new game. Children may want to share what they accomplished with the class during a show-and-tell session.

WRITING ACROSS THE CURRICULUM

Art Children can use sequential order to write directions for art projects they have completed.

Teacher Notes

MINILESSONS

Page numbers shown in boldface are for minilessons found in Unit 5 of the Teacher Resource Guide. Page numbers shown in lightface are for minilessons found in Units 1–4.

• **List continued on next page.**

MINILESSONS

Basic Skills

Handwriting—Manuscript

Introduce Show children a handwriting chart or make individual letter flashcards. Have them identify the letters as you flip through them quickly.

Model Write two words on the board, one neatly and one sloppily. Ask children to read the words and compare them. Explain that it is much easier to read the neatly written one and that writers should always be careful to form their letters and words as neatly as possible so that the reader can easily understand them.

Summarize/Apply Use a handwriting chart to demonstrate how letters should be formed. Give children the opportunity to practice forming letters correctly.

Margins

Introduce Hold up an empty frame. Discuss what a frame does. *(It highlights the important picture or words inside.)*

Model Create a large frame and place it on the board. Write several sentences inside the frame. Then remove the frame and show children how the newly uncovered area represents the margin. Invite children to make a similar 2"-wide construction-paper frame that will fit their handwriting paper and cover the margin area.

Summarize/Apply Encourage children to use their frame when they write. As they become better able to judge how much space to leave, they may choose not to use the frame.

Spacing Between Sentences

Introduce Ask children how they can tell they have reached the end of a sentence. Display a period, question mark, and exclamation mark. Discuss these ending marks and discuss what children should see at the beginning of every sentence. *(a capitalized word)*

Model Write two sentences on the board. Select a volunteer to tell where one sentence ends and where the next sentence begins. Point out the space between the two sentences. Tell children that in their writing approximately two fingers should be placed between sentences.

Summarize/Apply Point out to children that a little more space should be left between sentences than between words. Have children write two simple sentences to demonstrate.

Spacing Between Words and Letters

Introduce Write *space* twice on the board, first normally and then with large spaces between the letters. Ask children to compare the two words. Guide them to understand that the first is how a word should be written, with the letters close together.

Model Explain to children that one finger should always be able to fit between their words. Model writing on the board, pointing out that because your writing is so much bigger on the board, you will need to place several fingers between words.

Summarize/Apply Have children copy the sentences you wrote on a piece of paper. Remind them to use their index finger to make space between words.

Writing Process

Add Descriptive Detail to Support Main Idea

Introduce Hold up a classroom object, such as a puppet. Invite children to call out words that describe the object and list them on the board.

Model Write this sentence on the board: *The car races.* Invite children to suggest words to add details to the sentence: *The red sports car races fast.*

Summarize/Apply Ask children how adding descriptive details changes the sentence. *(They add information and keep the reader's interest.)*

Circling Spelling Errors

Introduce Hold up a magnifying glass and tell children you need them to be spelling sleuths. Spelling sleuths must be on the lookout for misspelled words.

Model Write these sentences on chart paper: *Do you kno how to swm? I tak swiming lessuns. I luv the watr.* Select volunteer sleuths to use a colored marker and circle misspelled words.

Summarize/Apply Invite children to copy this sentence from the board and circle the misspelled words. *Swiming keps you cul in the summr.* Help them spell the words correctly.

Conferencing: Reading Your Work to Yourself

Introduce Have children look at themselves in a mirror. Tell them they are their own best critic, since they alone know what they want to say.

Model Demonstrate how you conference with yourself. Read aloud a story you have written. Ask and answer the following questions: *Do I like how I started my story? Have I said everything I wanted? Are any sentences confusing? Are sentences about similar things together? Will the words I chose interest my audience? Do I have a conclusion?*

Summarize/Apply Remind children that asking questions about their writing will help them become better writers. Encourage them to reread their work often and to make changes they think are needed.

Conferencing: How to Be a Good Listener

Introduce Place two chairs facing one another. Invite two children to sit knee to knee. Explain to children that they will be learning about listening.

Model With the children, think aloud good listening strategies and write them on the board: *Look at the speaker. Pay attention. Listen to the story.* Invite one child to read something to the other. Encourage the listener to display some or all of the strategies listed. Then have children switch roles.

Summarize/Apply Pair children and invite them to practice good listening skills as they read to one another. Circulate through the room and praise good listeners.

Writing Process

Conferencing: How to Make Suggestions

Introduce Write these two sentences on the board: *Go wash your hands. Would you please wash your hands before lunch?* Read them aloud and have children tell which sounds nicer. Explain that when a suggestion is made nicely, it is received better by the listener.

Model Invite two children to role-play a peer conference. Give the listener cards with these phrases: *I really enjoyed… My favorite part was… I think it could be even better if … If I could change one thing, I'd change…* Tell children that they should start their suggestions with these phrases.

Summarize/Apply Encourage children to use these starters and other similar ones to make suggestions and constructively criticize each other's work. You may wish to post a list of ways to make suggestions in the classroom.

Conferencing: Questions to Ask

Introduce Walk around with a toy microphone asking children interview-type questions. Tell them that questions play an important part in a conference or interview.

Model Select a child to role-play a conference with you. Read something you have written to the child. Using the microphone, ask the child these questions: *What was your favorite part? Did my story keep your attention? Were there any parts that you didn't understand or that confused you?* Brainstorm other questions you might ask.

Summarize/Apply Write some of the questions on index cards. Pair children and give them an opportunity to read a piece of their writing to each other. Encourage children to use the cards to ask the writer questions about his or her writing.

Crossing Out Words

Introduce Explain to children that sometimes when authors reread a piece of writing, they decide that some words are not needed. Usually the way that those words are eliminated is by drawing a line through them.

Model Write these sentences on the board: *It was a sun sunny day. What a nice day to play outside today.* Read them aloud to the class. Select volunteers to find two unwanted words and cross them out with colored chalk.

Summarize/Apply Suggest that children read their writing aloud to find unwanted words. Encourage them to cross out any unwanted words in their drafts.

Deleting Unimportant Information

Introduce Ask children if every message on their home answering machine is saved or if they save every piece of mail they receive. Tell them that some information is not worth saving — it is not important or not needed.

Model Display the following sentences on chart paper. Invite children to track the print as you read them aloud: *My baseball team has green jerseys. We play sixteen games. I have a green frog. Every player gets to bat every inning.* Encourage volunteers to identify the sentence that does not fit with the rest and draw a line through it.

Summarize/Apply Have children copy the sentences from the chart paper onto sheets of paper, omitting the information with the lines through it.

Writing Process

Identifying Audience

Introduce Teach children these words to the tune of "Mary Had a Little Lamb":

Think about your audience, audience, audience.

Think about your audience.

The people you are writing for!

Model Ask children to identify the audience for these magazines: *Newsweek, Sesame Street, Highlights.* Explain that writers don't always write for the same audience, or group of people. Writers at children's magazines don't write the same when their audience is adults.

Summarize/Apply Remind children that before they begin writing, they need to identify their audience. Have them write something to an audience of their choice.

Identifying Purpose

Introduce Bring a colorful postcard to class. Ask children if they have ever written or received a postcard. Discuss reasons why postcards are written. *(vacations, business trips, short notes to family and friends)*

Model Invite children to think of other reasons why people write the things they do. Ask: *Why do people write letters?* (to keep in touch with a friend or family member) *Why do people write stories?* (to entertain someone — to share something interesting, funny, or scary) *Why do people write book reports?* (to share information about an interesting book)

Summarize/Apply Cut out sections of a newspaper (weather, comics, advertisements, sports). Encourage children to discuss the reasons these articles or sections were written.

Identifying Topic

Introduce Hold up several nonfiction books with illustrated covers. Read the titles and ask children what they think each book will be about. Write the word *topic* on the board and explain that the topic of a book or story is what it's all about.

Model List a few classroom story favorites on the board in a column. Have volunteers help you identify the topic of each story. List their responses in a second column. Encourage children to add items to the first column for additional practice.

Summarize/Apply Assign children to small groups. Invite several volunteers to read aloud pieces from their portfolios. Have the groups work together to identify the topic in each piece.

Inserting a Sentence by Drawing an Arrow

Introduce Make an oversized cardboard arrow or show a picture of a street sign arrow. Ask children what arrows mean. If they saw an arrow pointing left, in which direction would they move?

Model Explain to children that arrows can be used during the writing process to show where sentences should go. Write these sentences on chart paper. *Lunch is at 11:30. After lunch, I have recess. I brought a peanut butter and jelly sandwich.* Note that the sentences are not in the correct order. Circle the third sentence. Then draw an arrow from the beginning of the third sentence to the beginning of the second and point out that now the thoughts are in order.

Summarize/Apply Invite small groups to brainstorm three or more related sentences. Have them order the sentences with arrows.

Writing Process

Inserting a Word or Phrase Using a Caret

Introduce Show children what a caret looks like and teach them this song to the tune of "Found a Peanut."

Use a caret, use a caret, every time you add a word.

Use a caret, use a caret, every time you add a word.

Model Write this sentence on the board. *Today is the day of my life.* Model and think aloud how you would write a caret and a word you might add. *Today is the [^happiest] day of my life.* Ask children to suggest other words that could be added, and have volunteers draw the caret and the word on the board.

Summarize/Apply Write this sentence on chart paper: *I had for lunch.* Have children copy this sentence on paper and then add the caret and an additional word.

Making a Letter Lowercase Using a Slash

Introduce Write *SuNday* and *AnDy* on chart paper. Ask children if they can spot anything wrong with the words. Review that uppercase letters only belong at the beginning of a word. Draw a slash through the *N* and *D* and explain that this mark means to make a letter lowercase.

Model Write this sentence on the board: *I hAd peanUt butter aNd jelly for lUNch toDay.* Have volunteers draw a slash through the uppercase letters that should be lowercase.

Summarize/Apply Have children copy the sentence from the board onto paper, making the necessary corrections.

Making a Letter Uppercase Using Three Lines

Introduce Put on a superhero hat or mask and tell children you are Captain Capital. Your duty is to place three lines under lowercase letters that should be replaced with uppercase letters.

Model Write these sentences on the board and select volunteers to take turns as Captain Capital: *today is tuesday, february 8. it is adam's birthday.* Help children locate letters that should be uppercase and draw three lines under them.

Summarize/Apply Have partners each write two sentences with lowercase letters in place of those that should be capitalized. Invite children to trade papers and replace the appropriate lowercase letters with uppercase ones.

Managing Time in Writer's Workshop

Introduce Invite two children to exaggerate what happens during writer's workshop. They could drop and pick up papers, go to the pencil sharpener, stop and chat with several people, return to the table, fidget in their seat, and tap their pencil repeatedly without writing a word.

Model Explain to children that writer's workshop time is limited and needs to be used efficiently. Have children brainstorm a list of things that have to be done to prepare themselves for writing. *(sharpening pencils, finding paper, and so on)*

Summarize/Apply Select children to role-play efficient use of time during writer's workshop. Set a timer for five minutes for all "getting ready" things to be accomplished. When the timer goes off, children should be seated and ready to write.

Writing Process

Publishing—Book Dedication

Introduce Show children the dedication page of some of their favorite picture books and read the inscriptions aloud. Discuss with children who the people might be and why the author might have chosen to dedicate the book to them.

Model Think aloud how you would determine whom to dedicate a book to: *My mom really gave me the idea for this story. I wouldn't have been able to write it without her.* Take a sheet of paper, write a dedication, and share it with children.

Summarize/Apply Invite children to select a story they have written and add a dedication page to it. Have volunteers share their dedications.

Publishing—How to Make a Book

Introduce Show children a stack of 8½ × 11 pages and a copy of a published book. Discuss what changes have taken place to get from one to the other.

Model Share with children that there are many steps in the publishing process. Demonstrate putting pages in order, creating a front and back cover, writing a dedication page, and then publishing a book. Publishing may require using a computer or binding machine or simply stapling pages together.

Summarize/Apply Encourage children to select a story from their portfolio to publish. Create a class library of children's books.

Reading Old Pieces of Writing for Revision or New Topic

Introduce Show children before and after photographs of renovated houses or antiques that have been restored. Discuss how restoring a piece of furniture is similar to revising a piece of writing.

Model Invite a child to share an old piece of writing from their writer's workshop folder. Solicit suggestions for what might need to be done to make the piece better.

Summarize/Apply Assign children to small groups. Have children select an old piece of writing to share with the group and allow group members to make revising suggestions.

Rearranging Sentences So Similar Ideas and Facts Are Together

Introduce Display a collection of picture cards or photos of cats and dogs. Have children identify all the animals in each group. If children have difficulty, explain that it may be easier for them to separate the pictures into groups, with similar animals together. Point out that in writing, sometimes sentences need to be rearranged so that similar ideas are together too. This makes it easier for the reader to understand.

Model Display these four sentences on chart paper: *My father is a mail carrier. My mother works at a bank. He delivers mail downtown. The bank is near my school.* Read aloud and discuss which sentences should be closer to each other.

Summarize/Apply Encourage children to copy these sentences, with the sentences about similar ideas written one after another.

Writing Process

Rewriting a Confusing Sentence

Introduce Write the following sentence on the board and read it with the children. *Put the doll in the toy box with the broken arm.* Ask children if they can follow the directions. Point out that the sentence is confusing the way it is written.

Model Tell children you wanted the doll with the broken arm put in the toy box. Show them how to rearrange the words in the sentence so that it makes sense. Explain that it is important to make sure that all sentences make sense.

Summarize/Apply Have children review their writing by reading each sentence aloud. They can hear how each sentence sounds and make sure it is clear and makes sense.

Sequencing Events Using Time-Order Words

Introduce Teach children these words to the refrain of "B-I-N-G-O!"

> *First, Next, Then, and Last,*
>
> *First, Next, Then, and Last,*
>
> *First, Next, Then, and Last,*
>
> *Put ideas in order.*

Model Write these sentences on the board.

> *We ate pizza. We told ghost stories.*
>
> *We played a game. We went to sleep.*

Discuss the order of events and how adding time-order words would help the reader understand the sequence.

Summarize/Apply Give children word cards with the words *First, Next, Then,* and *Last* on them. Invite them to tape the word cards in appropriate places and then reread the sentences as a class.

Setting Up Workshop Rules

Introduce Display a picture of a traffic light. Ask children what the various lights mean. Ask children why there are rules. Discuss what might happen if we didn't have rules.

Model Brainstorm a list of rules that will allow everyone in the room the opportunity to work during writer's workshop. Suggested rules may include: *When you have finished, put your writing in your portfolio or get a piece of paper to illustrate your writing. Listen quietly when someone is sharing.*

Summarize/Apply Have children help you create a class poster listing the rules. Ask volunteers to illustrate each rule.

Using a Portfolio

Introduce Ask children if they ever look at pictures of themselves when they were younger. Tell children that looking at pictures of the past shows them how much they have grown. Write the word *portfolio* on the board. Tell children that a writing portfolio shows children how they have grown as writers.

Model Give each child an accordion-style folder. Have children each write their name on their folder and decorate it. Explain to children this is where they will keep all their writing — prewriting notes, illustrations, drafts, and final copies.

Summarize/Apply Show children the crate where the portfolios will be kept. Tell them to be sure to put their folder away at the end of writer's workshop so they will be able to find it when they write again.

Writing Process

Using Revising and Editing Marks

Introduce Write several editing marks on the board or display the editing marks chart found in the back of the Big Book. Tell children that they will become Evan Editor or Edie Editor when they use these marks.

Model Write these sentences on the board or on chart paper: *george washington was are first president his birthday if in february* Invite children as Evan or Edie to come to the board and write editing marks in another color chalk or marker. Model using editing marks first, if necessary.

Summarize/Apply Invite children to rewrite the sentences with the corrections. This will demonstrate children's understanding of the marks.

Using, Sharing, and Replacing Supplies

Introduce Tour the supply station in the writer's workshop area with children. Show them where the various supplies will be kept.

Model Ask several children to role-play using the supplies incorrectly. Have them take too many sheets of writing paper from the middle of the stack and use too many staples to assemble their books. Discuss with children how they should use supplies.

Summarize/Apply Remind children that the writing supply station is for the whole class and that supplies are not endless. Lead children to understand they must take responsibility for using and sharing the supplies.

Varying Sentence Beginnings

Introduce Invite children to imagine what it would be like if they ate the same meal for dinner every night. *(boring)* Discuss the importance of variety in meals, life, and of course sentences.

Model Write these three sentences on the board: *My bike is blue. My bike has a black racing stripe. My bike can hold a water bottle.* Model and think aloud as you change the beginnings of these sentences: *My bike is blue. It has a black racing stripe. A water bottle fits on my bike.*

Summarize/Apply Tell children that writers often make changes to the beginnings of sentences to make them more interesting. Encourage children to look at their writing and see if they need to vary some sentence beginnings.

Writer's Craft

Alliteration

Introduce Invite children to stand every time they hear a *b* sound. Sing the following tune:

> *My bonnie lies over the ocean. My bonnie lies over the sea. My bonnie lies over the ocean, so bring back my bonnie to me.*

Model Write the word *alliteration* on the board. Explain to children that alliteration is when two or more words in a sentence begin with the same consonant sound. Point out that alliteration makes words fun to read. Say "Peter Piper" or other tongue twisters to illustrate more examples.

Summarize/Apply Invite groups of children to create their own examples of alliteration using commonly used consonants, such as *b, p, m, n, s,* and *t.*

Writer's Craft

Dialogue

Introduce Invite two children to the front of the class. Encourage them to talk to each other about what they did over the weekend. Tell the class that conversations between two or more people are called dialogue. Adding dialogue to writing brings a story alive to readers.

Model Read aloud and then invite children to role-play *The Little Red Hen.* One child should be the narrator and read all parts except the dialogue. Invite the children portraying the animals to read their dialogue. For example, "Not I." Display and discuss the use of quotation marks.

Summarize/Apply Have small groups of children choose a favorite story with dialogue and act it out. Remind children to use dialogue in their own writing when appropriate to add interest.

Language—Purpose, Audience

Introduce Teach children these words to the tune of "The Farmer in the Dell."

Your audience is special.
Your audience is special.
Should you be friendly?
Or should you be formal?

Model Display a friendly letter and a newspaper article. Discuss who might be the audience for each and how the language used may be different in each. Which will be more formal? more friendly? Why do they think so? Remind children to think about how their audience affects their word choice and style of writing.

Summarize/Apply Have children choose an audience and write a short piece. Working in pairs, they can read one another's papers and determine if the style works.

Plot

Introduce Lead children in saying the nursery rhyme "Jack and Jill."

Jack and Jill went up the hill to fetch a pail of water. Jack fell down and broke his crown, and Jill came tumbling after.

Model Write the word *plot* on the board and tell children that the plot is the series of events that take place in a story. The *beginning* of the plot should introduce the characters. The *middle* has several events that build, and the *end* tells how everything turns out. Have children repeat the rhyme, identify parts of the plot, and label them *beginning, middle,* and *end.*

Summarize/Apply Display the nursery rhyme "Little Miss Muffet" or another familiar rhyme and invite children to identify and label its plot.

Point of View: First-Person

Introduce Invite a child to tell about a trip or vacation that he or she took recently. Select a volunteer to keep a tally chart of how often the child uses the words *I, me,* and *my.* Share the results of the tally chart when the speaker is finished.

Model Explain to children that when a person tells a story about himself or herself, it is written in the first person. The words *me, my,* and *I* are used in first-person stories. Pair children and have them take turns finishing this story starter: *It was a rainy day and I could not go outside, so I …* Encourage the partner to listen for clue words such as *I, me,* and *my.*

Summarize/Apply Encourage children to identify stories written in the first person and share what words or phrases helped them to determine this.

Sentences—Combining Short, Choppy Sentences

Introduce Invite one child to the front of the room. Then have another child come to the front of the room. Say the children's names with the word *and* in between. Explain to the class that using *and* is an easy way to combine words and sentences.

Model Select two volunteers to hold these sentence strips: *The sun is big. The sun is hot.* Discuss how adding the word *and* to these two short sentences combines them to create one longer sentence. Give another child a sentence strip with the word *and* written on it. Guide the child to stand between the other two children. Invite the class to reread the one long sentence with you.

Summarize/Apply Write these sentences on the board and invite children to combine them into one: *The train is fast. The train is noisy.*

Simile

Introduce Tell children that this morning your dog's fur was like a rat's nest. Ask them if they have ever heard that comparison and explain what it means if necessary. Then write the word *simile* on the board and tell children that a simile compares two unlike objects.

Model Display this frame in a pocket chart. *My hair is as _____ as _____.*

Invite children to compare their hair with something else by filling in the blanks in this frame sentence. For example, *My hair is soft as silk* or *My hair is as black as the night.*

Summarize/Apply Have small groups of children write similes to compare these objects: lake/glass, airplane/hawk, moon/plate. Remind children to use the words *like* or *as.*

Adverbs—Where, When, How

Introduce Write the word *adverb* on the board. Explain to children that adverbs describe action words and they often answer the questions *where, when,* and *how.*

Model Write these sentences on the board: *We camped out <u>here</u> in our backyard. We wake up <u>early</u> in the morning. We eat our breakfast <u>quickly</u>.* Underline the words shown and discuss how these words tell where, when, and how.

Summarize/Apply Review with children that most adverbs answer the questions *where, how,* or *when.* Have children brainstorm other adverbs that could be substituted in the sentences above and rewrite them.

Exclamatory Sentences

Introduce Write *I'm so excited! I'm so happy! I'm so mad!* on the board. Read each aloud, jumping up and down or stomping your feet. Then point to the exclamation marks. Explain that an exclamation mark shows strong feeling.

Model Give children each an index card and have them write a period on one side and an exclamation mark on the other side. Tell children you are going to read several sentences. Invite them to hold up the exclamation side if you read an exclamatory sentence and show the period if it is a declarative sentence.

Summarize/Apply Organize children into small groups and encourage them to write three exclamatory sentences. Have groups share their sentences with the rest of the class.

Grammar and Usage

Interrogative Sentences

Introduce Write and read aloud the following two sentences: *You have a dog. Do you have a dog?* Ask children to tell how the sentences are different. Help children conclude that the first sentence tells something and the second asks something. Explain that sentences that ask questions are called *asking sentences* and always end with a question mark.

Model Ask volunteers about pets they have or would like to have. Record the questions on the board and read them aloud with inflection, pointing out the question marks at the end. Then have volunteers ask pet-related questions and write them on the board.

Summarize/Apply Pair children and ask them to each write a question about a pet. Then have partners take turns showing and reading their questions to one another.

Nouns—Plural Irregular

Introduce On the board write: *Two mans were in the shop.* Read the sentence, and ask children what is wrong with it. Prompt children to tell you how to correct the sentence by substituting *men* for *mans*. Remind children that in many nouns the letter *s* often signals that a word names more than one person or thing. However, a few words like *man* are spelled in unusual ways when they name more than one.

Model Create a two-column chart on the board, with columns labeled *One* and *More Than One.* Write the words *man, woman, mouse, child, foot, tooth,* and *goose* in the first column. Guide children to help you fill in the second column.

Summarize/Apply Have children make a labeled drawing to illustrate one of the word pairs on the chart. For example, their drawing might show one mouse alone and three mice together.

Nouns—Possessive

Introduce Point to a poster in the classroom and ask a question such as *Whose tail is that?* Write and read aloud the response, such as *That is the cat's tail.* Point out the apostrophe and *s* at the end of *cat*. Explain that *cat's* is a word that names a person or thing that "owns" something.

Model Write and read aloud *Pat's house.* Explain that the house belongs to Pat and that by using *s* you can write this idea in a short way. Have volunteers come to the board and use possessive nouns to describe things that belong to them, such as *Lea's pencil* or *Mark's bike.*

Summarize/Apply Ask children to choose a picture that they have drawn and write a caption that uses a possessive form of a singular noun, such as *Can you see the boat's sail?*

Nouns—Proper

Introduce Write the word *child* on the board and read it. Invite several volunteers to print their first and last names below it. Point out that since *child* can be used to name any child, it is called a common noun. Explain that a noun that names a particular person, place, or thing is called a *proper noun.* Important words in proper nouns always begin with a capital letter.

Model Have volunteers come to the board and circle all the capital letters they see. Ask which letters in the names are capitalized. *(the first letter in each name)* Write the name of your school and your city on the board, without capitalization. Invite children to tell you which letters they think should be capitalized.

Summarize/Apply Have children create a cover for a piece of writing, including their full names, school name, and city name. Discuss why each word is a proper noun and how it should be capitalized.

Grammar and Usage

Nouns—Singular

Introduce Ask children several simple riddles about individual classroom objects, such as *What has hands and a face and is perfectly round?* Write the answers on the board. Then read the words aloud. Point out that they are all singular nouns, which name one person, place, or thing.

Model Read the following words and tell children to raise their hands each time they hear a singular noun: *book, tables, teacher, bakers, bridges, castle.* Write the words and point out that usually when a noun does not end in *-s*, it names only one person, place, or thing.

Summarize/Apply Ask children to write three sentences about individual items they see in the classroom. Then ask them to underline each singular noun.

Predicates

Introduce Have a volunteer mime a simple action, and have the rest of the class guess what he or she is doing. Write a sentence about the action, such as *Jim reads.* Tell children that every sentence has two important parts—one that tells who or what the sentence is about and one that tells what that person or thing does or is.

Model Help a volunteer circle the word in the sentence above that tells who the sentence is about. Underline the remainder of the sentence, the predicate, and explain that these words are the action words. These words tell what the person in the sentence does or is. Discuss why a sentence needs action words to make sense.

Summarize/Apply Have children work with a partner to review a piece of writing. Have partners point out the action words in their sentences and revise sentences that are missing action words.

Pronouns—Personal

Introduce Read aloud a passage about a storybook character, substituting his or her name for every personal pronoun. Discuss how the story became boring with the name repeated. Ask children what words you could have used in place of the name. Point out that writers use words like *he* and *she* in place of nouns to make their writing more interesting.

Model Write these pronouns on the board: *I, me, we, you, he, she, it, they.* Ask children questions such as *Which of these words would you use to talk about (yourself, your best friend, me)?* Review the pronouns and use them in oral sentences. Help children note that the pronoun *they* can be used to refer to either people or things.

Summarize/Apply Use tagboard to create pronoun cards and distribute them to small groups. Have them take turns choosing a card and using it to tell a sentence about themselves, someone in the group, or something they see.

Pronouns—Possessive

Introduce Write and read this sentence: *Liz looks great in Liz's red top.* Remind children that the apostrophe and *s* at the end of *Liz's* shows that something belongs to Liz. Prompt children to make the sentence sound better by substituting *her* for *Liz's.* Explain that there are several words like *her* that take the place of possessive nouns like *Liz's.*

Model On the board, write sentences with possessive nouns that could be substituted with the possessive pronouns *his, their, its, my, your,* and *our,* such as *This is Scott's coat.* Read aloud the first sentence, erase the possessive noun, and replace it with the correct possessive pronoun. Invite volunteers to repeat with other sentences.

Summarize/Apply Give a ball to a child and say, *This is [child's] ball.* Invite the child holding the ball to say, *This is my ball.* Then invite a classmate to point to the ball and say, *This is [his/her] ball.* Repeat with other individual children.

Grammar and Usage

Subject-Verb Agreement

Introduce Read aloud these sentences: *Mike likes running. He run every day.* Prompt children to correct the second sentence. *(change* run *to* runs*)* Tell children that if the naming part of a sentence tells about one person or thing, the action word in the sentence has to "match," just as it has to match when the subject is plural.

Model Have volunteers tell you about something that they, a friend, or a group of friends likes to do. Write and read aloud their responses in sentences that use the word *I* as well as singular and plural subjects. Point out subject-verb agreement.

Summarize/Apply Remind children that when the naming word names one person or thing, the action word ends in *-s*. When the subject of a sentence is *I* or names more than one, there is no *-s* on the end.

Subjects

Introduce Write the following sentences on the board: *The dog barks. The baby sleeps. The bell rings.* Point out the part of the sentence that tells who or what the sentences is about (subject) and the part that tells what that person or thing does (predicate).

Model On the board write *went to the show.* Ask children whether they find this sentence easy to understand. Discuss why the missing naming part makes the sentence impossible to understand. Invite suggestions for naming words you could use to turn these words into a complete sentence.

Summarize/Apply Write complete simple sentences on large strips of paper. Cut them in two just after the subject. Let children take turns picking out two parts that can be used together to make a complete sentence.

Verbs—Irregular

Introduce Ask volunteers, *What did you work on this morning? What did you see on your way to school?* Write their responses on the board, using the verbs *worked* and *saw.* Point out that many action words like work add *-ed* when they tell about something that happened in the past. Explain that some action words like see do not add *-ed* for the past tense; instead, they change their spellings.

Model Make a two-column chart with the words *see, do, say, come, eat, give, go,* and *run* in the left column. Write *saw* in the right column and review that it is the past form of *see.* Prompt children to suggest the past-tense forms of the remaining words to complete the chart.

Summarize/Apply Have children choose a word from the list and use it to write a sentence about something they have done in the past. Children can take turns reading their sentences aloud and asking classmates whether the action words are used and spelled correctly.

Verbs—Past Tense

Introduce Read aloud a passage in which the simple past tense of regular verbs is used. Ask children whether the story is told as if it were taking place right now or as if it took place in the past. Elicit that the ending sounds of the action words tell them that the story took place in the past. Identify the ending sounds /d/ and /t/.

Model Write some simple past-tense verbs from the passage on the board. Underline the *-ed* ending in the first word and explain that this spelling shows them that the action happened in the past. Have volunteers circle the *-ed* endings in the other words. Discuss why their writing might be difficult to understand if they accidentally leave this ending off some of the action words.

Summarize/Apply Have partners look through their writing portfolios. Have them read their sentences aloud to one another and correct any regular past-tense words that are missing *-ed.*

Grammar and Usage

Verbs—Present Tense

Introduce Ask children questions about one another, such as *What is Robbie wearing? Where does Kayla sit?* Write the responses on the board, using the present tense. *(Robbie is wearing blue pants. Kayla sits next to Ryan.)* Underline the verbs and explain that they tell about things that are happening now.

Model Write these sentences on the board:

> Jeremy _____ his new puppy.
> The dog _____ in the park.

Invite volunteers to suggest words that could complete the sentences. Write some of their sentences on the board using the present tense.

Summarize/Apply Have pairs of children interview one another about activities or hobbies they are currently enjoying. Prompt them to use present-tense verbs as they tell what they learned about one another.

Mechanics

Apostrophes in Contractions

Introduce On the board write *I do not have a dog. I don't have a dog.* Discuss whether the sentences say the same thing. Explain that the words *do* and *not* have been combined and that the apostrophe is used in place of the letter *o*.

Model Display a set of word cards for *do, not, can, is, it, I,* and *am* and another for *don't, can't, isn't, it's,* and *I'm*. Invite volunteers to choose two words from the first set that are used to make one word in the second set.

Summarize/Apply Have children work in groups to circle five contractions in newspaper or magazine articles.

Apostrophes in Possessive Nouns

Introduce Write these sentences on the board, underlining each possessive noun: *The <u>girl's</u> hat is dry. The <u>boy's</u> coat is wet.* Point out that most possessive nouns that mean "one" use an apostrophe before an *s*.

Model Write these sentences on the board: *The teachers desk is red. This is not my friends book.* Model where to place an apostrophe in each sentence. *(teacher's, friend's)* Have children suggest other sentences.

Summarize/Apply Encourage children to review a previously written narrative. Ask them to look for correct use of apostrophes in singular possessive nouns.

Capitalization—Pronoun *I*

Introduce On the board, write *i like to ride my bike. Today i ate three eggs.* Read the sentences aloud and ask children whether the sentences look right to them. If not, what is wrong? Point out that when the letter *I* is used to talk about themselves, it is always capitalized.

Model Invite volunteers to ask you questions about yourself. Write and read aloud your answers, using *I* when appropriate. Then ask volunteers questions and invite them to record and read aloud their responses using the word *I*.

Summarize/Apply Invite children to draw a picture of something they enjoy doing. Ask them to add one or two sentences telling about themselves. They can exchange papers to make sure they capitalized the word *I*.

Mechanics

Capitalization of States, Streets, Cities

Introduce On the board, write your school's address. Read it aloud and circle the capital letters in the street, city, and state. Review the meaning of the term *proper noun* and explain that the names of streets, cities, and states are proper nouns. Each important word begins with a capital letter.

Model Now write the address of a favorite meeting place for children, making all letters lowercase. Read the address and model how to capitalize the first letter of each important word in the street, city, and state. Repeat the activity, this time inviting volunteers to show how to capitalize the names of streets, cities, and states.

Summarize/Apply Invite groups of children to look up a favorite place in the telephone book. Ask them to write the address, including the street, city, and state using capital letters where needed.

Comma in Addresses

Introduce Hold up an envelope addressed to you. Show children that when an address is written on an envelope, the name, street, and city, state, and ZIP code go on different lines. Note also that there is a comma between the city and state.

Model Write this address inside the outline of an envelope, omitting the comma. Read it together and model how to insert the missing comma.

> *Tyler James*
> *415 E. Grant Street*
> *La Grange, Illinois 60525*

Summarize/Apply Give each child an envelope and a note card with their address (minus the comma between the city and state). Ask them to address the envelope with their own address, placing a comma in the correct place.

Comma in Dates

Introduce On the board write the following: *Ann was born on May 121994.* Read the sentence and stop when you reach the numbers. Ask whether it is easy to tell what day of the month Ann was born. Then erase and add a comma and space between *12* and *1994,* and point out that the comma and space make the date easier to read. Tell children that in a date a comma is always placed between the date of the month and the year.

Model Write the following dates on the board, omitting the commas: *May 11, 1999; June 9, 1996; March 2, 2001; June 22, 2002.* Read the dates aloud and invite volunteers to tell you where to put the missing commas.

Summarize/Apply Write the following on the board for children to copy and complete with dates that include the month, day, and year. *Today is _____. I was born on _____.*

Question Mark

Introduce Invite children to listen as you read aloud two sentences and tell which one asks a question. Say: *What a nice day this is! What day is this?* Write *What day is this* on the board. Then ask whether anyone knows what mark goes at the end of a question. Draw a question mark and explain that this mark always appears at the end of a question.

Model Write and read aloud the following:

> *Who has a cat*
> *What is your name*
> *When do we go outside*
> *Where are the boys*

Point out the "question word" in each and have volunteers insert question marks.

Summarize/Apply Have children write a question they have about something the class is studying. Partners can check one another's punctuation before you collect the papers and read their questions aloud.

Mechanics

Quotation Marks in Conversation

Introduce Write these sentences on the board:

> *The children saw two cats.*
> *"They look like Dan's cats," said Will.*

Read the sentences with children. Tell them that the first sentence describes what happened and that the second sentence tells what someone said. Point out the quotation marks and explain that these marks go around a speaker's exact words.

Model Write the following sentences on the board, omitting the quotation marks: *Dave asked, "Do you know Sara?" "She goes to my school," said Kim.* Add the quotation marks and discuss how difficult it would be to know who was speaking without them.

Summarize/Apply Have small groups select a book and look through it for sentences with quotation marks. Then ask them to read the exact words of the speakers to one another.

Compound Words

Introduce Write *cookbook* on the board. Challenge children to find two words in it and then write *cook* and *book* below. Explain that some words are made up of two or more smaller words and are called compound words.

Model Say the word *someone* and ask children what two words they hear in it. Write the words *some* and *one* and, below them, *someone*. Continue with words such as *anyone, daytime, butterfly*, and *cupcake*.

Summarize/Apply Write the parts of compound words on individual index cards. Let children take turns matching cards to form compound words.

Consonant Blends

Introduce Have children jump up and down until you shout *Stop*. Write *stop* on the board and read it aloud, emphasizing the *st*. Explain that *stop* has a consonant blend—two letters whose sounds are blended together. Have a volunteer circle the two letters that form a consonant blend in *stop*.

Model Point out that consonant blends are often at the beginning or end of words. Write these words on index cards: *sled, glad, step, find, best, felt, frog, clap, belt, hand*. Have children classify the words in these categories: consonant + *r* blend, consonant + *l* blend, *st* blend (at the beginning and end of a word), *nd* blend, and *lt* blend.

Summarize/Apply Have pairs of children brainstorm words that use the blends above. Invite children to share their words.

Consonant Digraphs

Introduce Teach children the tongue twister *She sells seashells by the seashore.* Write *sells* and *shells* on chart paper and discuss how these words are different. Help children understand that two consonants like *s* and *h* can stand for one sound, called a consonant digraph. Consonant digraphs include *ch, sh, th,* and *wh.*

Model Tell children that if they memorize the consonant digraph letter combinations, they will find it easier to spell words with the /sh/, /ch/, /wh/, and /th/ sounds. Slowly sound out and say the word *shut*. At the same time, model for children how to spell the word. Repeat with *Chad, why,* and *this.*

Summarize/Apply Challenge children to race to find ten words posted around the room that have these sounds. Have children point out any digraphs they see.

Spelling

Endings -s, -es, -ed, -ing

Introduce Review nouns and verbs. Tell children that nouns sometimes have special endings to show "more than one," and verbs sometimes have special endings to tell when something happened.

Model Write and read aloud this sentence: *Clocks and watches show time.* Invite volunteers to underline the nouns that name more than one *(clocks, watches).* Tell children that you add *-s* to most plural nouns and *-es* to plural nouns that end in *s, x, ch, sh,* and *zz.* Explain that *-es* can be added to action words, too. Write and say *wishes, fixes,* and *misses.* Tell children that action words can have the ending *-ed,* to tell about things that happened in the past, or *-ing,* to tell about things that are happening now.

Summarize/Apply Write the following on the board: *glass, cat, fox, cow, match, jump, reach, kick, hang.* Have children work in groups to add *-s, -es, -ed,* or *-ing* to the end of each word.

Endings -ed, -ing (Double Final Consonant)

Introduce Write and read aloud the following: *She batted the ball. (bat) The bird was flapping its wings. (flap)*

Underline *batted* and *flapped* and explain that they tell what happened in the past. Point out that when *-ing* or *-ed* is added to certain words, the final consonant should be doubled.

Model Tell children that an easy way to know if the last consonant needs to be doubled is when they see a word that ends in a single consonant just after a vowel. Write the words *rub, slam, nap, plan,* and *drag.* Have children help you decide how to spell them when you add *-ed* and *-ing.* Write the new words on the board.

Summarize/Apply Have children look in storybooks to find action words with letters that doubled when *-ed* or *-ing* was added. Children can share their findings with the class.

Endings -ed, -ing (Drop the Final e)

Introduce Write the words *use, uses, used,* and *using.* Read them with children. Demonstrate that when *-ed* or *-ing* is added to *use,* the spelling changes. Explain that when an action word ends in *e,* the *e* is dropped before adding *-ed* or *-ing.*

Model Write these words on the board: *bake, dive, love, close, glue.* Using *bake* as an example, add *-s, -ed,* and *-ing.* Point out that when *-s* was added, no spelling change took place. However, when *-ed* or *-ing* was added, the *e* was dropped.

Summarize/Apply Have volunteers take turns adding *-s, -ed,* and *-ing* to other verbs you write on the board. Make corrections as a class.

High-Frequency Words

Introduce Write the word *the* on the board and have children read it. Point out that *the* is not easy to sound out. Explain to children that they will sometimes come across words that are hard to sound out and spell because some of their letters make uncommon sounds. They have to learn to recognize these words.

Model Say: *are, been, does, great, have, off, once, is, was, you.* Ask volunteers to suggest how to spell each word. If volunteers don't suggest the correct spelling, spell the word for them as you write it on the board. Use the words in sentences to clarify the meanings if needed.

Summarize/Apply Create a year-round word wall of high-frequency words. Encourage children to add new words as they come across them.

Spelling

Long Vowel Sounds

Introduce Write *a, e, i, o,* and *u* on the board. Explain to children that when the vowel in a word sounds like the vowel's name, it is called a long vowel. Write *make, these, kite, home,* and *use* on the board. Tell children that a long vowel sound is often spelled with the vowel, a consonant, and a final *e.*

Model On the board write the following: *Take a big bite of cake. Those mice are cute.* Ask children to raise their hands to identify the long vowel sounds as you read the sentences aloud. *(take, bite, cake, those, mice, cute)* Underline the vowel-consonant-e patterns in the first sentence. Invite volunteers to underline the vowels in the second sentence.

Summarize/Apply Have children summarize what they learned about spelling long vowel sounds. Encourage them to suggest other words that follow the pattern.

Long Vowel Sounds in Letter Combinations

Introduce Write these sentences on the board: *Freight ships sail fast. What lies in the deep sea? Show us that coat.*

Underline *freight* and *sail* in the first sentence. Read the sentence and pause at each underlined word to ask children what long vowel sound they hear. Circle the *ei* and *ai* and tell children that these can all spell the long *a* sound.

Model Read the second sentence and have children raise their hands when they hear a long vowel sound. Underline the words they identify and ask them which letters you should write above the words. Invite a volunteer to circle the letters that make the sound. Repeat with the third sentence.

Summarize/Apply Remind children of the long vowel sounds associated with *ai, ea, ei, oa,* and *ue.* Then play a class game of "Hangman" using words that have those long vowel sound combinations.

Phonograms and Word Families

Introduce Have a volunteer spell *at.* Explain that if they can spell *at,* they can also spell many other words that end in the same sound. Encourage children to name a few and try to spell them. Tell children that looking for letter patterns will help them remember how to spell new words. Then review the phonograms *-ot, -an, -et, -in, -ad, -ick,* and *-ock.*

Model Write the following words across the board: *pot, pan, pet, pin, ad, sick, sock.* Call children's attention to the word *pot.* Invite volunteers to name some other words that have *-ot* and the /ot/ sound. Write the words below *pot,* such as *cot, dot, got, hot, lot, not,* and *rot.* Use the same techniques to focus on the other words.

Summarize/Apply Tell children that when they look at a new word, they should note whether it contains any letter combinations that are in words they already know.

Prefixes *un-, dis-, re-*

Introduce Write the word *happy* on the board. Have a volunteer read and define it. Write *un-* before *happy* to create *unhappy.* Ask a volunteer to tell what the word means. Point out that you changed the meaning of the word when you added a prefix. A prefix is a group of letters added to the front of a word.

Model Share with children that *un-* means "not." Some other common prefixes are *re-,* which means "again," and *dis-,* which means "the opposite of." Write several words using these prefixes and discuss their meanings.

Summarize/Apply Write the following:

> *un + fair =*
> *re + start =*
> *dis + appear =*

Have children write the equations and combine the prefixes and main words to make new words. Ask volunteers to tell what the new words mean.

Spelling

Rhyming Words

Introduce Write the following rhyming couplet:

*The moon's fat face
Looks down from _____.*

Read the lines with children and ask them to think of a word that rhymes with *face. (space)* Ask how they would spell the word *space,* have them sound it out, and write it on the line. Explain that sometimes writers know how to spell a word by remembering the spelling of a rhyming word.

Model Write *ate* on the board. Ask children how they could use *ate* to spell *date, late,* and *state.* Demonstrate sounding out the words. Repeat the procedure for *near (fear, hear, clear)* and *nose (rose, hose, chose).*

Summarize/Apply Have children look through spelling lists to find words that are hard to spell. Invite volunteers to identify rhyming words that can help them spell the tricky words. Be sure the rhyming words follow the same spelling rules.

Short Vowel Sounds in Letter Combinations

Introduce On the board, write the vowels *a, e, i, o,* and *u* and review the short vowel sounds. Then write *He read about the red fox,* underlining *read* and *red.* Read the sentence aloud and ask children how the underlined words are alike and different *(they sound the same; the /e/ sound is spelled differently).* Explain that short vowel sounds can be spelled by two vowels, such as *ai, ea,* and *ui.*

Model Write this sentence and have children read it and identify the words with short vowel sounds: *I said, "the Blue jay has built its nest."* Invite volunteers to underline the words in which the short vowel sounds are spelled with two letters. *(said, built)* Discuss the sounds made by each letter pair.

Summarize/Apply Write *bread, quilt, said,* and *weather* on the board and ask children how they would pronounce these words.

Short Vowel Sounds

Introduce Write *a, e, i, o,* and *u* on the board and have children pronounce the short vowel sounds after you. Invite them to suggest words with these sounds and write their suggestions in columns on the board. Ask whether they can see any patterns in how these words are spelled. Point out that many one-syllable words have short vowel sounds.

Model Draw attention to the one-syllable words and tell children that words with these sounds rarely end in e. Discuss what happens when you add an e to a word like *mat.* If children have suggested words in which a letter pair spells the sound, explain that a short vowel sound can sometimes be spelled by letter combinations.

Summarize/Apply Invite children to take an imaginary walk through their neighborhood. Have groups use clipboards and paper to make a list of short-vowel-sound words they see along the way, such as *stop, pass, milk, bump,* and *step.* Back in class, have them underline the letters that spell short vowel sounds.

Syllables in CVC and CVCe words

Introduce Write *pick* and *picnic* and tell children they are going to learn about syllables. Define a syllable as "a word or word part that has only one vowel sound." A syllable can have several consonant sounds. Say *pick* and point out that the whole word is pronounced in one chunk and that the only vowel sound is /i/. Do the same for *picnic* but draw a line between the c and n, and discuss why *picnic* is a two-syllable word.

Model Write the following words on the board and clap as you read them to show how many syllables each word has: *balloon, head, monkey, chair, backpack, house, rabbit, garden.* Discuss how children can count syllables, too, and have them identify the sounds heard in the syllables.

Summarize/Apply Ask children how saying a word to themselves and paying attention to its syllables will make them better spellers. *(Saying the syllables one at a time can help them figure out which letters belong in each syllable.)*

Reference Resources

Dictionary

Introduce Display a classroom dictionary and ask children what the book is used for. Tell them that the book lists the spellings and meanings of words in ABC order. Each word has its own entry, or section, which shows how the word is spelled and pronounced (syllable by syllable), what it means, and sometimes an illustration or example sentences.

Model On the board, write this entry:

> **cast** (kăst) *1. A case to hold a broken bone in place.* Her foot was put in a cast. *2. All the actors in a play.* The cast bowed at the curtain call.

Discuss the parts of the entry: the entry word, the pronunciation, and the definitions.

Summarize/Apply Discuss how using a dictionary will make children better writers. *(When they write, they can look up a word in a dictionary to check its spelling, pronunciation, and meaning.)*

Encyclopedia

Introduce Display an encyclopedia set and ask whether anyone knows its name and what's in it. Explain that an encyclopedia is a set of books that contains information on many subjects. As in a dictionary, the entries in an encyclopedia are in ABC order. Point out the guide letters on the spine of each encyclopedia volume. Explain that children can use information from an encyclopedia to write reports.

Model Ask children to name a science or social studies topic that the class has been studying. With the help of volunteers, model the process of finding an entry on that topic in the encyclopedia. Read the entry aloud.

Summarize/Apply Pair children of varying abilities. Have each pair select a topic that interests them. Tell them to find an entry in the encyclopedia on their subject and then find one interesting fact to share with the class.

Maps

Introduce Display a map of the school grounds or a local park. Explain that people mostly use maps to find out how to get from one location to another. Tell children that a map is a drawing of places as seen from above. Help children understand that most maps are drawn so that two distances that look the same on the map are also the same in real life.

Model Name and point out some locations on the displayed map. Then identify a starting point and a destination on the map and demonstrate how you would choose a route. Invite volunteers to take turns coming forward to trace a route on the map and read aloud some of the names along the route.

Summarize/Apply Have children work together in small groups to draw a map of the playground. Afterward, they can display their maps and point out routes between one piece of equipment to another.

Table of Contents

Introduce Display a nonfiction chapter book and turn to the contents page. Explain that many books list page numbers and general topics within it. This list is called the table of contents. The general topics divide the book into sections and are often the names of stories or chapters. Have children read the list of chapters with you. Then point to the page numbers and explain that these numbers show where the chapters begin.

Model Choose a chapter number or title from the table of contents, and model how to find the title and identify the number of the page on which the story begins. Have children turn to that page in their books and then back to the table of contents. Continue, letting other volunteers find titles and identify page numbers.

Summarize/Apply Provide pairs of children with a story anthology. Suggest partners take turns naming a story title and finding the story in their books by using the table of contents.

Index

V

Varying sentence beginnings, 206
Verbs, 129, 211–212
  action, 129
  agreement with subject, 211
  irregular, 211
  past tense, 211
  present tense, 212
Vowel sounds, 216–217

W

Webs, 98, 100, 123
Word families, 216
Word processing, 132, 177
Words
  descriptive, 63
  precise, 115, 131
  rhyming, 217
  sensory, 121
  syllables in, 217
  time-order, 188, 205
Writer's Block, 15, 17, 19, 21, 23, 25, 49, 51, 53, 57, 59, 61, 65, 67, 69, 73, 75, 77, 81, 83, 85, 111, 113, 115, 119, 121, 123, 127, 129, 131, 135, 137, 139, 165, 167, 169, 173, 175, 177, 181, 183, 185, 189, 191, 193
Writer's Craft, 67, 72, 75, 79, 83, 87, 121, 126, 134, 139, 195, 206–208
Writing Across the Curriculum, 15, 17, 19, 21, 23, 25, 49, 51, 53, 57, 59, 61, 65, 67, 69, 73, 75, 77, 81, 83, 85, 111, 113, 115, 119, 121, 123, 127, 129, 131, 135, 137, 139, 165, 167, 169, 173, 175, 177, 181, 183, 185, 189, 191, 193

Writing center, 4, 30, 92, 146
Writing forms, iii–iv
Writing process, xxix
Writing to describe, 89–142
Writing to inform, 143–195
Writing to learn, 1–26
Writing to tell a story, 27–88

Teacher Notes

Art & Photo Credits

Illustrations: Front cover, title page, v: Bernard Adnet.

Photo: All photographs ©Modern Curriculum Press unless otherwise noted.
v: *l.* Courtesy of Dr. Sharon Elizabeth Sicinski-Skeans. *r.* Courtesy of Dr. Lindamichelle Baron. xxxii: Steven Ferry for Modern Curriculum Press. xxxviii: Nancy Ferguson for Modern Curriculum Press.

Big Book of Writing Models Acknowledgments

Excerpt from *Grandmother's Dreamcatcher* by Becky Ray McCain, illustrated by Stacey Schuett. Text © 1998 by Becky Ray McCain. Illustrations © 1998 by Stacey Schuett. Reprinted by permission of Albert Whitman & Company.

"Kat's Good Idea" from *Kit and Kat* by Tomie dePaola, copyright © 1986 by The Philip Lief Group, copyright © 1994 by Grosset & Dunlap, Inc. Used by permission of Grosset & Dunlap, Inc., a division of Penguin Putnam Inc.

"Thank-you note" from *Manners* by Aliki. Copyright © 1990 by Aliki Brandenberg. Reprinted by permission of HarperCollins Children's Books.

ZB Font Method Copyright © 1996 Zaner-Bloser.

NOTE: Every effort has been made to locate the copyright owner of material reprinted in this book. Omissions brought to our attention will be corrected in subsequent editions.

Big Book of Writing Models Art and Photo Credits

Illustrations: Front cover, 1 *t.*, pencilperson: Bernard Adnet. 17–27: Tomie dePaola/Penguin Putnam Inc. 32–33: Stacey Schuett/Albert Whitman & Company. 36: Kristina Stephenson. 40: Aliki/William Morrow & Company, Inc.

Photo credits: All photographs ©Modern Curriculum Press unless otherwise noted.
8, 34: Elliott Smith for Modern Curriculum Press. 17: Suki Couglin. 28: *l.* Steven Lott for Modern Curriculum Press, *r.* Ron Kimball Photography. 30: Andrews Photography for Modern Curriculum Press. 36: Courtesy of Lindamichelle Baron/Harlin Jacque Publications. 37: Bruce Hucko for Modern Curriculum Press. 38: Steven Ferry for Modern Curriculum Press. 40: Courtesy of Aliki. 41, 48: Bob Boyer for Modern Curriculum Press